The Archer Method
An Expert's Guide to

WINNING AT POKER

John Archer

Published by
Melvin Powers
WILSHIRE BOOK COMPANY
12015 Sherman Road
No. Hollywood, California 91605
Telephone: (213) 875-1711

Printed by

HAL LEIGHTON PRINTING COMPANY
P.O. Box 3952
North Hollywood, California 91605
Telephone: (213) 983-1105

Library of Congress Catalog Card Number: 78-62718
Printed in the United States of America
ISBN 0-87980-362-2

CONTENTS

INTRODUCTION: WHY THIS BOOK?

Most poker players have heard the tale about the fellow who lost half his inheritance drawing to inside straights—and then lost the other half when he finally filled one. If you have played much poker, you must have encountered the type of wild gambler who wins a huge pot by drawing two cards to complete a flush—and predictably loses night after night thereafter trying to repeat such luck.

Abundant good advice in print could have saved these players from their blunders. The famed Albert Morehead,[1] the man people are often quoting when they declare something is "according to Hoyle," once wrote that he had never read a bad book on poker—and he had read just about all of them. When I began to contemplate devoting my time to writing an addition to the extensive literature on this fascinating game, I had to ask myself whether a further contribution would serve a useful purpose. As a professional writer, I had no interest merely in a rehashing, and several good books on poker certainly do exist—plus some not so good but still containing a degree of worthwhile advice.

A New Approach

I think my decision to make this undertaking was dictated by an appreciation of something that may have led me to ponder the matter in the first place. From the viewpoint of the reader, the *user* of information on poker, most books on the game seem to be written backward. No, I do not mean backward in the sense of logic or sound organization. It is reasonable for a book to begin with fundamental principles and an explanation of the simpler forms of poker, roughly as these developed historically, and then to progress to more complicated or more recently evolved variants. Over the decades, the game has progressed from the classic Draw Poker for high, to Stud for high, to varieties of low poker, and then to high-low split games—with an interspersion of wild-card games, widow games, and a challenging array of variations that range from whimsical to ingenious. A book on poker must begin somewhere, and I do not disparage a textbook-type format that instructs first in High Draw and Stud and then proceeds to the other forms.

v

But how is poker played today? While it includes the traditional forms, if you have sat in with several different private poker groups in the past decade or so, the odds are great that you played more high-low deals than anything else—most likely with the Seven-Card Stud variety predominating. The popularity of this poker form, while possibly a fad to some degree, did not occur by accident. Good players, experts, hustlers, have manipulated dealer's-choice poker sessions to give themselves added advantage over their naive opponents. These superior players know that a complicated game gives them added opportunity to exploit their skill.

Paradoxically, the bad players, who pursue the game for excitement and with a vain hope for luck, accepted high-low poker with the same enthusiasm as that of the hustlers who imposed it on them. Habitual losers, devastated by the inexorable toll extracted by good players in traditional Draw and Stud, embraced the "wild" game with the notion that it was less demanding of skill and discipline.

Simultaneously, many devotees of traditional poker have largely abandoned the game. They are discouraged by varieties they do not understand and frustrated by the inability to find enough players to form a poker group that will restrict itself to the simpler games. Thus, as many people who basically enjoy poker have found themselves out of the mainstream of modern developments, the game is bypassing them further as exciting new varieties are evolving.

This book embraces both the older and the newer poker forms that are now commonly played. My aim has been to develop a presentation that will be useful either for a player who has never studied the game seriously before or for one with a good fundamental knowledge that needs the polish required to win against modern competition. To serve the two purposes, I have devised a format that departs from the usual design of poker instruction—but in a way that I believe will be much to the reader's advantage.

If at the outset I can make you competent at the relatively difficult game of High-Low Seven-Card Stud, this basic knowledge will become highly adaptable, with appropriate modification, to most other games. It is common to find in poker books, after they have presented instruction on high and then low poker almost in a manner of litany, a statement or implication that all previous advice must be ignored when high-low is considered. To whatever extent that precept is correct, the converse is not. An initial mastery of Seven-Card High-Low provides excellent equipment for adaptation to the nuances of other poker forms.

A Realistic Assumption

A valid and useful book on poker must specify the circumstances under which the game is played. I am thinking now primarily of the stakes and betting limits. Good playing strategy in one type of game may be unsound in another. While most writers on the game recognize this fact, some presentations still let the matter get out of focus at times. Some poker is played for very high limits— where bets at least the size of the pot are common, or perhaps no limits at all prevail beyond each player's bankroll. Some other games are played with *very* low limits, in which bets are unrealistically low in comparison with the ante—or the total amounts involved are so small that players have little concern for the money *per se*. Appropriate strategy for these latter games could be disastrous in more serious poker.

While I do not disparage poker played for matchsticks and pennies by those who find it entertaining, this book is written primarily for a different type of audience. The book is intended for the serious player of games where the money really counts.

On the other hand, the recommended strategies are not designed for the type of "go-for-broke" games played by "Amarillo Slim" Preston in the World's Series of Poker. Poker comparable to that is uncommonly seen. Also, I would not even want to try to advise you on whether to bet several thousand dollars on a poker hand in a table stakes game unless you happen to be a millionaire.

I personally enjoy pot-limit, table-stakes poker if the stakes are within my budget. Nevertheless, if we disregard the frivolous forms of poker played purely for social entertainment, by far the most common games today are for a set limit that is appropriately related to the size of the ante. Accordingly, I have assumed that type of game for most of the instruction given in the book.

For each game described, I shall specify some particular dollar amounts for the limits. In actual games, of course, the poker group may agree on larger or smaller stakes. However, the ones I have chosen are within ranges that are reasonably typical in modern games played by serious but non-professional players.

I do not mean that I shall totally ignore games with other types of limits. Often it will be convenient to point out variations of strategy appropriate in such games, and I have no intention of withholding such information from the reader. At the moment, however, I am merely explaining the basic thrust of the book.

An Additional Ingredient

Many of the games explained in this book are played in legally sanctioned casinos, such as in Nevada and California. The casino versions, however, have certain features of their own that distinguish them somewhat from the comparable games typically played in private sessions. Little attention has been paid in most books to the nuances that can be highly important to the player in adapting to the casino games.

I have played often and with reasonable success in casinos. For readers with a wish to do the same, this book contains a substantial bonus. I have made a particular study of casino poker, especially that played in Nevada, and shall include in the book considerable information that will prepare you for that game and advise you of what to expect.

Some Ground Rules

I am confident that the great majority of readers of this book already know something about poker. Those who do not will find the glossary near the back (pages 148-159) helpful in explaining the technical terms and jargon of the game.

The rules and mechanics of the game can readily be explained as the presentation unfolds. I am avoiding the undue tedium of a long chapter devoted to such matters at the beginning. Still, I want to make the presentation understandable to all readers. Accordingly, I shall include just enough of a description of the game early in Chapter I to get us quickly underway into material that is directly useful at the poker table. As implied earlier, the organization of the book was not designed so much to be "logical" as to be practical and useful. Numerous variations and subtleties of rules will be interspersed elsewhere.

One thing you must understand: successful poker is based on applied mathematics. Precise tables have been constructed to provide analyses in depth of the probabilities of a myriad of results in playing poker hands under a variety of conditions.[1-5] Such tables are worth studying as you continue your poker eduction, but I have elected a didactic presentation in this book that does not really require that you do so. In recommending certain tactics, however, I shall often give a capsule explanation of the mathematical odds that led to the advice.

Before We Proceed

At the risk of offering advice that may seem obvious, I regard three items related to the material in this book as so important that I must begin with some brief reference to them.

First, you must never gamble with money you cannot afford to lose. While I plan to make you a probably winning player, almost surely one in the long run, there are good reasons for this advice. They are given in my previous book on Blackjack,[6] and are equally applicable at poker: "Chance fluctuations in the run of the cards can overcome a statistical advantage, and there is no absolute guarantee of winning. Besides the obvious folly of risking money that is needed for something else, doing so compounds the danger by leading to bad play. It can affect judgement in various harmful ways. At best, mental concern about the money on the table is distracting and induces errors. At worst, some players, after a series of losses, abandon sound play and begin foolish, wild gambles in the hope of being suddenly lucky. Others, while not yielding to such harmful impulses, may nevertheless be intimidated into overcaution and fail to press advantages when they appear—fail to [bet, raise, call, or bluff]* when indicated. For best prospects, the player ordinarily should allocate a specific sum of gambling capital that he can well afford to lose and, for practical purposes, consider it already spent."

Second, the advice given in this book assumes an honest game. You *can* be cheated at poker. Thus, you must use some discretion in choosing the company in which you play.

Third, gambling winnings are taxable. Although the Federal Government does not permit an income-tax deduction for losers, it wants a share whenever you have a net win throughout a year. This requirement may assume new meaning for you when you become the type of expert this book is intended to develop.

---

*Paraphrased from the original quotation to fit the present context.

Chapter I
THE GAME OF TODAY

Many habitual poker players disdain games of "High-Low Split." But these people are seldom good players, and practically never experts.

I suggest that if you have any prejudices against this form of poker, you set them aside—at least temporarily. I am satisfied for the moment to say *temporarily,* because I am perfectly confident that once you have digested the material of this chapter, you will abandon any idea you may have had that split poker is a frivolous game. It is probably true that a few decades ago, High-Low was seldom played outside of nickle-dime poker circles. Today, however, this is a poker form embraced and dominated by the experts.

I have chosen to begin my instruction in poker with High-Low Seven-Card Stud for a variety of reasons, some mentioned in the Introduction. First, it is very frequently played. Second, mastery of this game provides an excellent base of knowledge to adapt, with proper modification, to other games. But third and most important, winning at this form of poker probably involves less of the element of luck than at any other frequently-played variety of the game.

This latter statement may come as a surprise to many readers. But at few other games does the skillful player have as great an advantage over the ordinary player as at High-Low Seven-Card Stud.

The Elementary Structure of Poker

Readers who are already familiar with poker may skip this section and begin on page 4. In fact, if you know the basic rules of high-low poker, you may skip to page 8. (Be certain, however, that you are familiar with the jargon of poker, much of which is introduced in pages 1-8.)

In order to explain the elementary structure of poker for readers approaching the game for the first time, I shall digress from my plan to begin with Seven-Card High-Low Stud and instead describe the simplest form of poker that can exist. This is called Showdown.

1

Showdown requires no skill whatever; it merely involves the knowledge to recognize which hand wins.

Suppose it is late in the evening, the serious poker session has broken up, and players A, B, and C have some loose change and decide to amuse themselves for a few minutes with some hands of Showdown. A standard, 52-card deck is used (no Bug or Joker).

Each player puts an equal amount on the center of the table to form a "pot." One player acts as dealer and shuffles the deck, the player to his right cuts, and the dealer gives each player one card at a time in clockwise rotation until everyone has five cards.

The three hands are then compared to see which wins. The cards rank in descending order as follows: Ace, King (K), Queen (Q), Jack (J), 10, 9, 8, 7, 6, 5, 4, 3, 2. Suits have no rank.

Suppose the hands are as follows:

Player A: Ace,J,4,3,2
Player B: K,Q,9,7,2
Player C: Ace,7,5,4,3

If under the rules the players have adopted the high hand wins the pot, then player A would win. His Ace tops B's K. His Ace ties C's Ace, but his J tops C's second highest card, the 7. (When two players have *two* identical highest cards, then the third determines the outcome, and so on.)

Suppose, instead, it has been determined that the lowest hand wins. Under most prevalent rules, player C would win, as the Ace is usually regarded as either a high or a low card, whichever is to the advantage of its holder. C's highest card is thus a 7, better than A's J (or B's K . . .).

If the game were High-Low, A and C would split the pot. If the pot cannot be split equally, it is customary in High-Low for the high hand, A, to take the odd coin or chip. In the variation in which an Ace *must* rank high, A and B would split the pot. In this book, however, I am assuming the much more common rule in which an Ace ranks low for purposes of a low hand.

Assume another deal with the following hands:

A: K,K,4,3,2
B: Q,Q,10,8,5
C: Ace,K,Q,9,7

A's pair of Ks is higher than B's pair of Qs. Their other cards are immaterial. C, with no pair, has the low hand.

Another deal:

A: 9,9,3,3,2
B: 8,8,7,7,5
C: K,K,Q,10,8

A's two pairs are higher than B's two pairs, as the 9s are higher than the 8s. The fact that B's 7s are higher than A's 3s is immaterial. C's hand is low with only one pair.

Again:
> A: J,J,J,9,8
> B: Ace,Ace,K,K,3
> C: Ace,Ace,K,K,2

A, with three of a kind, is higher than B and C with two pairs each. C is low; since his two pairs are identical to those of B, the fifth card determines the outcome. (It would be overly tedious for me to give a specific example of hands showing that, say, three Ks would rank higher than three Js; I am confident that is obvious to you by now.)

Still another deal:
> A: Q,J,10,9,8
> B: 10,9,8,7,6
> C: Ace,Ace,Ace,K,Q

Notice that A and B each have five cards in uninterrupted sequence. These hands are known as "straights." They rank higher than C's three of a kind.* A's straight is higher than B's.

Suppose instead of the hands just given, the straights of A and B had been identical (except for the suits, which have no rank). In High poker, they would tie and divide the pot between them. In High-Low under rules probably most prevalent, C would win half and A and B would win one-fourth each. (For the moment, let us not bother with the Solomon-type problem of how a three-coin pot might be split under circumstances like these; I am merely illustrating the ranking of hands and prefer to keep things simple.)

Again:
> A: K,10,6,5,2 (all clubs)
> B: Q,J,10,7,6 (all spades)
> C: Ace,K,Q,J,10 (varied suits)

A and B have "flushes," which rank higher than C's straight. Note that at this point suits take on importance; a hand made up of five cards of the same suit ranks quite high in poker. But still, one suit, per se, does not outrank another suit. In the preceding hands, A's flush is higher than B's flush because A has a K and B's highest card is a Q.

Another deal:
> A: 8,8,8,2,2
> B: K,K,7,7,7
> C: Ace,J,10,7,4 (all hearts)

A and B have "full houses." A's full house is higher than B's because the three 8s that help make it up outrank B's three 7s. The fact that B's two Ks are higher than any of A's cards is immaterial. The full houses are higher than C's flush.

---

*For simplicity at this point, it is better to defer discussion of a rules variation in which B's hand would win low in Low or High-Low poker.

And finally:

    A: 7,6,5,4,3 (all diamonds)
    B: Ace,Ace,Ace,Ace,K
    C: Q,Q,Q,J,J

A has a "straight flush," a straight with all cards of the same suit. This ranks higher than B's four of a kind. (Imagine losing with four Aces!) B's hand containing four of a kind is higher than C's full house.

The highest hand possible is called a "royal flush." This is a straight flush consisting of Ace,K,Q,J,10.

In summary, the relative ranking of hands in poker is: straight flush, four of a kind, full house, flush, straight, three of a kind, two pairs, one pair, high card.

I hope you will understand that the game I chose to illustrate these fundamentals (Showdown) is absurd. Unlike all other poker, it depends entirely on luck, and I hope you will never play it except in frivolity. Poor B did not win a single hand—high or low. Well, naturally I invented the whole thing, but perhaps a moral can be found in the illustration. I can assure you that if B learns to play poker according to the instruction in the remainder of this book, he will fare much better.

How High-Low Seven-Card Stud Is Played

At the beginning of a deal, the start of a pot must be established by an ante. Several methods exist for making this ante, but for the present explanation, we shall assume that each player contributes an equal amount before the deal.

In a manner to be described, each player will eventually receive seven cards. The object of the game is to obtain five cards among the seven that either make a better high hand or a better low hand than that of any other player.

Each player initially receives two "hole cards" (face down and thus only visible to their owner) and one "up card" or "open card" (visible to everyone). The player with the highest up card may then make a bet, within the established limits for the game, by adding money to the pot. Alternatively, he may announce "Check," thus declining to be bet for the moment. (Rules of many games do not permit that player to check at this particular time, but I shall defer discussion of such variables.) When the highest up card is tied, the elder of the two hands "acts" first (i.e., bets or checks). The "elder hand" is the first one to the dealer's left.

After the initial bet or check, each player acts clockwise in turn:

1. Also checking, if that was the previous action.
2. Betting, if he wishes, when all previous players have checked.
3. "Calling" any previous bet (i.e., "staying") by contributing the same amount to the pot.

4. "Raising," by calling any previous bet plus adding an additional bet.
5. "Passing" (or "folding") by abandoning his hand and tossing his cards, face down, in front of the dealer or somewhere near the center of the table, as discards. Obviously, this action should not be taken if no previous bets have been made and thus the player may check along. However, a player *must* pass unless he is willing to call any previous bet plus any raises.

On the uncommon occurrence when every player checks, the action is over for that "betting interval," and another card is dealt (up) to each hand. Usually, however, betting occurs, and this continues in rotation until every "active player" (i.e., every player who has not passed) has acted on all bets and raises.

(Suppose, for illustration, that a player bets and then every other player folds. Well, the bettor would win the pot, but at high-low poker, that simply will not happen. Under highly unusual circumstances, it *can* occur during the last betting interval, but that matter involves nuances far too advanced for the present stage of instruction. At other forms of poker, it is quite common to win pots for lack of a call, but we are now discussing High-Low.)

If a raise has occurred, any active player may reraise in his turn (i.e., call the bet and the raise and add still another bet). This includes the player who has made the initial bet. (Rules of some games forbid a raise by a player who has previously checked, although he may *call* any bets and raises.) A player who has raised may raise again, but only if his initial raise has been reraised. In other words, the betting interval is over after every active player has acted on the last bet or raise preceding him.

Rules of most games place some limit on the total number of raises permitted during one betting interval. Three is a common limit. Some such rule is practically essential for any acceptable high-low game—for reasons eventually to be made clear.

The preceding fundamentals of poker may best be summarized and illustrated by reference to a figure (see page 6).

Seven-Member Poker Group

1. Suppose A bets first. B through G must at least call in order to continue to compete for the pot on this deal. If no one raises, the betting interval is over after G has called or folded.
2. Suppose A bets, B calls, C folds, and D raises. Unless E, F, and G elect to fold, they must at least call the bet and the raise. A and B then, unless they fold, must call the raise. If no one reraises, the interval ends when B acts. (C is now a nonentity, as he has already folded.)
3. Suppose A bets, B calls, C folds, D raises, E calls the bet and raise, F folds, and G reraises. To stay in, A and B must call both

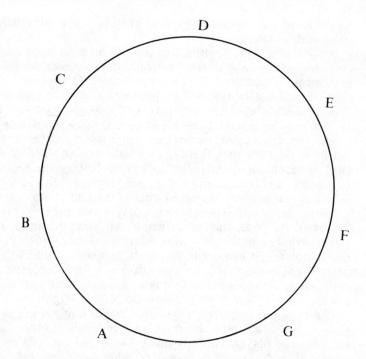

raises. C is already out. D and E must call the reraise or they must "drop" (another term for *pass* or *fold*). F is already out. If no further raises occur after G's reraise, the betting for this interval ends when E acts.
4. In the example just preceding, A, B, D, and E were each eligible to raise still again in their turns. However, if a three-raise limit prevails, once any of these players has made that last available raise, the remaining players may merely call the raises that they have not already called. The betting interval ends when the active player to the last raiser's immediate right has called or folded.

Remember that we have been discussing the first betting interval or "betting round," when each player has two hole cards and one up card. When this betting round is complete, each player receives one more up (or "open") card, and another round commences.

Again, the high open hand acts ("speaks") first, by betting or checking, and players then act in rotation as before.* However, note that the player with the high open hand (or "high board") may change as additional cards are dealt.

---

*I am familiar with a game at the Sahara Hotel on the Las Vegas Strip in which the turn to act first is shifted to the *low* board on the fourth and subsequent cards, but that rule is uncommon.

For example, on the first round player A may have been high with an Ace showing. His fourth card (second up card) may be a 7, D at this point may show a higher hand with Ace,K, and G may be even higher with a pair of deuces. Accordingly, G would speak first on this second round.

After the second betting round is completed, a fifth card is dealt to each player—up once again. Another betting round occurs, and the sixth cards are dealt—still up. These are the last open cards. Each player has an open hand of four cards. Another betting round occurs.

Finally, a seventh card is given each player. Like the first two, this one is dealt down as another hole card. The last betting round occurs. Note that whoever was "high" for betting purposes on the sixth card must remain high on the seventh.

In summary, in High-Low Seven-Card Stud, five betting rounds occur, and at the end, each player who has continued to compete throughout has three hole cards and four open cards.

After the betting is completed, the winners are determined. The player having the highest five-card hand among his seven divides the pot equally with the player having the lowest.

In many games, before the cards are shown, players must declare whether they intend to compete for high or low, and they are entitled to win only in the way they declare. The manner in which these declarations are made varies with the rules in force. At the moment, however, I shall defer discussion of these poker forms; my intention in this section is to present only the barest fundamentals of High-Low Seven-Card Stud. Accordingly, I shall assume that "the cards speak for themselves" and that to have a chance to win high, low, or both, the players who have called all bets need merely expose their hole cards in order that all hands may be compared. This comparison is called the "showdown," reminiscent of the terminology of Showdown poker described in the previous section.

Suppose players A, B, D, and G have active hands at the showdown. (C, E, and F have dropped out somewhere along the way.) The hands may be as follows (but arranged *not* necessarily in the order the cards have fallen):

A: Ace,Ace,Ace,J,7,6,2
B: Q,Q,4,4,7,5,3
D: K,K,8,7,4,3,Ace
G: K,7,5,4,3,2,2

A wins high with three Aces and splits the pot with G, who wins low with his "7-low" hand.* B and D lose, wait for the next deal to begin, and watch enviously while A and G divide the money.

---

*More accurately, the hand is *7 high* **for** *low,* but is more likely to be called "7 for low" or merely "7 low."

Whether A, B, D, and G *should* have played out their hands to the showdown is immaterial to the present discussion. However, I have constructed the example in a way that all individuals may have played with excellence or incompetence, depending on circumstances.

These circumstances include the order in which the cards fell, the open hands of each player's opponents, the vigor of betting and raising, position at the table in relation to other players' hands and actions, the size of the pot at any particular moment, the number of players still competing, and many other considerations. But all that must wait. I have merely been describing the structure of the game. I shall make you an expert later.

Please notice that in High-Low Seven-Card Stud, one player may win the entire pot. For example, he may have a hand like this:
J,8,7,6,5,4,Ace
An 8-high straight is present in this hand. A different selection of the five best cards provides a 7 low. The J helps neither way.

The hand wins high unless someone has a higher straight, or a flush, et cetera. It also wins low unless it confronts something like a 7,5. . .or less!

By custom, the turn to act as dealer rotates clockwise from player to player from one hand to the next. The dealer has certain leadership obligations at stud poker. He is expected to call attention to who is high on each round and thus first to act. When three-card straights or flushes appear, the dealer should announce, "Possible straight," or "Possible flush." However, for reasons to be explained on page 26, he should not announce possible *straight-flushes*.

Let's Play for Money

I now shall really begin the book. We shall assume that seven people are to play High-Low Seven-Card Stud ("Seven Hi-Lo"), "Cards Speak."

Cards Speak is the form of the game in which players do *not* have to declare, before the showdown, whether they are competing for high hand or low hand. The winners are determined simply by which players hold the best five cards in the two directions. (In the declaration forms, to be considered later, a player must declare high to win high; he must declare low to win low.)

The total ante for the game we shall assume will be about $2. Several methods exist for making the ante. The most common is for every player to contribute a small amount. Twenty-five cents by each player would, of course, make a $1.75 ante. Alternatively, since in the game we assume the deal rotates clockwise from one player to the next after each hand, it is fair and simpler to have the dealer, in his turn, make the total ante ($2).

A common custom is to have a smaller initial ante by the dealer or by each player, but then to *require* that on the first betting round, the player with the high card make some minimum initial bet (a "forced bet"). Or, the high card hand might have to make the entire $2 ante—again perfectly fair, as during a prolonged session, this obligation will usually average out fairly well between the players.

For our game, however, we shall assume one of the first two methods: the dealer antes $2 *or* each player antes 25¢. Thus, the player with the high open card may check if he wishes.

The initial limit on bets and raises will be $1. After an open pair shows in any hand the limit increases to $2. Even if no pair shows, the limit increases to $2 after the sixth cards have been dealt (i.e., on the final two betting rounds).

The minimum bet permitted will be 25¢. (Thus, if chips are used instead of cash, the smallest chip will be worth 25¢.)

A maximum of three raises per betting round will be allowed. The exception is that the "right-to-bet rule" prevails. That rule means that during any round, no player may be deprived of the privilege of raising at least *once,* merely because three raises have been made ahead of him. Although the situation rarely occurs, it is unfair to permit three players with speculative hands to make successive raises of, say, 25¢ each, and thus prevent another active player from raising $1 or $2 if he wishes.

Many poker games have a rule that a player may not check and later raise if another player bets. This practice is called "sandbagging," and it offends many people to have a player trap an opponent by "lying in the weeds" in this manner.

Not long ago, I was in a game (not Seven Hi-Lo) in the Stardust Hotel on the Las Vegas Strip, and a famous entertainer was one of the players. He became enraged and left in his fury (with two of his friends who also were in the game) when another player made him the victim of such a "check-raise."

The tactic was perfectly legal in that game, and I cannot understand such objections to it. I fully subscribe to ethics at the poker table. If a poker group wishes to outlaw check-raising, that is its business. However, I regard poker to be a competitive game. It is a game of skill. To forbid the sandbagging tactic is to remove much of the excitement and subtlety from the game.

The rules of the game to be discussed assume the check-raise, or sandbagging, to be legal and proper. (If you happen to be in a game where it is forbidden, and you wish to trap players into betting into your good hand, just make the smallest bet possible. That is practically like checking, but it puts the potential victims on notice that you may come back with a raise. Later in the book, I shall discuss some highly advantageous uses of this tactic. At the moment, however, let us get on with our business. Sandbagging* *is* legal in the game we shall assume.)

Finally, a word must be said about the ranking of hands. While rules of a few games require that an Ace be treated only as a high card, the great majority permit it to "swing" and thus be treated as high *and* low. Thus, a combination of Ace,K,10,6,5,3,2 counts as an Ace-high hand and a 6-low hand. For our game, we shall assume that the Ace plays this dual role.

But what about straights and flushes? Some games permit a hand like Q,7,5,4,3,2,Ace to count not only as a straight for high but also as a 5 for low (which would be the best low hand possible). Traditionally, however, a straight is always a straight with its normal high value; thus, in the hand just illustrated, the 5 would have to be disregarded for purposes of low, and the 7,4,3,2,Ace combination would have to be used.

To simplify a similar example, let us assume that all seven cards in a hand happen to be clubs. If straights and flushes "swing," the highest five cards would be used as a flush for high, but the suit feature could be disregarded in counting the lowest five for low.

I personally prefer to let straights and flushes swing. This makes for a bit livelier game and also gives a slight additional edge to the better player.

However, tradition dies hard, and I must not allow my personal preferences to compromise the value of this presentation. It is safe to say that a modern *trend* is to permit the dual role for straights and flushes. Appraisals of just how *widespread* it has been adopted vary with the book you read. I suspect, however, that if you play in a variety of poker groups, you will more commonly find that these hands are assigned only their high value. Certainly most of my playing experience has been with the traditional rule. Accordingly, I shall assume for this book that straights and flushes do not swing in High-Low ("Hi-Lo"). Occasionally, however, I shall point out a slight variation of strategy that might be indicated if the different rule were in force.

(It is easy to understand why the concept that *Aces* should swing in Hi-Lo has been much more readily accepted than that straights and flushes should do so. The game has evolved from regular high poker, and in that game, Aces universally swing in a sense, in the one type of hand where it matters: straights. Ace,K,Q,J,10 is the highest straight; 5,4,3,2,Ace is the lowest.)

Sandbagging is an ambiguous term. It does not necessarily imply a check with the intent of raising. A "sandbagging" check may be used merely to avoid advertising a good hand prematurely. In that case, the plan is to bet strongly on later rounds, after opponents have been deceived about the value of the hand. No one questions the legality of the tactic when employed in that way. Some authors distinguish this latter tactic from *sandbagging* by calling it "slow-playing" a hand.

Seven Hi-Lo—Cards Speak

Although many precepts of sound poker are firm and applicable to all circumstances, an essential ingredient of overall strategy is appraisal of the opposition. For our game, we shall assume a rather typical group.

In addition to yourself, the other six players consist of: two good players (not necessarily experts, but they win more often than they lose); two average players (not complete suckers—they have some judgment and a fair degree of experience—but they have never really bothered to *study* a book like this); and two inept players.

All start with three cards and a chance for half the eventual pot (occasionally all of it), which at this point has been begun by the ante. The way you play these first three cards, hand after hand, is the key to your success as a poker player. This is the time when you consider your eventual prospects for winning.

A straight will win the high half of most pots. Three-of-a-kind is borderline. (I do not mean that most pots will be won *by* a straight specifically, but that if you have one, or something better, you will usually win.)

A 7-high hand ("7 low" or "7 for low") will usually win the low half by the same token.

Accordingly, after you have seen your first three cards, you should continue to play (betting or calling bets) only if the cards give a reasonably good prospect for a winning hand. Four more cards are yet to come, and every player who matches your bets gets four of his own.

But what is a reasonable prospect when you are just beginning a hand and you will end later competing (usually) for only half the pot? It is a hand that offers prospects for developing into *either* a high or low winner (occasionally both).

A three-card beginning of, say, a pair of Ks with a J has no such prospects. No four additional cards can possibly produce a decent low hand. You have a potential only to compete for high.

On the other hand, three very small cards, with four to come if you stay all the way, provide wide-range possibilities. Two more non-matching small cards can give an excellent low hand. If the cards begin pairing each other, you may make "trips" (three of a kind) for a reasonable chance at high, or occasionally a full house (great). If just the right cards fall, a straight (occasionally a flush) may develop.

In short, if you begin with good prospects for low, you are not only competing in that direction, but you may "accidentally" win high. If you begin competing strictly for high, you can never win low except under fluke circumstances.

That fact leads to a concept frequently advised for good play of Seven Hi-Lo: at the beginning of a hand, "Always play for low."

That generalization is a bit simplistic as we shall see. Exceptions do occur. Nevertheless, it is an excellent principle to bear in mind. If you ordinarily get out of hands that do not have low possibilities, you will generally be playing only those that have a chance of winning either way.

"The Rule of 7."

I have mentioned that a 7-low is usually good enough to win the low half of the pot and have explained that in early stages of a hand, it is most desirable to begin aiming for that half. Accordingly, we shall now consider the types of three-card hands that are worth betting and staying for at least one more card.

Three cards all 7 or lower, none pairing another, are greatly desirable and obviously should be played (e.g., 7,5,Ace;6,4,2). Unfortunately, however, such a fine combination is the exception and not the rule, and you must recognize the more common playable hands. Very simply, two unpaired cards in the Ace-to-7 range make a starting hand better than average in quality. Examples include K,7,Ace and J,6,4. Such hands should be played.

Conversely, a hand *without* two unpaired cards in the Ace-7 range is inferior and should be "dropped," or folded (exceptions to be discussed). In other words, K,8,7; Q,9,Ace; or J,10,2 should not be played, because all these hands contain only one card in the Ace-7 range and thus offer only dim prospects of ever developing into a competitive low hand.

In fact, the particular examples just shown do not give any reasonable prospects for high either. However, many seasoned players of poker for "high only" cannot accept the concept that something like Q,Q,J should be dropped fast in Hi-Lo. Unless they do, they will never become successful Hi-Lo players—at least not if their opposition is competent. Even if their opposition is not competent, they will win less than they would by following sound principles.

If the high hand could win the whole pot, a player would ordinarily be pleased to start with a high pair. But with a moral certainty that half the pot will go to someone else, he should not try for merely the other half with such values. He will not be getting his money's worth in comparison with players with low cards that have the potential for competing either way—depending on how subsequent cards may improve the hands. K,K,Ace is only slightly better than Q,Q,J; it has only one card in the Ace-7 range, and is definitely not worth playing.

Note that a pair in the Ace-7 range can count as only one card for the purpose of low. Thus, the third card must be in the range for the hand to conform to the "rule of 7," i.e., the principle that in the early stages you should only play hands with a reasonable potential for developing into a 7-low or better. For example, 5,5,8 is not playable, as the 5s pair one another, and thus only one may count for low.

However, 5,5,7 is playable, as two cards are in the Ace-7 range for low.

Even a pair of Aces is not worth playing unless the third card is low. With Aces, however, I may slightly relax the rigidity of the rule of 7 and play with an 8. That leads to the subject of a few exceptions to the rule of 7.

Exceptions—Instead of doggedly insisting on two in the Ace-7 range, I will stay with precisely an Ace and an 8 plus a high card provided the hand has *some* further redeeming feature. One such feature would be for the third card to pair the Ace or 8. [Note that the second Ace (or 8) can only be regarded as a "high" card in this circumstance.] Before I toss the money into the pot, however, I am going to look around at the other players' exposed cards. If I see another card that matches my pair, or more than one that matches my other card, I will not play.

Note that at this point I introduce a feature of the game on which I shall frequently concentrate later—paying attention to cards besides your own. Also, notice that I am staying with my principle of playing three-card hands that give some chance of developing either high or low. While I prefer to play for at least (or perhaps I should say *at most*) a 7-low, an 8-low does have a fighting chance. That feature of an Ace,8 combination, *plus* a pair that gives some start toward high, provides a barely sufficient justification to stay for another card. Note carefully, however, that for an 8 to be regarded as a satisfactory "low" card, its companion must be the versatile Ace. 8,2, for example, is simply not worth playing if the other card is high.

Another adequate compensating feature of an Ace,8 and higher-card hand is for two of the cards to be of the same suit. No, I do not really *expect* to make a flush from this start. But I am not committed to stay for seven cards. I am merely paying for one more card at this point, to see how things start developing. And that moderate chance, for example, that the fourth card may be a nice low card of the same suit, to continue *both* the flush and the low-hand possibilities, justifies the play. Again, however, you should take a look at the open cards. If other players show more than one or perhaps two of your suit, toss the hand away.

Any three to a flush are ordinarily worth playing, regardless of rank. This is a major exception to the principle of "always playing for low." Naturally, you would prefer that the three-flush contain two or three cards in the Ace-7 range. But even three high ones may be played unless you see an abnormal number of the same suit among the exposed cards. If, say, your three-flush is in clubs, and you see three other clubs elsewhere, only seven more remain in the deck. Your chances of eventually completing the flush are significantly less than if nine or ten remain, and three high clubs should not be played.

Also worth playing are three to a straight no higher than Q high.

The reason three to a K-high straight are not worth playing involves the lack of versatility. If the fourth card is an Ace, the only way to complete the straight will be to draw a 10—and you know that only four cards of a rank are available among the 52 in a deck.

Finally, I advise that any three of a kind be played. To some readers, this recommendation may seem too obvious to mention. They will be surprised to learn, however, that some experts regard this hand, so magnificant in strictly High poker, as not worth playing in Seven Hi-Lo—Cards Speak. The reason is that any chance for low is greatly remote—almost nil with high trips (except for Aces, which, of course, are also low).

I side with those who play "trips," but a full discussion of the strategy is most conveniently deferred until a later section. At the moment, merely bear in mind that three of a kind are not as good a hand as they might seem.

AN INTRODUCTION TO BETTING TACTICS

In Seven Hi-Lo, betting on the first round usually tends to be fairly uncomplicated (not much raising). That fact, however, makes it convenient to introduce the subject of betting tactics at this point.

Remember that in our game, the limit is $1 on the first round (and the sum of the antes in the pot is about $2). Since you are only going to play hands with sound values (normally at least two low cards), you ordinarily will start with an advantage over average players. Thus, you have two logical desires at this point: you want as many competitors as possible in the pot, eventually to get their money; and you want the size of the pot built as large as possible.

Unfortunately, a degree of incompatibility exists between these desires. The more expensive it becomes to stay in, the fewer the players there will be who are likely to do so. Accordingly, you must balance these two factors to your best advantage.

When my exposed card is "high on board" and thus I am first to bet, or when the betting has been checked around to me, it is usually my practice to bet the full $1 limit (provided, of course, the hand is otherwise suitable to play). There is a fair likelihood that players who would have called, say, a smaller bet of 50¢ will go ahead and call the limit bet too. And I surely do not want to let everyone in for something cheap like 25¢.

Usually, of course, you will not have the first bet, and your decision will be whether to call someone else's bet. You should have little problem; in our limit game, if your hand meets the criteria we have established for staying, you should call regardless of the size of the bet.

Also, at this stage of the betting, when you call any bet, you should be willing to call a subsequent raise. Conceivable exceptions would be too uncommon, too borderline, and too tedious to discuss at the moment.

This does not mean that you necessarily must be prepared to call a raise and *re*raise that may occur before the time to act returns around to you. For example, suppose you have properly called an opening bet on a hand of 7,6, and high card. If then there are two raisers who act after you and both have very low cards showing, the odds are quite high that you do not have the best hand. And it is becoming too expensive to try to overcome this newly discovered handicap. Even if your next card is ideal, and neither of the raiser's cards helps his hand, you *still* may be third best.

That introduces one of the most vital principles of poker. Just because you have put some money into a pot, do not think this gives you any special interest in either. Once money is there, it is not yours any more. Your interest in the pot is based entirely on your prospects of winning part of it. If the prospects are poor, get out!

It is true, as we shall see, that the size of a pot can often determine whether you should call bets on marginal or speculative hands. But the size of the *pot* is what counts, not the amount you have contributed to it.

Just as you do not stubbornly call reraises, you often should not call *both* a bet and raise ahead of you, even though you would have called the bet alone. If a player has bet with an Ace, and someone between you and him has raised with a 2, your hand of a 7 with a lower card and a higher card no longer looks so good.

This brings us to the question of when *you* should raise on the first round. Some disagreement exists among good players on this point. My experience, however, persuades me that sound raises are uncommon at this stage of the betting.

I virtually never raise in early (or "poor") position—i.e., when I am near the left of the first bettor. The reason is that if I hold a promising hand, I do not want to drive other players out of the competition.

When we discuss High poker, we shall see that situations occur when it is good tactics in poor position to make the price too high for later potential callers to stay. At Hi-Lo, however, the danger in this maneuver is that you may drive out the wrong players. These would be the ones competing against each other in the opposite direction from you. You want their contributions to the half of the pot you hope to win.

Also, with just a moderately good hand, while you are pleased to play, it is well to keep things at least relatively inexpensive until you see another card or so. While you are willing to call a maximum bet at this point, if you raise, you are subject to a *re*raise by someone behind you who may have an exceptionally good starting hand.

If *you* have an excellent starting hand of three low cards, you surely do not want to scare off players still waiting to call. About the only time I raise on the first round is when the opening bettor is very near my left and thus I am the last or perhaps penultimate player to act. In this "good position," the other callers' money is already in the pot. They will likely call the raise in this event, and with three in the Ace-7 range, I want them to put more there.

Remember the Folded Cards—You will recall that I have mentioned that the exposed cards around the table should sometimes influence your decision of whether to stay. By the same token, cards you have seen folded may sometimes be important to a later decision, and thus they should be remembered.

Many inexperienced or casual card players complain that they cannot remember cards. I contend that with alertness and a bit of practice, almost anyone can train himself to remember at least most of the cards he sees folded during the early rounds—particularly cards that are potentially important to his own hand, such as low cards, cards that match his own, or cards of a suit in which he holds a potential flush.

Particularly on the first betting round, an attentive player should have no problem in remembering the folded cards: rather typically in a seven-handed game, only about two will be folded at this point. I do not mean that five players will ordinarily have *sound* calls. But in the usual poker group, a few players will likely be present who will stay for the fourth card on just about any excuse, especially when no raises occur ahead of them.

THE FOURTH CARD

With the great majority of hands, sound play on the second betting round—in other words, after the fourth card is dealt—will involve the continued strategy of playing for low. Thus if you have started with a three-card hand of two low and one high (the commonest staying hand), the fourth card must help to justify staying further. The commonest "busted" hand will contain two low cards and two high cards; a hand like that should be folded.

Playable four-card hands are as follows:

At least three cards in the low (Ace-7) range. (Remember that if two cards are paired, only one can be considered as a "low" card. By the same criteria, two pairs are not worth playing.)

An 8,Ace, and one card in the 2-6 range. (8,7,Ace,X* is not quite worth a play unless the odd high card happens to be a 9, or unless the total hand contains three to a flush.)

---

*X indicates an indifferent card—in this example a high one.

Four cards to a flush.
Four cards to a straight.*
Three cards to a straight flush.
Three of a kind. (Needless to say, this criterion would include that *rare* circumstance when you may catch four of a kind.)

Some of these criteria should be modified when the other players' exposed cards alter the normal prospects for improving the hand with subsequent cards. For example, if you are drawing to a flush, it is generally better to abandon the hand if more than two cards of your suit have been shown in other hands.** Four to a straight should not be played if more than *one* card needed to complete it has been exposed.**

Three of a kind ("trips") should usually not be played further if more than a single card that would improve the hand has been seen. For example, K,K,K,2 should be folded if the other K and a 2, or two 2s, are no longer available. (Trip Aces are an exception: play this hand regardless of other cards.)

In good position, raise on the fourth card with four in the Ace-7 range. Any of three more cards can give you a probably winning low, and you may "accidentally" fall into a good high hand if the later cards are right.

Also raise on a four-flush with three of the cards in the Ace-7 range. You have good prospects at least for making either a good high or low, and sometimes you will make both.

At the risk of becoming tedious, I shall mention three other rarely-held four-card hands always worth a raise in good position: four to a straight flush; precisely 5,6,7,8 (note the four-straight with three cards in the low range); and obviously four of a kind.

In poor position, raising is generally inadvisable with the preceding good hands. You do not want to frighten potential callers from contributing to that pot in which you expect to share.

Once again, exposed cards may alter your strategy. For example, suppose you hold 3,4,5,7 and are in good position to

---

*Here and elsewhere, when I speak of four (or three) to a straight, I mean cards in exact sequence, such as 6,7,8,9. A holding of 6,7,9,10, missing the 8, would involve drawing to an "inside straight," an unsound play in any but unusual circumstances not under consideration here. In Hi-Lo, of course, we *do* draw to an inside straight such as 5,6,7,9, but that is because three cards are in the Ace-7 range. The possibility of hitting the straight is merely a bonus feature.

**Unless, of course, the hand contains a compensating feature of other criteria for staying, such as three cards in the Ace-7 range.

raise. However, suppose you have seen a couple of the 6s and three or four of the Aces and 2s. Your chances for improvement are greatly diminished, and you should do no more than call. In fact, if you have seen half the cards you need and a raise has been made ahead of you, you might even consider folding this normally fine hand—particularly if the raiser appears also to be playing for low.

On the other hand, if the exposed low cards consist mainly of other 3s, 4s, 5s, and 7s, your hand becomes even better than ever. Several cards are eliminated that you would not want to catch.

THE FIFTH CARD

The fifth card represents something of a pivotal point in a hand. It should be noted first that the expert player, which you plan to be, will not even be in the majority of hands at the fifth card. (In fact, he will have played his first *three* cards little more than half the time.)

If a hand is played beyond the fifth card, however, it usually will be one with such possibilities that it should be played to the end. I certainly do not mean that you should always stay around stubbornly beyond that point if things develop badly. I am simply mentioning that a five-card hand worth playing will normally continue to remain worth playing until the seventh.

A generalization can be made that you should play the fifth card only when you need but one more to make a probably winning hand.* However, the appraisal of a probable winner now depends more than before on the other players' exposed cards.

Four in the Ace-7 range should practically always be played. Exceptions do occur, however, when a couple or more opponents show nothing but *very* low cards and someone is betting as if his hand is already made. On the other hand, a potential 8 for low can begin to look rather good at this point if the other players show predominantly high cards and have begun to pair their low ones.

Recall that I advised at the beginning of the hand to play "trips," even though some controversy exists among experts on this matter at Seven Hi-Lo—Cards Speak. The reason for my stand on this issue is best explained now.

It would not be worth playing trips from the beginning on

---

*Obviously you will continue to play, and raise in good position, in the rare circumstance when your hand is already made: 7 or better for low, a straight, a flush, etc.

the lone prospect that by themselves they will win half the pot. However, they will often do so. And about two chances in five exist that four more cards will improve the hand to a full house. This will only rarely fail to win.

At the time a five-card hand is obtained is the most important point to reappraise the prospects for a full house. This will be true both in the circumstance when you had trips from the beginning and when you happen to have caught them along the way. It usually will have been relatively inexpensive to stay until now. On the next two betting rounds, however, remember that the limit doubles; raises also will be likely.

Usually when you receive your fifth card, you will have seen about 20 cards altogether (your five plus all other exposed cards and those you have seen folded). If you have three of a kind and two unmatching cards, there now are seven more that will make a full house. If these all remain in the deck, you have two more chances to catch one. Also, if you fail to catch on the sixth card, there will remain three additional cards that would help. In a sense, then, the odds are about 17 in 32 that you eventually will make the full house (or rarely four of a kind)— provided the cards that will help remain undealt.* If only one card that would help has been seen, the chances are still almost even. However, if more than two have been seen, the chances of completing the full house become quite a long shot. In this case, you should consider abandoning the hand.

Before folding, however, it is well to appraise the possibility of winning with only the trips. Are pairs showing that are higher in rank than your trips? Are any three-card straights or flushes exposed?

Also, in a borderline decision, does your hand retain at least *some* chance, albeit small, to develop into a good low? Still another feature of your trips can influence a borderline decision: namely whether the trips are completely concealed. By this I mean that two of the three are in the hole. Trips under that circumstance are far better than when a pair (or more) is in sight, because the competition will have little reason to suspect the true strength of your hand. At the end, players may stay in with mediocre high hands merely because no other high strength is showing.

Finally, half the pot may be large enough that a long-shot try for four of a kind may be an influence if you can call cheaply and your position relieves the fear of a raise.

At the fifth card, a four-flush or four-straight should

---

*Or, more accurately, remain *unseen*. The hole cards in folded hands cannot be appraised, and for purposes of figuring the odds, they must be included among the 32 cards outstanding.

normally be played. Three to a straight flush are not worth playing unless nearly all the potential helping cards are still available and your position is so good that little or no danger exists of a raise behind you.

Two pairs are usually not worth playing. The chances of making a full. house are too slim, and the chance of winning high without such help is not sufficient to make the play worthwhile. Observe, however, that if you have played properly to this point and happen to find yourself making two pairs, you probably will also have three cards in the Ace-7 range. Thus, if the opponents' "boards" (exposed hands) appear weak, do not *automatically* abandon two pairs. While the individual chances for high or low are small, the combined chances can sometimes make a call a reasonable gamble in late position.

With few exceptions, raising is seldom indicated on the fifth card unless the hand is already made. However, if I do happen already to have drawn a probable winner, I will raise at every opportunity. Position becomes less important at this point. Although I *may* drive someone out that I want to play, more commonly players who will stay on a five-card hand will call a raise too.

A few other five-card hands also merit raises. These are four-straights and four-flushes with four of the five cards in the Ace-7 range.

THE SIXTH CARD

While exceptions occur, the criteria for playing the sixth card generally resemble those for playing the fifth. Bet and raise strongly if you have already made a probable winner. Stay with four in the Ace-7 range unless the betting and exposed cards make it highly apparent that an opponent has already drawn a better low than you can hope to make. If the opponents show generally high cards and pairs, appraise the possibility that you may win low with a hand higher than 7. Even a 9 can occasionally begin to look good.

If three of a kind have been played to this point (or if the sixth card makes the trips), the draw for the full house is usually justified. The odds of making this good hand will generally be only about one in three now, and perhaps not quite that good, but the money in the pot will normally justify the try. However, if too many of the cards you need have been exposed, and if opponents convince you with their betting and exposed cards that trips will not win without improvement, accept the bad luck and fold the hand.

Four to a straight or flush should normally be played. Again, however, if the raising and exposed cards convince you that you will not win even with a good draw, save your money. Your opponents will make things expensive for you, not only on this round but on the last one also.

At this point of the game, consideration should sometimes be given to winning high with two pairs if no other pair is showing. You may even think of staying if you do see another pair, lower than your highest, held by a player who is not raising. Two pairs are usually not worth playing, however, if it appears that you *must* draw a full house on the last card to have a chance at winning. The odds are just too slim under most circumstances.

During the late rounds of betting, a common occurrence is to find two players raising each other at every opportunity. Typically, one of these will have an evident high hand and the other a low one. On the sixth card, you will sometimes find yourself the "man in the middle" of this situation. If your hand is not yet made, but you have an excellent draw to a hand that will probably win if made, you may want to keep that draw as inexpensive as possible.

Remember that the rules we assume involve a $2 limit at this stage, but a 25¢ minimum, and only three raises are allowed. You can use one of these raises with a 25¢ bet, thus depriving the opponents of at least one opportunity to make you pay more for your speculative draw.

The preceding note may give insight into why some limit on the number of raises is a desirable feature of poker rules—and virtually a necessity at Hi-Lo. Otherwise two people with excellent hands could take a totally unfair advantage of a third player—wiping him out on a single hand or depriving him of a legitimate opportunity to compete in the hand.

THE SEVENTH (AND LAST) CARD

The last card is dealt down, as a third hole card. Thus, you have already seen all the exposed cards that you will see. Little needs to be added about strategy at this point. If a "made" hand has been played to this point, it virtually always is worth calling all bets on the final betting round. Occasionally, a good hand one way will be made even better by the last card. Occasionally an excellent hand one way (particularly when you started with a potential low) will be converted into a two-way winner—such as by completing a straight or flush.

You should generally raise, and reraise if possible, if you know you have a probable winner. Now and then, however, some restraint may be expedient if you expect that overly vigorous raising may drive out a potential loser who might otherwise call.

Obviously if you took the last card on speculation, your action will depend on whether the card helped. With a mediocre hand, it generally is worth continuing to play at this stage unless you are absolutely convinced that you are beaten both ways. Remember the maneuver of the minimum raise (25¢ under the rules we assume) when you suspect you are *likely* beaten but do not want to give up at this late point.

Occasionally there will be four competitors at the showdown in a hand of Seven Hi-Lo, and rarely even more. In the typical hand, however, the showdown will involve three competitors, usually one with a good high, one with a good low, and the loser—whichever way he happened to be going. But while that is the commonest situation, some oddities occasionally are seen, especially at Cards Speak.

For example, all players may have been playing low hands, and just a small pair or even an Ace may win the high half of the pot. In rare situations, everyone may turn up with high hands, e.g., full houses or trips, but no flushes or straights. In this situation, a *pair* may turn out to win low. Remember that the best five of the seven cards are selected for the winning hand. It may be that no one can find five cards not containing a pair. The lowest pair would, of course, win low. For this purpose, a pair of Aces can be used as the lowest pair—even if these same Aces work as high cards in the other direction.

An actual hand that I once played may illustrate the type of strange development that can occur in this game. I never expect to see this *exact* one again, but it did happen.

I began to play for low, started pairing, but continued to play because of a good possibility for a flush. Instead of the flush, I made Ks full. Exceptionally heavy betting by several players during early rounds made the pot quite large. At the end, however, only one other player remained—with exposed cards suggesting an excellent low. The raising by the two of us had driven everyone else out.

I was astonished at the showdown to see my opponent turn up his hole cards to complete a hand of four Aces. This permitted him to win the entire pot. The hands:

> His hand: Ace,Ace,Ace,Ace,5,4,3
> My hand: K,K,K,2,2,4,3
> His high hand: Four of a kind
> His low hand: Ace,Ace,5,4,3
> My high hand: Full house
> My low hand: 2,2,K,4,3

It is uncommon, but not rare, to have a full house beaten for high. But I was beaten *both* ways by a *single* opponent!

By further coincidence, that particular opponent happened to be one of my closest friends. Well, except for normal courtesy, friendships are suspended during a poker game. But the next day, he bought me an excellent lunch at the fine Su Casa Mexican restaurant in Chicago.

A Few Rules and Common Customs •

"LET'S SPLIT"'

Fairly often only two players will find themselves competing for the pot. From that point on, if the pot is eventually split, any additional money won will simply be what each contributes. Very commonly, the two players will simply agree to split the pot and not play out the hand further.

Under strictest rules,[7] this practice is considered unethical; it suggests the possibility of a partnership arrangement—illegal in poker by any standards. However, such splitting is often tolerated— even encouraged to speed the game—in groups in which the players know each other well. I have no objection to it prior to the final betting round provided there is no reason to suspect that any particular two players have an advance agreement that they will try to drive competitors out of pots for the purpose of dividing the money.

Such a voluntary splitting is fairly routine in Hi-Lo poker in some groups during the early betting rounds. Note that at *any* time, the only reason why a player should insist on playing out the hand against a single opponent is the prospect of winning both high and low. And naturally, a player who follows this course usually runs some risk of the disagreeable development in which he turns out *losing* both ways.

During early rounds, my advice is to refuse to split only if you have an excellent start for low. For example, suppose on the first round you have three very low cards to an Ace. Almost always, you will have the single opponent at a severe disadvantage; with four more cards to come to both of you, you will seldom lose both ways, and a reasonable prospect exists for a two-way winner. You should make that opponent call maximum bets if he wants to stay in and try for half the pot. During these early rounds, I recommend this tactic only if you have one of those versatile Aces, which can swing both high and low. During late rounds, you should refuse to split if you are reasonably sure of having the best hand one way—plus some prospect of winning the other way too.

If *you* are the potential victim of a single opponent who insists on your paying to draw against his potential two-way winner, you must judge whether enough money is already in the pot to justify your bucking the odds to try for half of it. I will return to this matter briefly when we consider Hi-Lo with declarations.

PLAYING LIGHT

Under the rules of some poker games, a player is forbidden to take money from his pocket for betting purposes during the play of a hand. Once a deal has started, his stake is limited to his money (or chips) on the table. The term for this limit is "Table Stakes."

It will be more convenient to postpone until a later chapter the discussion of settling the pot when the table-stakes rule applies and a player runs out of money on the table before he can call all bets. In most private games with fixed betting limits, such as we are primarily discussing now, players are permitted to play "light."

Under this custom, a player is permitted (and normally expected) to use money in his pocket for betting if he wants to play out a hand beyond his monentary resources on the table.* Ordinarily, the player will likely be permitted merely to owe the pot until the winners are determined and not be required actually to produce the cash during the middle of the hand. To keep account of the amount owed, when the temporarily deficient player makes or calls a bet, he takes that amount from the pot and sets it aside on the table just in front of his hand. If he eventually loses the hand, that sum set aside is, of course, still part of the pot, and he must match it from his pocket (plus replenishing his stake on the table for use in future hands if he continues to play).

"'LIGHTS' GO TO THE OTHER WINNER"

If the player who is light wins half the pot, a convenient means of settlement is available without the use of cash from the pocket. The other winner merely takes *all* of the money set aside as "light." Then, the two winners divide the remainder of the pot.

The equity of this arrangement can readily be seen through an example. Suppose a pot contains $25 in actual cash (or chips), but one of the two winners is $5 light. Thus, the pot really is worth $30. $20 is in the center of the table, $5 is aside, and $5 is owed. The light player *could* add $5, and then each winner would receive $15. But it is just as well for the non-light player to take the $5 that was set aside, plus $10 from the middle. The light player takes the other $10 from the middle; his $5 is still in his pocket, and thus he has really "received" his fair $15 share. He has merely avoided the bother of putting the extra $5 in and then taking it back. This custom speeds the game and is a convenience.

Occasionally both winners will be light—ordinarily by a different

---

*Naturally, the time can come when a player may exhaust his total resources for a session and thus be unable to play light. In this case, when his money runs out, he will be permitted to compete for a reduced portion of the pot. Again, however, detailed discussion of the settlement is deferred until a later chapter.

amount. In this circumstance, each will take the *other's* light stack of chips, and then they will divide equally what remains in the middle. If you have any doubts about the equity of this custom, you can readily work out an example that will illustrate that it automatically creates a fair settlement.

THE CARDS SPEAK FOR THEMSELVES

Standard rules of poker require that every player active to the showdown expose his entire hand for the purpose of determining the winner(s). This rule is often waived. A losing player, after calling all bets and then seeing that he is beaten, may simply fold his open cards and never show his hole cards. A player may keep one or two hole cards hidden if they are not relevant to his winning the pot. This tactic is employed to prevent the opponents from gaining insight, for purposes of future hands, into the player's method of play. (It may also be employed by a loser simply from embarrassment over his sorry hand.)

If no one asks to see these hidden cards, the matter is moot. However, *any* player, whether still in competition or not, has a *right* to see every card that is played to the showdown.

That fact leads to another facet of the rule. A positive advantage can occasionally accrue to a player who voluntarily exposes his cards. Namely, he may have misread his hand and have a winner he failed to see.

Naturally, a player will not be allowed to win or share in a pot unless he proves his right to it by showing his cards. But if a player's hand is in view, anyone at the table may point out a winning five-card combination that the owner may have overlooked among the seven. It is, in fact, a duty of other players to call attention to such oversights when recognized.

No player should resent losing a pot to someone who initially failed to recognize a better hand. Regardless of what hand a player *thinks* he holds, the cards speak for themselves—provided anyone at the table recognizes their value.

If, instead of exposing his hand, a player tosses it among the discards, virtually no poker group will allow him to retrieve it for reconsideration; he has surrendered any right he might have had to win. That fact can create a rather Solomon-like dilemma if efforts are made to enforce rules strictly. While another player has a "right" to see the hand, it is improper to look through the discards, and the hand has now become, in effect, part of the "discards." I suggest that you avoid all such problems by exposing your cards at the showdown.

This may be the time to mention that a mere onlooker, or "kibitzer," has neither the duty nor the right to point out oversights or discrepancies. Anyone who watches a poker game without playing in it is nothing but a tolerated guest. He should maintain silence and participate in no way.

(To avoid confusion, I will point out that a player who fails to call a bet has no requirement or need to reveal his cards: he is not *involved* in any showdown.)

AN IMPROPRIETY FREQUENTLY COMMITTED

Please recall from page 8 that the dealer has certain obligations at Stud Poker. He calls attention to the high hand on each round and thus to the player with the first turn to act; he announces the appearance of three-card (and four-card) straights and flushes. However, I mentioned that he should *not* announce possible straight-flushes.

I deferred discussion of the reason because many readers will choose to skip that section—yet many experienced poker players are unaware of the rule about this impropriety. It is improper to announce "Possible straight-flush," because one may or may *not* be possible—depending on whether one or more necessary cards have shown around the board—and perhaps but not necessarily have been folded. If the dealer has failed to notice, he should not announce a possibility that may not exist. If he knows a necessary card *has* appeared, he surely should not mislead less observant players. And even if he knows the cards are still in the deck, he should not be so helpful as to inform the unobservant and penalize the more watchful players.

When a "possible" straight-flush is on board, the dealer should merely announce "Possible flush." It is up to the players themselves now to determine whether a straight-flush is also possible.

THE EIGHT-PLAYER GAME

For convenience, I have assumed seven players for our Seven Hi-Lo game. With that number (or less), no possibility exists for the 52-card deck to be depleted even if all players stay to the end and take seven cards (7 x 7 = 49).*

You undoubtedly have observed, however, that the usual poker table for home and club use is octagonal and thus conveniently accommodates eight players. Seven-Card Stud is often played with eight players, and problems only rarely arise. The problem that *can* arise, because of the lack of 56 cards in a deck, is easily resolved if anticipated: if, when the betting is completed after the fifth card is dealt, and it is evident that insufficient cards remain to give everyone a total of seven, the dealer announces that the winner(s) shall be

---

*At least there is no such possibility as the game is usually dealt; in some games, a card is "burned" before each round, but I will defer discussion of this.

decided by a six-card hand. No one will receive a seventh card.*

The possibility of this occurrence is often eliminated early. After all, if two of the eight players fold on the first two rounds, sufficient cards will remain. However, the dealer must become alert to the possibility of insufficient cards when seven players remain active after two rounds.

It is important to mention now another rule of poker: *the last card is never dealt*. Thus, while the deck contains 52 cards, only 51 are playable.

USE OF TWO DECKS

Serious poker players prefer a fast game—or at least one in which unproductive delays are avoided. Clearly, the time involved with shuffling the cards between deals is unproductive time. Some poker groups in which I have played employ an innovation borrowed from Bridge: the use of two decks of different color.

When player A (see page 6) is dealing the red deck, player C will shuffle the blue deck. Immediately after the round with the red deck is finished, the blue deck will be ready for player A to cut and for player B to deal. While player B deals the blue deck, player D will shuffle the red deck. And so on.

TABLE-STAKES LIMIT AND POT-LIMIT POKER

I have mentioned previously that in some games, during the play of a particular hand, the player is restricted to betting only the money he has on the table. Some high-stake games place *no* limit on the size of bets except these table stakes. Regardless of the size of the ante or the pot, a player may bet as much as he wishes—providing he takes no money from his pocket between the beginning of a hand and the showdown. Thus, there are no *fixed* limits.

Some other games employ a pot limit: a player may bet any amount not exceeding the size of the pot at that moment. As the pot builds, the limit rises. If play is aggressive, it is evident that bets can rise to astronomical levels in relation to the ante. Note that if the ante is $2 and player A bets $2, matching the pot, player B may call the $2 and raise $6, because his call brought the pot to $6. Player C may now call the bet and raise ($8 total) and reraise $20, bringing the pot now to $40!

Usually, pot-limit games will also employ the table-stakes feature: regardless of how large the pot becomes, each player is further limited to betting no more than he has on the table. If a player runs out of money during the play of a hand, he competes for only that

---

*Another method of dealing with the problem will be given when the casino version of poker is discussed, but the one above is the commonest used.

part of the pot to which he has contributed his share. Further explanation of this latter feature of table-stakes play is given later.

Please recall that the instruction in this book is generally oriented to the more common fixed-limit game.

OBSERVE THE AMENITIES

One of the commonest irregularities at poker, usually committed accidentally, is to act out of turn. This is universally resented by serious players, and you should be cautious to avoid it. It usually is to the disadvantage of the player who makes the improper call, but it also can penalize others in the competition.

Many other "standard" improprieties are probably as often honored in the breach as in the observance. We have noted, for example, that rules require all hands involved in a showdown to be exposed and that no one look through the discards. It is also improper for a player who has folded to look into active players' hands as play continues. It is improper for one player to bet for another one who has temporarily stepped away from the table.

However, if your group tolerates these irregularities, and many do, I suggest that you not object. I merely point them out to advise you not to be *first* to commit them if you are a new member; some people will insist on certain proprieties.

I suggest *Official Rules of Card Games*[7] for a useful guide to the many formal rules of poker, including the correction of irregularities. Even there, however, you will find that many rules are left to the option and custom of the particular group. Most disputes in private poker sessions are settled amicably by arbitration.

One rule of considerable importance and rather generally accepted is that each player is responsible for his own hand. If it contains too many cards, through the dealer's error or otherwise, it is dead and cannot win the pot. (Of course, no one is required to accept an extra card accidently dealt, but he must note the error and refuse the card immediately—without looking at it.)

An accidentally exposed card must be played by its holder. However, if the dealer accidently exposes a hole card, the player's next up card (if any) should be dealt down.

Seven Hi-Lo with Declarations

Many poker games require that before the showdown, all active players must announce whether they are competing for high, low, or both. A player cannot win in one way unless he declares in that way. A player who declares in both directions must win in both directions or he loses *all* the pot. Even if he is tied in either direction, the fact that he may have the best hand in the other is immaterial: he wins nothing. Note that if all players declare in the same direction, the winner takes the entire pot.

SIMULTANEOUS DECLARATIONS

Two forms of declarations exist, and the game is quite different depending on which is used. Simultaneous Declarations is regarded by most experts as a superior form of poker, and I shall discuss it first.

After the last betting round and before the showdown, all active players must designate simultaneously whether they are attempting to be the high winner, the low winner, or both. The customary and convenient way to make these announcements is for the players to hide (or pretend to hide) chips (or coins) in their closed fists. This hiding is usually done with the fists under the table. The fists are then held over the table and opened at the same time. While a poker group can devise any code it chooses, the usual one is for an empty fist to indicate that a player is going low. One chip indicates high. Two indicate both ways.

Representation—The reason Consecutive Declarations (or "Chips Declare") requires superior skill to Cards Speak is principally because of the influence of deceptive representations. A player's four exposed cards may strongly suggest either a high or a low hand when in fact the three hole cards turn the true strength in the other direction. While this feature of Hi-Lo is not absent in Cards Speak, its only influence in that game is to lead players into betting against hands that are misinterpreted. In Chips Declare, it may also lead a player with a potentially winning hand to declare in the wrong direction. Sometimes a player who successfully misrepresents his hand may win the entire pot after declaring in only one direction—provided all other players have been led into declaring the same way.

A related feature involves two-way winners. At Cards Speak, a player with a good winning hand in one direction may accidentally win in the other direction too with mediocre values—merely by exposing his cards. If a declaration is required, a player with a near-certain winner in one direction must use great discretion if he calls in the other direction. While this feature of Hi-Lo is not absent in ways must win both ways or he loses the entire pot.

Obviously, most hands will not lend themselves to effective misrepresentation. The player has no control over just how the exposed cards may fall. Thus, the majority of hands will be won or lost in about the same manner either at Chips Declare or Cards Speak. However, the player who is alert to the opportunities that appear from time to time will frequently be rewarded at declaration poker.

For example, suppose you start with three 6s, and the next (exposed) card is a 2. Since your trips are concealed, your hand will appear to be a good start for low. You should raise vigorously. This reasonably good start for high would warrant nothing more than a call at Cards Speak. But with declarations, it has enormous potential.

Suppose the next card is a mediocre 8. Whether to raise or merely call depends on the board. If the opponents catch high (non-pairing) cards, continue to bet enthusiastically; if they catch low cards, feign some disappointment and merely call.

Suppose now that the sixth card pairs the 8—or the 2—or that even it is the fourth 6! The trap is set. You have apparently busted your "low" hand. If it is your bet, you check; you call other players' bets—seemingly with the hope of drawing a lucky seventh card.

After the seventh card (which is down), you resume aggressive betting and raising. Everyone at the table will think you have completed your low. At least half the time, all other active players will call high—just as you will do. Very seldom will your full house fail to win. And unless someone has luckily (or perceptively?) called low, you will win the entire pot.

Similarly, a low hand may occasionally appear to be high. A summarized illustration assumes that cards have fallen in such a way as to justify your staying all the way. You started with Ace,2 concealed. You caught, say, three 5s up—or perhaps two low pairs—and bet aggressively as your high hand developed. If the seventh card happens to complete an excellent low hand, you may take the entire pot when everyone else calls low. And when this fortunate opportunity for a misrepresentation fails to develop, you are still very much in the competition for high.

During the middle of a hand, a misrepresentation, or "bluff," may sometimes be used to drive a dangerous opponent out of the competition. The ploy is somewhat risky but effective often enough to be remembered.

Suppose you have started with three low cards but the next two match each of your hole cards to make two pairs. Say two opponents have nothing but high cards showing and each has made a high exposed pair early (not Aces). Both remain in the hand—perhaps betting strongly. (These are likely poor players, but that is beside the point.) A fourth player, who started with a 2 up, has caught a mediocre 8 and then a 9.

You have essentially ruined your hand. Your chances either of drawing two good low cards or of making a full house are rather slim. Equally cogent, the board shows a fair possibility that even if you made a full house if would lose to a higher one.

However, the player with 2,8,9 very probably started with a low hand like you. He likely is equally disappointed by his draws. Nevertheless, if you play your hand timidly at this point, he may suspect something and hang around. If you raise aggressively, he will probably be intimidated by your *apparently* excellent low and fold his hand. Thus, you have eliminated your most threatening competitor. You now expect eventually to take the low half of the pot and let the two remaining high players fight each other for the other half. And normally you should continue to raise consistently to the bitter end—both to make the high players contribute to your share and to intimidate either from trying for low on a busted high hand and mediocre low values.

(Note that at Cards Speak, your initial raise to drive out the low competitor would have been a more doubtful play. Even if it succeeds, without the necessity to declare there is too much danger that at least one of the high players may "accidentally" beat you for low.)

It should be noted that when you have succeeded with your misrepresentation in limiting your competition to high players, one of these may see at the end that he is beaten for high on board—i.e., that his other high competitor's exposed cards alone beat his entire hand.* In this case, his only chance whatever would be to call low against you. In this circumstance, however, if you have continued your bluff by betting and raising aggressively after the seventh card, he will very probably throw away the hand without calling.

Other examples could be given of circumstances when you may misrepresent an excellent hand or a relatively poor one to your advantage. Further discussion could become wearisome. The preceding illustrations were presented to give insight into the principles of such strategies. You must remain alert to take advantage of opportunities to outwit your opponents in specific situations as they arise. The counterpart of the strategies is to keep aware of the possibility that another good player may employ such deceptive practices against you. However, if you are more skillful than most of your opponents, you will deceive them successfully far more often than they will deceive you. Knowledge of your opponents' habits and relative ability, through prior observation, will give you a further edge.

"Swing" hands—Two-way calls (or "swings") are obviously very risky. Even the best high hand that also contains a perfect low (6,4,3,2,Ace) can lose the entire pot if someone ties the perfect low. Thus much discretion must be used, based both on the opponents' exposed cards and the vigor of the betting.

If I have a reasonable probability (no certainty) of winning in each direction, I will try for the entire pot. I am much less likely to do so, however, if I have a certain or near-certain winner for half and only that "reasonable probability" for the other half.

In other words, if I know that half of the pot can be mine, but must risk it to *try* to win the other half, I must feel that my chances of winning that other half are well above even to make the gamble worthwhile. On the other hand, if I know I *may* be beaten in either

---

*We assume for the continuation of the example that your sixth and seventh cards have failed to give you either a good high or good low.

direction but do not expect to be, then I am willing to make two separate gambles at once to try for everything. I am not potentially sacrificing any half of which I can be *sure*. And if I do happen to be beaten in one direction but not the other, and have timidly tried in only one direction, about half the time I will have guessed wrong and lost the whole thing anyway.

The commonest swing hand is one containing a low straight. (E.g., Ace,2,3,4,5,6,K contains a perfect low and a 6-high straight.) Caution is necessary against a player with exposed cards suggesting a higher straight—or a flush—particularly if he is betting as if he has what you fear. If you can probably win low and also have a straight, be very careful if an opponent has an evident high hand with a pair exposed. If he has been raising, you had better believe he has a full house. True, he *might* raise on trips, but this is unlikely except as a bluff, as *your* exposed cards *must* have alerted him to a possible straight.

Be sure to note a situation in which an opponent with a high straight could deign not to raise. Suppose your exposed cards contain four in the same suit—or even three. If you can win low and see a strong possibility of a straight against you, you had better actually *have* that flush if you intend to swing.

I mentioned earlier that, despite the rules we assume in this book, I prefer rules in which straights and flushes swing—i.e., they can count high, low, or both. This dual evaluation is sometimes called the "California scale." As you play Hi-Lo poker, you will be surprised by the number of Ace,2,3,4,5 hands you will see—just a straight under traditional rules, but also a perfect low by the California scale. Less common but not rare are low flushes that can be used only in competition for high.

With the California scale, more swing hands occur. This favors the expert at declaration poker, merely because he can use his judgment more often in situations recently discussed, while the weak players have the opportunity to make unsound two-way calls more often.

The greater frequency of swing hands with the California scale can create some situations in declaration poker that are highly unusual with the traditional scale. Suppose three players remain at the end, Players A and B both have perfect lows (which are also straights), and both swing. They tie, and player C wins the entire pot *regardless of what hand he holds.* (Note that at Cards Speak, however, A and B would have split the pot unless C could have beaten them high. If C *did* beat them high, he, of course, would take half the pot and A and B would take one-fourth each; I mention this merely as a review of previous instructions on how pots are split.*)

---

*When a tie occurs for half and the pot contains an odd chip, the sole winner of the other half takes the chip.

A bit more common, the tie of a swing hand may allow a relatively poor hand to take half the pot from a better hand. Suppose A has played trips—or has busted a try for low by making two pairs. Player B swings with a low straight. Player C wins (or ties) for low and takes the low half. Player A calls high and wins the other half—just through the good fortune of C's low hand. In similar vein, a mediocre low hand may win against a good one that swings and is beaten for high by another player.

When to Stay—Declarations vs. Cards Speak—Declaration poker is so different in some ways from Cards Speak that many experts make subtle distinctions between the requirements for playing a hand during the early stages. In the fixed-limit game that we assume in this book, I believe the requirements at Declarations remain the same as those I recommended at Cards Speak. However, you should be aware that a particular hand at one game can be slightly better or worse at another. This fact can become especially important if you happen to find yourself in a pot-limit or table-stakes game.

Practically everyone agrees that early trips constitute a good hand that definitely should be played at declaration poker. I also recommended that they be played cautiously at Cards Speak. In high-limit games, however, I would *not* play high trips at Cards Speak unless they were Aces (which is a quite good hand because of the swinging nature of Aces). Three of a kind in the 2-7 range are borderline.

At *high limit* Cards Speak, in fact, I would not play any three-card hand that failed to offer *some* prospect for an eventual low. (The possible exception is a moderately high open-ended straight flush.) The competitors with low hands have chances ultimately of completing a good low *or* drawing out against your high. If you have only a good start for high, you have no such dual possibilities.

Thus, the highest three-card straight that should be played is 7,8,9 (at least you have *one* in the Ace-7 range). A three-card flush, which is more difficult to complete than a straight, should probably have two in the Ace-7 range—or certainly no more than one card higher than 8.

The preceding leads to consideration of a few early playable hands at Cards Speak that should be folded at *high-limit* Declarations. The 7,8,9 just discussed should not be played in the latter game. Even 6,7,8 is doubtful.* No three-card flush should be played without two in the Ace-7 range.

The reason these middle-sized straights and relatively high flushes should not be played at the beginning in pot- or table-stakes limit

---

*Note that in the high-limit game under temporary consideration, if your only two cards in the Ace-7 range are precisely 6 and 7, their playable quality is quite borderline in declaration poker.

involves a fairly common dilemma that can occur at the end of the hand when you find yourself with a straight (or flush) and about an 8 or 9 for low. Often you will be fairly confident you can win one way or the other, but not know which. At Cards Speak, you can call the final bet(s) and merely turn over your cards with a reasonable prospect that you will win half the pot. With declarations, you will have to guess, and with the betting very high on the last rounds, only a 50-50 chance of guessing right to win merely half the pot will offer very poor odds.

Perhaps the simplest illustration at Chips Declare involves the situation in which you remain at the end against a single opponent. Suppose you hold 3,6,7,8,9,10,Q—a 10-high straight with a 9 for low. Suppose the opponent's up-cards are Ace,2,K,K. He may make you pay the entire size of the pot if you want to stay in. (If he is clever, he may make it slightly less expensive just to tempt you to call.) The opponent *knows* whether he has, say, a full house or a perfect low. You may have no idea. You are certain you can beat him one way, but you must guess which. If you guess right, you get your money back. If you guess wrong, you lose the entire pot.

I do not suggest that more than a relatively few hands, starting with the values under consideration, will have endings similar to those just discussed. However, in view of the many ways there are to lose a hand, borderline hands should not be played at the beginning when they threaten the additional possibility that such a dilemma may develop. Similarly, if you have started with sound values but the fall of subsequent cards are such that, at about the sixth card, you see that you are eventually going to have to make a 50-50 guess at the declaration, fold the hand promptly in a high-limit game.

These considerations apply much less drastically in the fixed-limit game we generally assume for this book. Commonly there will be enough money in the pot that a 50-50 chance of winning half will justify the expense of calling to the end. Remember that when opponents are raising, you can "kill" one raise by raising the minimum (25¢), thus reducing the expense.

Thus, while I recommend playing the first three cards in a fixed-limit game in about the same manner whatever the type of Seven Hi-Lo, knowledge of the variability of the values of some hands can be of help. For example, three of a kind do not have to be played quite as cautiously at Declarations as at Cards Speak.

CONSECUTIVE DECLARATIONS

When declarations are made consecutively (i.e., in rotation), the method for calling high, low, or both is different from Chips Declare. The player who has made the last bet or raise on the final round must declare first. He does so merely by announcing orally "High," "Low," or "Both ways." Then, the other active players make their declarations orally, each in turn, in clockwise rotation. If everyone has checked on the final round, the player with the highest exposed hand must call first.

The Importance of Position—In general, the principles already discussed for declaration poker also apply in Consecutive Declarations. However, position is often of vital importance in Consecutive Declarations and will frequently dominate the betting tactics on the last round.

Half the pot is more often "stolen" with poor values in Consecutive Declarations than in Chips Declare. Particularly in our fixed-limit game, it may sometimes be advisable to stay in near the end, say at the sixth card against two players, even with a very doubtful hand—especially if there is *some* remote chance that a lucky seventh card will complete a good hand.

While exceptions will be discussed, it usually is an advantage to be last to declare—or as near to last as possible. This feature of Consecutive Declarations induces much checking, or deigning not to raise, on the last round. Remember: the last player to take aggressive action (bet or raise) must declare first. This timidity, and the frequently reduced betting action it induces on the last round (sometimes there will be none at all), is one reason why many experts consider Chips Declare a superior game. The last round is the logical climax to a poker hand, and there is something disagreeable about having everyone become reticent about betting at this point. Nevertheless, Consecutive Declarations requires some special tactical skills that must be mastered for successful play.

The great advantage of declaring last is that *any* kind of a hand can fairly often win half the pot. This can happen whenever all earlier calls are in the same direction. The last player to call can merely declare in the opposite direction and win half regardless of his hand.

Less common but not rare, if you can declare last you can sometimes win the entire pot with a good hand in only one direction. For example, if your board (exposed hand) appears low, but you actually have a concealed full house, players ahead of you may call high with trips, straights, flushes, or lower full houses. Your full house can win the pot with a similar high call.

(Of course, an early caller *can* win everything with a one-way call; rarely, everyone will go the same way and he will have the best hand. But notice that if you can call last, you have a *choice:* settle for half *or* try for everything. If you call first and have a good hand in only one direction, you *must* call in that direction to have any remote chance for the whole pot. And except as an occasional bluff, to be discussed later, you must call that way to have a chance for even half.)

Further, with mediocre values in both directions, the opportunity to call last may allow you to make a good guess in choosing which opponent to contest. Suppose you have trip 9s (two of them exposed) and a 9 for low. (You were trying for a *good* low but caught the third 9 on the last card.) You are against two opponents and are last to call.

Suppose further that the first player calls high and very much appears to have a flush. (He has four exposed clubs and he bet on the last round after you checked.) The second player calls low with a motley board (2,6,6,10).

Your only hope of winning now is that at least one opponent is making a bluffing declaration—trying to take half the pot with a busted hand against opposite calls. You must decide which is more likely attempting that tactic. While either (or both) *may* be, it is considerably more likely to be the second caller. Usually in situations like this, your educated guess should be to contest the second caller for low. Similarly, if the first call has been low and the second one high, with mediocre values both ways you should normally try for high.

The preceding leads to consideration of why, if you cannot call last, it often is better at least to be able to call second—asssuming two other players remain. (And in the typical hand, there *will* be exactly three players total at the declaration.) If you are second and hold mediocre values in both directions, you normally should call in the direction opposite to the first caller, whichever that may be. You *may* have the third caller beaten. Or he *may* be going against the first caller.

There are, of course, exceptions. Sometimes it will be obvious that the third player can beat you and almost equally clear that he will call against you if you call opposite to the first player. In this situation, about all you can do is hope that the first player has busted his hand and is making a bluffing declaration. You may, in fact, be wondering why you should still be in the hand to this point. In our examples, however, we are assuming that the betting, size of the pot, and other considerations have justified your staying. Remember: some strange situations can develop in declaration poker.

After reading the preceding portions, you may have become aware that *sometimes* there can be an advantage to calling first. If your board *appears* very strong in one direction, but you really do not have a decent hand either way, you should bet or raise aggressively. If this tactic succeeds in making you first to call, you declare in whichever direction your apparent strength lies. This may lead your opponents, even with fair hands in your direction, to call the opposite way. Even when your betting tactics fail to make you first to declare (someone else has taken the last allowable raise), your deceptive board may still intimidate everyone from calling against your apparent strength. With much raising, a player with a fair hand may have been driven out of the competition altogether. Naturally, this bluffing is less likely to succeed if someone else has an exceptionally strong board in the direction you are representing; the bluff should not be attempted if that opponent has already bet or raised aggressively.

The preceding tactic would rarely work if there were not a more frequent and normal correlation to it. That is, you should not strive unduly to call last unless you *need* that positional advantage.

For example, if you hold a very strong hand that also appears strong on board, and two or more players show strength in the opposite direction, you should bet and raise to build the pot. Make the other players contribute to your half of the pot while they fight it out for the other half.

Even if another player shows strength in your direction, you usually should bet strongly if you are reasonably sure that you can beat him. Make him pay to be the "man in the middle" between your strong hand and another strong hand the other way. The time you *might* sandbag in this situation (i.e., merely call other bets instead of raising yourself) is when you fear you would drive your potentially losing opponent out of the action. In other words, if other players are betting and raising "for you," your reticent behavior may trap an opponent going your way on borderline values.

In summary, with a near-certain winner one way, the only time you normally will strive to declare last is when your board misrepresents your true strength and your opponents' boards and actions suggest that you may win the entire pot by this positional call. And obviously, if you are confident you can win both ways, you should have no reluctance to call first: make the opponents pay if you can.

Another important tactic for the last caller with a busted hand in Consecutive Declarations involves the situation when the first caller declares both ways. If the third caller realizes that he cannot beat anyone, he merely declares in the opposite direction from the second—hoping that the second can win in his direction.

In a similar situation, *you* may be second behind a two-way call. In that circumstance, you should try to anticipate from the open strength of the third player which way he will call. If he can win in his direction, and this proves in fact to be opposite from yours, you will split the pot with him regardless of your hand.

Imagine the same thing, except that there are *two* hands behind you, one apparently high and the other low. Well, at this point, I must leave you on your own. Make the best guess you can and wait for the next hand. You can't win them all. I should point out further that only under highly unusual circumstances would you have any business even being *in* for the declaration when such a situation could arise.

A further point involves a fairly common one-on-one situation in Consecutive Declarations. The second caller then has an enormous advantage; if he plays safe, the only way he can fail to win half the pot is for the first caller to declare both ways. With a well concealed strong hand, he can win the whole pot by calling the same way as his opponent. Note that when you know you can call second in this situation, the only reason at all to initiate the betting is that you intend to declare both ways.

This brings up a matter introduced on page 23: a mutual agreement to split a pot before the final round when only two players remain.* If you can anticipate that your opponent will eventually have to declare first before the showdown, you should refuse to split unless you strongly suspect that he may have a two-way hand. Crafty players often make a "friendly" offer to split early when they realize they are going to have the disadvantage of calling first.

Before closing this chapter, clarification should be made about the requirement to show all cards upon request at the showdown. If a player wins his half of the pot uncontested in Hi-Lo (no one calls in his direction), he is not involved in any "showdown." If he wishes, he may merely throw in his hand and collect his money.

I will add that it is usually good practice *not* to show your cards when unnecessary.

---

*Unless this splitting is accepted practice by your group, please ignore the discussion. Recall from page 23 that splitting before the showdown *can* be considered unethical.

Chapter II
SEVEN-CARD STUD—
HIGH ONLY

Another of the more popular forms of poker (and reasonably so) is dealt exactly like Seven Hi-Lo just discussed. However, pots are not split;* the high hand wins all. Again, the best five cards among the seven are selected to determine the strength of the hand.

To recapitulate, the first two cards to each hand are dealt down and the third up. The first betting interval then occurs. Three more cards are dealt up (for a total of four), with a betting interval on each one. The seventh card is dealt down (for a total of three), and a final betting interval occurs before the showdown.

At each betting interval, the highest exposed hand bets (or checks) first. If exposed hands are tied for high, the first to the dealer's left bets first. Turns to bet rotate clockwise. The deal rotates clockwise between hands.

We shall continue to assume, unless otherwise noted, a game with seven or eight players and a total ante of approximately $2. The limit is $1 (25¢ minimum) until either a pair shows or the sixth card is dealt. Thereafter it is $2. A maximum of three raises per betting round applies except that the "right-to-bet" rule is employed (see page 9).

General Strategy

In Seven Hi-Lo recently discussed, eventual success demands that you win substantially more than half the times you remain active until the showdown. The reason is that on the average, you will have contributed about one-fourth of the money in the pot. Thus when you win the pot, you have only about doubled your investment.

Superficially, this rough analysis might suggest that winning half the showdowns should put you about even. But not so: you must win enough extra ones to make up for those many more hands when you

---

*Except in the unusual event of a tie.

have made some contribution to the pots (at least your share of the antes and sometimes more) and have dropped out along the way.

At Seven-Card Stud for High (Seven Hi), you can win something less than half your showdowns and still be successful, because you take the whole pot whenever you win. Once again, however, you must win often enough to make up for those contributions you make to pots when you fail to contest all the way. Thus, to be a successful player at high poker, you must still win something reasonably approaching half the hands you play to the end. A corollary to this discussion is that you must keep your contributions as small as possible to pots you do not win. You should fold hands early that fail to show reasonable possibilities of eventually winning.

A high three of a kind will win most pots. (Three 9s or so is about the *average* winning hand.) A moderately lesser hand will win often enough to be frequently worth playing, but I shall briefly postpone discussion of these matters.

At Seven Hi, somewhat fewer straights and flushes will occur than at Seven Hi-Lo. The reason is that at Hi-Lo, many such hands are made "accidentally" by players trying primarily for low. Many of these unlikely straight and flush possibilities are not worth playing at Seven Hi.

Before we proceed to the specific tactics for sound play of Seven Hi, a memorable experience I once had will illustrate the value of restricting yourself to sound play. I am referring most particularly to the principle of keeping your overall contributions low to pots you do not win.

I was in an eight-player game for almost five hours. I would estimate that about 120 hands were dealt. Stakes and limits were roughly comparable to those we usually assume for this book.*

With eight players participating in 120 deals, the "fair share" for each to win would superficially seem to be 15 (120 ÷ 8 = 15). I won exactly five pots all night (during one period, I did not win a single pot for more than two hours). Yet I still came out ahead! In fact, I *would* have come out slightly ahead if I had won only four of those five.

Admittedly, this was an unusual result. The pots I won happened to be large ones. Among the 115 I did not win, the early cards to the hands contained an abnormally few combinations to tempt me to play from the beginning. As luck had it, my busted hands tended to bust early. Thus, my overall investment in the pots remained sufficiently low that I was successful at the end even after a rather long session with generally bad cards.

---

*Actually, this was not strictly a Seven-Hi session. A modified form of "Dealer's Choice" was played; all games were high poker, but two or three forms besides Seven-Hi were occasionally dealt (these will be presented later). Nevertheless, Seven-Hi greatly predominated. And the same basic principle I am discussing applied equally to the other forms.

A poor player, however, would have played many of those hands that I refused to play. Undoubtedly he would have luckily drawn out now and then and would have won several more individual hands than I did. But he almost certainly would have been an overall loser at the end. You simply must disdain the play of hands that do not offer a potential advantage over your opponents.

When to Play

So many variables can occur in poker that it becomes impossible to discuss every nuance involving the playability of all hands. The relative value of a hand may depend greatly on the strength or weakness of opposing boards, the availability of cards you need—or those the opponents evidently need, the vigor of betting and raising, concealment of values, and position in relationship to the last bettor.

Sometimes I can point out how certain of these variables may affect your play. Sometimes I can indicate hands that should always be played—and others that should never be played (except on a "free ride" when the betting is checked all around). In many marginal situations, however, you must appraise the variables just mentioned and use judgment.

In the following sections, unless variables are specifically discussed, recommendations assume relatively normal circumstances.

THE FIRST BETTING INTERVAL

Obviously, on the first three cards, you should stay with trips.* With this fine start, you normally expect to stay for all seven cards. High trips will win more than half the time without improvement. And with any trips, you have about two chances in five of eventually making a full house.

Three cards of the same suit should be played. The exception would be the rare occurrence when you see about four of the other cards to your flush showing around the board.

Three cards to a high straight should certainly be played. Three to a low straight are less attractive (i.e., less than 8,9,10), but in our fixed limit game, they are still worthwhile.

---

*Theoretically, I could invent a situation in which you might consider folding low trips on the first round. I might imagine a situation in which a bet and three raises ahead of you could convince you that you have a poor start against higher trips. But the matter is too fanciful for serious consideration. Among other things, a player with an early three of a kind would normally not want to drive out the competition with premature raises. Also, there is only about one chance in 500 that any one hand will consist of trips with only three cards.

In pot limit, etc., I would not play three to a low straight*—for a variety of reasons. First, it is no cinch to win if you complete it. Second, other players with good hands will likely make you pay highly to try to complete it. Third, the low three-straight does not offer the attractive dual possibilities for improvement that exist with a high three-straight.

That is, when drawing to a straight, you may instead begin pairing and eventually make two pairs or trips. High trips are above average and a high two pairs gives a fighting chance. Low trips are a bit below average, and a low two pairs are markedly inferior. (Note how this principle of "two-way" possibilities is reminiscent of Hi-Lo, although now we are thinking only of dual possibilities for making a high hand.)

A pair of Aces or Ks should certainly be played. (Note how this contrasts with Seven Hi-Lo, where the pots are split and these pairs are merely traps for inferior players.)

In fact, you should normally play any pair 9s or higher. One exception would be when a raise is made ahead of you, and your moderately high pair is accompanied by a third card lower than K. Another exception is the appearance of a couple of cards around the board that you would need to improve.

With these moderately high pairs, the element of concealment becomes important. I would even call a raise if the 9s (or whatever) were both in the hole—unless cards that would help are exposed. The reason will eventually become evident; if you make a good hand later, its true strength will be hidden, and you may win a lot of money.

Low pairs (8s or less) are more problematical. They are normally worth playing if completely concealed. However, if one of the cards is exposed, a low pair should be folded unless the odd hole card is an Ace. (A K is acceptable if no Ace shows elsewhere.**) A low-pair combination like this becomes borderline if any card is seen around the board that would help the hand, and it should definitely be folded if two such cards are seen. The only time I would play an unconcealed low pair with less than a K as the other card would be with perfect position (sitting immediately to the right of the opening bettor, with no raises having been made, and thus no subsequent raises possible).

---

*Unless it contained *some* elements of a straight-flush possibility (and this is a potential straight *or* flush).

**Well, suppose *three* Aces show around the board and you hold 7,K,7. In this case, the Aces are just one card away from being "dead." The exposed low pair is then worth playing. I add this footnote only to re-emphasize that many exceptional circumstances can modify the advice I give, that I cannot feasibly explain them all, and that judgment is required in poker.

Also playable on the first round is Ace,K in the hole if none of these cards is in sight elsewhere.

On this first betting round, I would raise only in good position and with an excellent hand. Such would be trips or a concealed pair of Aces or Ks. And even in excellent position, I often would sandbag for a round.

THE FOURTH CARD (SECOND BETTING INTERVAL)

Trips naturally should be played. Raise in good position. In poor position, merely call (trapping). If you are high on board, normally bet to build the pot. (It is a bit early at this stage to use check-raise strategy.)

Play two pairs.* In good position, raise with *high* two pairs (Qs up or better) unless a higher pair is exposed against you. Also, sometimes raise with two pairs in poor position (i.e., first to the opener's left). You probably have the best hand at the moment, but it is hard to improve. You would like to drive out speculative hands that may draw out against you. However, do not *always* make this play against the same opponents, or they will eventually learn to "read" you.

If you have started with a low pair and low card, do not play further unless the fourth card is an Ace or K or otherwise improves the hand.

With three more cards to come, a four-flush is almost always worth a raise in any position. You plan to play this hand all the way. A three-flush is normally worth playing unless about four of the cards you need have shown around the board.

Similarly, four to a straight usually make a raising hand. Just call, though, if you see a couple of cards out that would complete the straight. If you see about four such cards, consider folding the hand.

A three-straight at this point requires delicate handling. Normally call if seven of the eight cards remain that will produce a four-straight.

A high pair (9s or better) should continue to be played unless it is beaten on board. If exposed cards appear favorable, raise with concealed Aces or Ks, regardless of position.

THE FIFTH CARD (THIRD BETTING ROUND)

When the fifth card is drawn (three up, two down), a pivotal point is often reached in Seven-Card Stud. If you started initially with sound but speculative values, you usually must now toss the hand if you have failed to improve.

---

*I am sure that by now you will recognize exceptions: you see cards you need, and raising is occurring by hands you suspect are already better than yours.

Three-flushes and three-straights should be abandoned. The odds are too great against catching two perfect cards with only two more to come.

A great deal of your poker success will depend on how you play two pairs at this point. A high two pairs should normally be played. However, nothing lower than Ks up should ordinarily be played if a higher pair shows around the board. You might even consider tossing Ks up if a pair of Aces shows and you have seen neither of the other Aces.*

Occasionally with two pairs, your high pair may be tied in sight. Say you hold Aces up but see a pair of Aces elsewhere. It will be very difficult to improve this hand. Whether to play should depend on your lower pair. If it is lower than 9s (8s are borderline), the hand should probably be abandoned. In close decisions, the size of your odd fifth card, and whether others like it have shown, can influence your play.

A low two pairs (8s up or less) should ordinarily be played only if *no* pair shows elsewhere and you have seen no more than one card you need to help. The size of your odd card becomes important in close decisions. If it is an Ace, and no other Aces have shown, the hand may be worth playing if only one low pair is showing against you.

Note that at this point (and in the subsequent rounds to be discussed), the appearance of cards that your *opponents* need can become a distinct influence. For example, an exposed pair by an opponent becomes much less intimidating if both of the other cards like it have shown. With two small pairs in this circumstance, a crucial decision in whether to play may depend on whether your odd card is higher than the opponent's exposed pair.

With only a single high pair after the fifth card, the number of players remaining in the hand becomes a decisive influence on whether to play further. No pair lower than Qs is worth playing, and that only against a single opponent showing no pair. Aces or Ks are worth a play against two opponents unless the hand is beaten on board. Against three or more opponents, I would not even play a pair of Aces. The exception might be if the Aces were completely concealed, neither other Ace had shown, and no opponent showed a pair. Even then, I would want some additional dual possibility for improvement, even if remote, such as a three-flush or three-straight—or an abnormally high number of my unmatching cards remaining in the deck.

Occasionally your hand will already be "made" on the fifth card, e.g., contain a straight, a flush, or rarely a full house. In this circumstance you should raise to build the pot. And you should continue to bet and raise on subsequent rounds unless the

---

*In pot limit or table stakes, you should surely do so.

appearance of the board and betting by an opponent lead you to believe you are beaten.

A high three of a kind is similarly worth a raise. Even low trips may warrant a raise against only one or two opponents evidently drawing to straights or flushes. If you and an opponent both fill, you can win a large pot. If no one fills, your trips are still good. Of course, your opponents may help while you fail to do so. But poker is a gamble. With trips against a four-flush or four-straight, the odds favor you, and you should make the opponents pay to draw.

The only time three of a kind should not be played further is the rare circumstance when higher trips are exposed against you. Four-straights and four-flushes should continue to be played; if you have seen almost none of the cards you need, normally raise with them.

THE SIXTH CARD (FOURTH BETTING INTERVAL)

The criteria for staying, betting, and raising differ only moderately after the sixth card from those after the fifth. No longer raise with trips if a four-flush or four-straight shows *on board*. Stay, however, in the hope of filling plus the possibility that the opponent does not really have the hand he represents.

Do not raise now with an unfilled straight or flush,* but stay for the seventh card unless almost every card you need has been exposed. If a two-pair hand or a single high pair has been worth playing to this point, it usually will continue to be unless the sixth card drastically changes the potential strength of the board or your chance for improvement.

THE SEVENTH CARD (LAST BETTING INTERVAL)

The seventh (last) card is dealt down. Because everyone has three concealed cards, a player can only very rarely be certain he has the winning hand. You can sometimes be certain from the exposed cards that you are *beaten,* but otherwise you must make informed guesses as to when to call, bet, or raise.

You cannot really expect a pair to win. Nevertheless, against a single opponent, the size of the pot may make a call worthwhile on a high pair in the hope that he is bluffing. The same can be said for two small pairs. Sometimes, two small pairs may even win against two

---

*Although a raise is unwise, if your unfilled straight or flush is completely exposed and everyone ahead of you checks, it is sometimes good tactics to make a bet. This ploy has dual possibilities: it builds the pot if you do happen to hit; it sets the stage for a bluff if you do not. Please note, however, that unless much checking has occurred on previous rounds, you will not often have stayed long enough to have this board, and virtually always you will have some type of additional hidden values to have kept you playing. Conversely, if you *see* such a board by a competent opponent, you must know that he has *something* more than a bobtail or he would have dropped before ever getting it.

opponents if you sit third and can call a bet without a raise.

Although any two pairs are normally an inferior hand, Aces up can even be worth a bet in good position when weak boards have been checked to you—provided your board has no show of strength. Small trips are similar. However, if a player who has checked in poor position then raises your bet, you had better believe you are beaten. You have been trapped by a check-raise; it takes much courage and skill for a player to bluff with a check-raise.

This leads to reference to a fact implied earlier: there is a counterpart to every maneuver in poker. Note that with three hole cards, a full house can be held with no pair showing. In this circumstance, suppose you are high on board with an Ace and strongly believe an opponent or two have made straights or flushes, or perhaps have concealed trips (after all, they stayed on something). If you check, someone will probably bet; then you can raise and perhaps increase your profits. However, you must judge your opponents. If you bet, someone may make an unwise raise. Then, you can reraise for an even larger win. In prolonged play, it is best to vary your play in similar situations to keep everyone guessing.

By far the best time for a check-raise is when you have filled a hand on the seventh card and an opponent has bet or raised strongly on the sixth. Particularly, say you have bet an open pair of Qs on the sixth card, with a third one in the hole, and an opponent has raised. His board should offer some suggestion as to whether he has raised on higher trips, a straight, or a flush. At this point, the pot odds will normally justify a speculative call. Then, suppose you make a full house on the seventh card. If you bet now, the opponent will rarely raise, but if you check, he will almost surely bet. Then you can reraise. (Of course, there can be some risk that the opponent has simultaneously made a higher full house, but that is uncommon and merely part of the game.)

If check-raising is forbidden by the rules, a minimum 25¢ bet can be used with almost the same effect. While it puts the opponent on notice that you may be planning to reraise, he usually will interpret your bet as merely a desperate gesture to try to avoid calling a larger bet.

A moment ago, I mentioned the check-raise bluff. Say you have failed to fill what would have been a well-concealed straight, are high on board with an Ace, and check. If an opponent bets, you may consider raising—hoping he will regard himself as beaten and fold. Admittedly, he will usually call, but if you can occasionally succeed with this bluff, the pots will usually be adequate to make the effort worthwhile. Also, even when you are caught bluffing, opponents will remember your play, and you may later get unsound calls when you do have a good hand.

However, you should never bluff purely for this "advertising" motive. You want your bluffs to succeed. Never try the sophisticated check-raise bluff against a bad player: he will *always* call. But it may succeed against a good player.

The type of strategy I have just been discussing plays more of a role in high-limit poker than in the fixed limit game we are generally considering. However, the maneuvers are worth bearing in mind even in fixed-limit poker.

It should be mentioned that bluffing is usually less effective in Seven-Card Stud than in some of the games we shall consider later. This is because so many excellent hands can be well concealed—and also because all players know that boards that appear strong often will not have been helped by the seventh card.

A successful bluff is unlikely if you have merely played along and then try to appear to have filled your hand with the last card. That leads us back to a bet I recommended with the sixth card. If you have played a completely exposed four-flush or four-straight strongly during the fourth betting interval, opponents will suspect that your hand was already made. If, after the seventh card, they end with mediocre hands that cannot beat the hand you represent, a bluff with a busted hand has a quite good chance of success. I will practically always bluff with that type hand and in the manner just discussed.

I repeat, however, that every tactic has its counterpart. When you suspect an opponent of using the ploy just discussed, you must make an informed guess—based on your estimate of his skill and some rough appraisal of whether the size of the pot makes it worthwhile for you to try to outguess him.

It should be noted that bluffs rarely succeed against more than one or occasionally two opponents. I repeat, however, that with the boards I have just discussed, a competent player without sound values will not be *in* to the sixth (and seventh) cards against more than very limited opposition unless much checking has occurred. The situation can develop, though, when you start playing for a flush and fail to fill it, but a four-straight comes up on board.

The skillful play of hands that do not develop as you hoped is a major factor in success at poker. Almost a platitude: "It isn't the cards you get that count, it's how you play them." Nevertheless, the *cornerstone* of success is to play only sound values in the first place.

Seven-Card Stud—Casino Version

"The casinos of Nevada, and everywhere else, are designed to take a visitor's money like boll weevils take cotton."[6] All but a small fraction of casino gamblers, or at least those on the customers' side of the tables, have no statistical chance whatever of eventually winning. The only casino game in which a skillful player can compete against the house and reasonably expect to win is Blackjack —or Twenty-One. Several other authors and I have described methods by which Twenty-One can be beaten by an intelligent student of the game.

That, however, is a different subject. Many casinos offer games of poker, and in these, players compete against one another—not against the house. The casino's profit comes from either a fee for playing or from a "house cut," i.e., a fraction taken from the pots. Except in a few high-stakes games, the latter method is generally used in Nevada, the only state in the U.S. where Stud poker is played legally in casinos.*†

Thus, in addition to Twenty-One, the "Card Rooms" (poker areas) of casinos provide another possibility for a customer to play with a reasonable prospect of winning. The necessity is to be sufficiently more expert than the average player to overcome the compromising effect of the house cut. This *is* feasible, as I have been able to demonstrate to myself. But an intimate knowledge of the casino game is required for success.

All Nevada casino games are dealt by a professional employee of the house. This dealer does not play. He or she deals the cards, sells chips, referees the game, maintains control over the pot until the winner is determined, and extracts the house cut.

Besides the necessity for being a good player, success at casino poker requires choosing a game in which the cut is not so large as to wipe out the advantage your skill gives you. In a nutshell, this means avoiding the low-limit games. A typical such low-limit game is Seven-Card Stud with betting limits ranging from $1 to $3.

Admittedly, players in these low-limit games tend to be less skilled, and thus more vulnerable to defeat, than in the more expensive games. However, since the money action obviously is relatively low, the casino must extract a rather high percentage of the pots to make the operation of each table worthwhile. Casinos vary somewhat in just how much they take. However, a fairly common cut in small games runs around 15%. Now, you may be a very good poker player, but you just cannot expect to win in the long run if you must give up 15% of every pot you win. In prolonged play, a rather normal result would be for *every* player to lose, with the only "winner" being the casino through its inexorable cutting.

Casinos are required to post somewhere in or near the playing area the percentage amount of their cuts. They often do this,

---

*By local option, *Draw* Poker, a game to be discussed in later chapters, is offered legally in California. A California gambling statute specifically bans *Stud* Poker. Since the statute makes no mention of Draw, the inference has been made that the legislature had no intention of banning this form of poker.

---

*†I do know one Las Vegas Strip casino, the Silver Slipper with games of this type, that takes *no* cut; a charge is made for time at the table. This is quite reasonable, and I have won nicely there.

however, in quite vague terms, giving broad ranges to cover any eventuality. For example, a casino might post a range of 1/4% to 50% house cut! It is absurd to think that any poker game is really going to be cut anywhere near 50%; the posted figure, however, would presumably provide legal protection against any claim that a posted percentage were ever exceeded on a pot. Further, you could look in vain for any game in the room with an average cut anything nearly as low as 1/4%. Still, the figure would be defensible, because some individual small pots are not cut at all; these are ones in which no one calls the opening bet and only the ante is won. (By similar token, a casino may post its range down to 0%. But you can be certain that you are not going to be allowed to play free.)

Posted ranges tell little about the variation in cutting from game to game. If you are scouting an unfamiliar card room before playing, somewhat more specific information can usually be obtained from one of the floor men (supervisory personnel who oversee the games in general). These people vary in their candor. They are anxious to have customers at the tables, and some will be vague, dissembling, or actually untruthful in disclosing how much the casino takes. Others will be entirely forthright.

One of the latter explained the policy of his particular casino—one of the larger ones on the Las Vegas Strip. He said that in the $1 to $3 games, the dealers are instructed to average cutting about $35 per hour. Thus, depending on whether the table is full (eight players) and on the overall vigor of the betting, the cut might range from 10% to 20% (an absolutely unacceptable range for a serious player).* In the less numerous higher-limit games, however, the house settles for a bit less than $35 an hour, and thus obviously a much smaller *percentage*.

Observation proved him honest. Dealing about 25 to 30 hands an hour, the dealers in the small games were cutting about an average of $1.25 per pot (more or less depending on its size). In the $3 to $6 game, the cut was about 5%; in the $5 to $10, about 3%.

Some casinos simply advertise that no game is cut beyond some stated amount. Even there, the larger games may be cut less than this amount; sometimes the cut may be held down by never exceeding a particular *sum* (e.g., $2)—as well as never exceeding a particular percentage.

I will not attempt to cover all variations in house cutting I have observed, but the policy of one more Strip casino may be illuminating. On my first visit to it, two types of games were offered: $1 and $3, and $5 and $10—both Seven Card Stud. In the smaller games 10% was cut up to a maximum of $3 (i.e., a tenth of the first $30 in each pot). In the larger games, 5% was cut to a maximum of

---

*At more recent observation, that particular casino was posting a maximum 10% cut. Competition forced moderation?

$1.50 (i.e., only one twentieth of the first $30); then, an extra 50¢ would be cut *only* if the pot reached $70. Accordingly, the cut averaged well below 5%, as pots generally ran substantially above $30. Again, not only was the *percentage* cut much less in the larger game, but the *total* was less. Thus, to a degree, the small games tend to subsidize the large games for the serious players.

Cutting is done in stages, from one betting interval to the next, to maintain the desired percentage as the pot builds. It is interesting to observe the difference in the simple mechanics of cutting between different type games. In the small games with the devastating percentage extracted, the dealers usually deftly and quickly finger coins or chips into a slot in the table and thus to a box underneath. These repeated maneuvers are accomplished with practiced, near-sleight-of-hand motions—almost as if the dealer felt he were stealing the money. The casinos simply do not like for players to realize that something like 15% or more is being taken: this could discourage many customers from playing.

Commonly, however, in larger games with their more acceptable cuts, the money is stacked forthrightly in front of the dealer for all to see. It is eventually dropped into the slot when the cutting for an individual pot is completed. The casinos realize that knowledgeable players do not expect to play free. When the percentage cut is reasonably low, it seems wise to demonstrate to the players just what this is.

In alluding to cuts of 15% or more as "unreasonable," I do not mean to imply criticism of the casinos. They are in business. They must pay the salaries of dealers, floor men, cashiers, and waitresses. They must pay for the "free" cocktails, soft drinks, cigarettes, and cigars furnished to the players. They must pay the rent. And they must then make a profit. If they are to offer the popular low-action games, they simply must take enough to pay these expenses, and that requires a high cut.

One of the most surprising discussions I have read, by a man who writes in all seriousness on gambling, is the account of his apparently first experience at casino poker in Las Vegas.[8] To kill a bit of time, he got himself involved in a nickel-ante, dollar-limit game of Five-Card Stud. He contradicts himself in his description of the action, but by his own account, he threw a temper tantrum in public, verbally abused a dealer who was merely working for a living, accused a floor man of "cheating," left in a rage, and later wrote that the dealer was "robbing" the pot. He seems unable to realize that casinos have over-head expenses: what could he possibly expect in such a low-action game?

The entrepeneurs of major Nevada casinos, by the way, do not regard poker as an important money-making game like Craps, Twenty-One, Slot Machines, Keno, and to some extent Roulette and Baccarat. In some casinos, the poker area is subleased to outside operators: the management prefers not to bother with running it personally. Nevertheless, the game is clearly important to the serious players at the tables—and to the managers of the "Card Rooms." Also, the same State laws against cheating apply as elsewhere in the casinos, and surveillance to avoid violations is intense. Thus, poker is the "other"* casino game that can be beaten.

I regard a 5% house cut as just about the maximum to be tolerated. That means that $3 to $6 limit is normally the smallest game in which you should play. In a sense, the cut must be regarded as the player's overhead expense. However, it is not quite all; tips to the dealer must be included in the overhead.**

TIPPING

Unlike other casino games, in which tipping is highly inconsistent from player to player, with many players not tipping at all, the tipping custom in poker games tends to be rather structured. I do not mean that you will be forbidden to play if you fail to tip, but in most games you will be considered with disdain by all present. Also, not only is the player who does not tip regarded as a curiosity, a player who tips at the wrong time or too much is a similar curiosity.

With exceptions to be noted, you should tip the dealer each time you win a pot. Except in very large-ante or small-ante games, the amount of the tip is normally the amount of the individual's ante. Thus, if each player's ante is 25¢ (as typically in a $3 and $6 game), 25¢ is the customary tip.*** If the ante is 50¢ (as in a $5 and $10 game), the tip is 50¢. In the small $1 and $3 games, the ante is likely to be only 5¢. A nickle tip would be insulting. A quarter is the appropriate tip in these games.†

No tip is expected if only the antes are won, i.e., if no one calls the opening bet. Some option is permissible in other circumstances when the pot won is exceptionally small. For example, suppose only one player calls the opening bet, and then he folds on the second round. Failure to tip in this circumstance is socially acceptable.

When leaving the game, a winning player may choose to leave an additional tip of whatever size he wishes, which like other tips will be

---

*Besides Twenty-One (Blackjack).

**The concept of *overhead* in poker can really become a mind-boggling matter. A somewhat different appraisal of overhead will be presented later.

***Some players may tip 50¢—particularly if they win an especially large pot.

---

†I *have* seen an occasional low-limit game in which no one was tipping. However, this will usually be one of the "tourist-type" games with inexperienced players.

shared by the various dealers on the shift. This is purely an optional matter.

Almost needless to say, the waitress should be tipped when she serves you. The amount is rather optional. The drinks themselves, however, are free. This matter introduces another element into success at the game. Many players avail themselves of these "free" cocktails to the point of impairing judgment. If you confine your refreshments almost or exclusively to the non-alcoholic variety (equally available), an added advantage over your opponents will frequently accrue to you.

STRUCTURE

The betting in casino poker is highly structured, although specific rules vary considerably between games and casinos. In almost all games there is a forced opening bet of a specific amount. We are now discussing Seven-Card Stud for High. A fairly typical $5 and $10 game may serve as an example of the structured betting.

The player with the highest card on board *must* open the betting for exactly $1—no more and no less.* He cannot check. He cannot fold. He is required by the rules of the game to bet the $1.

As an alternative, depending on the casino, this forced bet may be required of the *lowest* card on board (an innovation that I like). Although I noted earlier that suits have no rank in determining the winning hand in poker, they do play a role for the purpose of the forced bet. Suits rank as in Bridge: clubs lowest, then diamonds, then hearts, and then spades highest. Thus, suppose the lowest card must bet, and one player shows the spade deuce and another the club deuce. The club must bet. Similarly, suppose no deuce shows, but three 3s appear: the spade, the heart, and the diamond. The diamond must bet.

When the high card must bet and ranks are tied, the spade is high; the club is low.

Note that in a sense, this forced opening bet may be considered as part of the ante, as it is automatically part of the pot before any optional betting occurs. Some players with only a knowledge of the commonest type of private game tend initially to resent the concept of a forced bet. However, it is completely reasonable and fair: in prolonged play, the burden of the mandatory bet will fall about equally on all players.

After the opening $1 bet, other players may fold, call, or raise in usual fashion. However, the first raise is usually for a specific, predetermined amount—typically $3 in the five and ten game under

---

*Thus, the name "$5 and $10" may seem slightly incongruous but its meaning will be clarified momentarily.

consideration. Subsequent raises, if any, will then be $5—no more and no less on this first betting round.

On later betting rounds, the high hand on board is first to act. Its holder may then check or bet as he wishes, but he may bet only for the set limit. Initially this is precisely $5 in the game under consideration. Typically this limit increases to $10 on the third, fourth, and final betting rounds (and bets of less than $10 are not allowed). Alternatively, the increase in limit may occur on the last two or *four* rounds. In any event, it may also occur after a pair shows. Rules vary between casinos.*

With three or more active players, a limit is set on the number of raises permitted per betting round. In our private game previously discussed, we set a limit of three raises. Different casinos set this limit at three, four, or five. Ordinarily, however, *no* limit on the number of raises applies when only two active players remain. With no "man in the middle" to victimize, these two may raise one another, if they wish, until one of them runs out of money on the table.

The table-stakes rule applies at casino poker. No player may reach into his pocket to buy more chips during the play of a particular hand. That brings an exception to the rule in which bets must be "exactly" $5, $10, or such. If a $10 call, for example, is normally required, but a player with an active hand has less than that amount left, he merely puts whatever remains into the pot.

Such a player is "in for the pot." He continues to compete for that portion of the pot in which he has matched other players' bets. With two or more other players active, a side pot is created, as they continue to bet (and perhaps receive cards) against one another.

The bankrupt player receives his usual allotment of cards—just like the others. If he has the best hand, he wins the pot to which he has contributed; the side pot goes to whichever player has the next best hand.**

To avoid an undue number of occurrences in which players cannot call all bets, the casinos require some minimum "buy-in." In a five-and-ten game, for example, a player may be required to start with at least $50 on the table. If he loses this, or if his stake on the table becomes lower than he desires, he may buy in again between hands.

Whether a player may buy in again for less than the initial

---

*Some games, usually of the one-to-three variety, do allow discretionary variations in the amount of bets and raises—always, though, within certain limits.

**Note that *two* or more side pots can occasionally be created if more than one player goes "in for the pot" for different amounts. Casino dealers are quite proficient in managing these complicated situations.

minimum varies with the casino. One casino I know permits one "short buy" but not a second. However, the matter would not always be easy to control, as it is common for players simply to add cash to a low stack of chips on the table. I have never seen an objection even if this was a relatively small amount.

Other games have counterparts of the preceding rules. In a three-and-six game, for example, (25¢ ante), the forced opening bet is usually 50¢. The first raise (if any) on the initial betting round may be $2.

BURN CARDS

Note that with the house dealer dealing all hands, including doing all shuffling and even cutting of the deck, there is ordinarily no reason for a player even to touch any cards except his own. Thus, a would-be cheat at the table, or "card mechanic," is deprived of his usual opportunities to manipulate the deck. Seemingly, however, a technique would remain of surreptitiously marking cards during play.

I say *seemingly* because it is highly unlikely that a cheat could mark cards and escape the expert scrutiny in a casino for any substantial period. However, to whatever extent he might be successful, he could make most frequent use of his maneuvers if he could indentify the top card on the deck before the beginning of a betting round.

To avoid any danger, real or imagined, of this latter possibility, the dealer routinely discards ("burns") the top card immediately before dealing the cards for the second through the fifth betting intervals.

Thus, in a complete deal of Seven-Card Stud, four cards altogether will be burned. Since the last card cannot be dealt, only 47 cards in the deck are available for play. As most casino poker tables accommodate eight players, note that a real possibility exists that so many players will stay that insufficient cards will be available to give everyone his full seven-card allotment. (Even with only seven players present, a slight chance of this development exists.)

Remember from our discussion of the private game, the commonest way to cope with such an eventuality is to anticipate it after the fifth card and for the dealer to announce that the hands must be considered completed after six cards. The casinos have a more satisfactory method of dealing with the problem.* If, after the sixth card is dealt and the penultimate betting round is completed, insufficient cards remain for every active player to receive a seventh, a single final card will be turned up in the middle of the table. This

---

*The method is equally adaptable to the private game, and I recommend it, but from my experience, most poker groups are unaware of it.

becomes a "widow" card, or one that is considered the seventh card in every player's hand.

Note, however, that even with this excellent innovation, when a full complement of eight players is present, a rare situation could occur when 47 cards would not last even for the six-cards-per-player allotment plus the single widow card. This exceptional event would not only require that every player stay through the opening betting round but that most stay to the bitter end. A floor man at one casino told me that his dealers would then use the discards to ensure that every player receives a complete hand (including the widow card).*
It occurs so rarely that a dealer told me he had never seen it happen. A floor man at a different casino said that the correct way to handle the situation is for the dealer to anticipate it after the fifth card when circumstances make it possible and to deal only a sixth card (to each player if exactly enough remain or a widow sixth card otherwise). However, another dealer said he had seen the event occur twice during his career, and both times the casino rules had failed to provide for it—with the result that utter chaos developed as players, dealer, and floor men tried to resolve the problem.

Thus, even with the highly organized professionalism with which casino poker is conducted, lapses in perfection occur. I can bear witness to at least one more. A man at the other end of the table from me played to the hilt a hand that showed little on board. When an opponent eventually turned up an excellent hand, the man simply conceded by folding his exposed cards. A woman sitting near me, who had dropped from the action near the end, asked him what he had held, and he tossed his hand to her face down. She looked at the cards, I said I wanted to see them too, and in fact looked at them.

With some displeasure, the man told me, "I was showing them to *her.*" Well, I knew that standard rules of poker provide that any player can demand to see any hand active to the showdown, and I repeatedly had seen the rule invoked in casino poker. I knew my act was proper and appealed to the dealer to confirm the fact.

Rather nonchalantly, the dealer said, "Naw, he doesn't have to show them." He saw that I was astonished (and very surely knew that he was wrong). Somewhat lamely, he explained, "House rule."

All right, but I am certain there was no such "house rule"— except as the dealer conjured it momentarily to assuage the other player. The man evidently was a frequent player whose presence bore some weight with the management.

Although occasional minor disruptive incidents do occur in casino poker, I should emphasize that the norm is extreme orderliness and exactitude. The brisk efficiency of a casino operation is ordinarily a thing to admire.

---

*Another casino would use the discards *first*—then a widow card if necessary.

Admittedly, the business-like zeal has been known to become excessive. I have a secondhand account of one episode on the Las Vegas Strip that illustrates a callousness to which the casino milieu can lead. A player in a game suddenly gasped, turned pale, slumped in his chair, slid to the floor, and turned blue. About the only solicitude shown the dead man was to convey him away on a stretcher with utmost dispatch. The dealer then had a single remark: he turned his head and called to the room, "Seat open."

STRATEGY

Most sound poker principles vary only moderately, if any, from one game to another. However, some subtle differences exist between the casino game and the fairly typical private game previously described that dictate for the expert a somewhat more conservative style in the former—particularly during the initial betting intervals. In general, strategy at this time should largely resemble that of a high-limit game—i.e., the type of game we have mentioned in which betting limits greatly exceed the amount of the total ante.

Of course, the usual casino game does have fixed limits. For a variety of reasons, however, the usual eventual pot (and the size of your contribution to it if you stay) tends to be considerably larger than its counterpart in a private game with a similar ante.

For one thing, the forced original bet has at least a slight influence in getting an additional player into the action initially; this is particularly true in those rather common games in which the *low* card must bet. Naturally, the player with the forced bet without sound values should get out quickly thereafter, but he will be in for the fourth card, and that will sometimes help him enough to induce him to stay longer. (True, if an opponent simply "gets involved" and stays too long with a weak hand, this will work to your overall advantage. But often he will have a good hand, and the fact that his initial play was mandatory can make his hand harder to "read.")

More important, even though bets are limited, the maximum limit is also usually the minimum limit. You do not have the frequent small bets below the limit that are common in private games. Even in those games that allow some discretion in the amount of a bet, "cutting of raises" is forbidden. In other words, any raise must be for at least as much as the original bet—or as any previous raises.

Further, the limit often rises sooner in the casino game. It commonly doubles (e.g., from $3 to $6 or $5 to $10) with the fifth card; in private games, this usually occurs only with the sixth card unless a pair has shown earlier.

Finally, instead of restricting raises to three per betting round, four or five are often allowed. This can greatly increase the action in a pot.

All this can make it very lucrative to win a pot, but comparatively expensive to lose one. As in all poker, your prospects in the pots for which you compete must be appraised in relationship to the overhead for the game.

Overhead is commonly used as simply another term for the total of your antes. Certainly this is correctly considered as mandatory overhead. Figuring such overhead in the casino game becomes more complicated, as two small amounts must be added.* These include your share of the mandatory opening bets that you ordinarily would not make in the absence of the force, plus your tips to the dealer on winning pots. In a sense, *total* overhead, more difficult to estimate, includes the mandatory overhead plus all bets you make voluntarily based on your card values. Obviously, to be a successful player, your return from winning pots must exceed the overhead.

The reason serious players are so sensitive about mandatory overhead is that they know they will get back less than their share. That is simply because they will be in fewer pots than their inferior opponents and thus will win fewer than their numerical share. The compensating factors, of course, are that their discretionary overhead will be relatively low and that they will win more than their share of the pots for which they do compete to the end.

Theoretically, the total returns to all players should be the sum of all overhead, but in the casino game, the return is diminished by the house cuts (and dealers' tips).** Thus, a further influence is involved in the strategic approach to this form of poker. For the purpose of analyzing your *return* from pots, it is convenient to regard the ante (including the forced bet) as somewhat less than it appears. In the size game we are considering, the cut and tip from a typical pot will consume roughly a third of what was anted. Thus, in appraising the pot in relation to the ante, still a further disparity from our private game may be included as a practical matter in playing strategy.

From all the preceding, it becomes evident that you must keep your discretionary or voluntary overhead somewhat lower than in the private game used as our previous model. In other words, you should compete in somewhat fewer pots. And the time to take this more conservative approach is usually at the very beginning of a hand.

---

*These sums cannot be predicted exactly, as they will vary with the luck of the game. For the good player, however, they will probably add about 20% to mandatory overhead in the long run.

**Actually, even in private games, pots are sometimes cut a bit, but this is normally merely to cover the expenses for refreshments, snacks, cards, etc. For practical purposes, it generally can be ignored. If anyone cuts pots for a profit, the game, in a sense, becomes a professional one.

On the first three cards, I simply will not play a small pair (smaller than 9s)* unless it is accompanied by a very high card. That usually means an Ace, although a K is acceptable if the board shows no other K and no Ace. The reason is that if I make two small pairs on the next card, I will have no interest in playing them in these games; making trips with one more card is too unlikely to make an investment worthwhile. True, if the fourth card were an Ace, that plus the small pair and odd card would probably be worth staying for another round, but *having* this speculative hand is a different thing from spending money in an effort to get it.

I will not play a three-straight lower than 8,9,10 unless the concealed cards are of the same suit. You play beginning straights because of the dual possibility of making pairs. But I do not want to aim for low pairs.

Except for a forced opening, I will not play an Ace,K, even in the hole, unless I am at least in fairly good position and conditions are otherwise perfect: my other card is higher than any other card on the board.

I relax these restrictions only if my position is perfect and thus I can "buy" the fourth card for only the small price of the forced bet that has been made to my immediate left.

Except for the preceding, playing requirements are essentially as previously described. In later rounds, however, remember that reraising is often less restricted than in private games; you must be very careful with speculative hands if the action becomes vigorous.

SOME PRACTICAL MATTERS RELATED TO STRATEGY

Strategy at casino poker can involve more than appraisal and play of your cards. Because of the shape of the table, the mere matter of position can have some influence on your efficiency.

A Nevada casino poker table is elongated, flattened on each side and curved on each end. The dealer sits in the middle of one of the flat sides. Necessarily leaning forward with forearms outthrust, he tends to obscure the cards of the player immediately to his one side from the player at the other. I dislike either of these positions and avoid them if I have a choice.

A place on the other side, essentially across from the dealer, is best. A seat at one end is not particularly objectionable, although distance can be a minor problem with hands at the other end unless your vision is excellent.

If I must sit beside the dealer, his (or her) right side is better than the left. The reason is that the action proceeds clockwise, and you are expected to make routine decisions rather promptly. It is often more inconvenient to have to make your plays immediately after a

---

*Well, I might play *concealed* 8s.

hand than before one if you must engage in contortions to see it.

Of course, you cannot always have the seat you prefer. Sometimes you must register with the floor man and wait a while for a seat in the type game you prefer. However, once you are at the table, you should remain alert and ask immediately to move to a better seat when one is vacated.

In a casino, always remember that the dealer runs the game. He should be asked about any questions of rules or other conduct of the game.

The dealer is responsible for determining the winner of each hand. Experience teaches dealers to read the value of hands very well. However, if a player at the showdown looks at an opponent's exposed hand and simply acknowledges himself as the loser, the dealer will not himself turn the hand up. In fact, if a player folds his hand, it is "dead" for purposes of winnng.

Thus it is generally wise policy to turn up all your cards at the showdown. More than once I have seen an experienced player fail to recognize some unexpected value in his hand—or more commonly misread an opponent's hand turned up at the far end of the table.

I recognize, of course, that you may sometimes want to conceal a losing hand, provided no one asks to see it, in order to disguise your method of play. If you do so, however, be very certain that you have not overlooked or misread anything anywhere. I once won a nice pot with three Ks when another player thought he saw a full house in my hand and tossed away a straight. He realized his mistake before the cards were gathered in, but the dealer would not permit him to correct it after he had already folded his cards.

I should mention that despite their skill, dealers do occasionally make mistakes in reading hands. Rarely you may need to speak up when a dealer is preparing to push your pot to someone else.

In any poker game, it is necessary to appraise your opposition, and this certainly is true in a casino. One thing may be said with confidence: in virtually any serious casino game (i.e., one with stakes sufficient to permit an acceptable house cut), some excellent players will be present. A substantial number of expert and near-professional players (or perhaps *true*-professional is the word) habitually frequent the Nevada casinos. You must be at least approximately as skillful as most of these, but even so, probable success demands that you get out of games in which *too* many other experts are present. If more than half of the opposition plays equally as well as you, success becomes difficult. You need about four inferior players at the table (three are all right if two of them are downright incompetent). It is essential, then, that you pay attention from the outset as to what type hands the opponents will play and how they manage them during the betting.

Conceivably every player at a table could be an expert, but this is most unlikely. The reason is that *they* would not remain long in a game in which everyone had about equal talent.

It is legal for casinos to use shills—employees who play for the house. Not all casinos use them, and the custom seems to have declined during recent years, but it is hard to obtain a good appraisal. Shills must be identified if anyone at the table asks about the matter, but otherwise they remain anonymous, and a player would make too much of a curiosity of himself if he repeatedly asked whether a shill was present as other players drifted in and out of the game. Usually no shill will be playing, but be aware that in some casinos you occasionally may be at a table with one. You may be sure of one thing: if a shill is playing, he will be an expert. But that does not mean that he necessarily has to be better than you.

The fact that you recognize casino employees in the games by no means identifies them as shills. Many dealers (Blackjack dealers, Craps dealers, etc.) play poker during their off hours and entirely on their own behalf. These tend to be good players, some expert, but they are not invariably so. As might be expected, the *poker* dealers are generally the best among this group, but even these do not routinely play a sound game.

Usually, the poker dealers who play will do so in a casino where they do not work, but sometimes they play in their own establishments. Once I saw a floor man finish his shift of duty, quickly take off his green felt apron (but not his casino tie), and immediately sit down at a seat that was open and begin to play with his own money.

With the professionalism and greed that pervade casino poker, it is natural to wonder about the possibility of being cheated. In Nevada, with the strict regulation of the Gaming Commission and its enforcement arm, the Gaming Control Board, it would be seriously risky business for a casino to sanction cheating. Certainly there must be temptation for a dealer with the ability to manipulate cards to team up with a confederate at the table and help him win. However, with both the open and surreptitious surveillance that is present in a casino, it is highly unlikely that such a conspiracy could long succeed.

With human nature what it is, there is almost surely some cheating somewhere sometimes. However, the chance of cheating by the house in any given game is so small that it can be virtually ignored. The danger of cheating is very real in an illegal game in which you play with strangers. (John Scarne's book[9] is recommended reading for advice on that subject.) However, I have not once had reason to believe that a casino cheated me in a legal game.

Perhaps the greatest danger involves team play by two opponents. Typically this will involve theoretically unsound raises by one player to help an opponent get more money into the pot—or to drive you out of the action with a fair hand. Beware of two opponents who repeatedly raise each other under unnatural circumstances. True, you may sometimes turn the tables by sandbagging an excellent hand. Another facet of team play, however, is for a member with a normal call to fail to make it, knowing (from signals) that his partner has a better hand. Thus, when you win a pot, it may not contain as much as it normally should. You should get out of the game in which you have strong belief that this practice is taking place.

Another obvious precaution to take is to avoid holding your cards in easy view of spectators. Onlookers frequently watch games from just outside the "poker pit"—perhaps from behind a rail surrounding it. While they are normally just innocent observers, you must be aware of the slight possibility that one may be signaling your hand to a confederate in the game.

Although I said I have never suspected that a casino poker dealer had cheated me, I shall relate an incident one of my acquaintances once observed. A rowdy drunk was at the table, much to the annoyance of the dealer. The drunk was lucky at first, but soon began to lose steadily as expected. However, he won a fair number of individual pots, simply because he played in practically all.

Every time this player won, the dealer amused himself by taking an extra cut. The drunk noticed nothing.

Eventually exhausted of chips, the drunk took a large bill from his stack and tossed it into the pot. The dealer made change and set it aside—but just a bit toward the player, who failed to reach out and retract it.

The drunken player won the hand. The dealer leaned over the pot with his forearm, and with his free hand pushed the man's change to him as a decoy, simultaneously fumbling with it a bit to make further change for the next ante. Then, the dealer pulled the real pot toward himself and deliberately dropped it all into the slot. He cut the entire pot!

(On the other hand, I know of one incident in which a dealer was fired for "overcutting" a pot. Why he did it I don't know; only the management had anything to gain. But the manager would not tolerate the practice—even if in behalf of the casino.)

A further word may be added about small-stakes games, e.g., of the $1 and $3 variety. I mentioned that sometimes you must wait for a while for a seat in the better games. Sometimes I may play in a small game briefly (perhaps unwisely) during such a wait.

While the percentage cut is very high, the ante is usually almost trivial: a nickle or dime, plus an occasional small forced bet. If you do play in such a game, you can give yourself a gambling chance by keeping your play of the first three cards *very* conservative.

I recommend playing no pair lower than Aces or Ks—or perhaps Qs if no one shows a card higher than J. I recommend playing no three-straight less than 9,10,J, and then only if two of the cards are in the same suit.

I will admit that I have not always followed my own advice (initially partly because of lack of experience). Perhaps that is why, when I said I am usually a winner at casino poker, I was not including games of less than the three-and-six variety.* However, I am not sure that these small games with a 10 to 20% house cut can be beaten in the long run under any circumstances.

It is possible that you could reasonably expect a profit if you happen to find yourself in a session with a full eight-player complement, with relatively heavy action, in which you observe that virtually all the opposition is incompetent.

In later chapters, I shall describe other poker forms played in casinos. With the detail given in the present chapter, the novel features of the casino versions, as contrasted with usual private games, can be more eaisly and quickly pointed out.

----

*Please see footnote, page 48, for an exception.

Chapter III
RAZZ—SEVEN-CARD STUD FOR LOW

Just as Seven-Card Stud may be played high-low or strictly for high, it may be played with the low hand winning the entire pot. This poker form is commonly called "Razz," or frequently "Seven-Card Lowball." It is played in Nevada casinos, usually for relatively high stakes, and is popular with some private poker groups.

The cards are dealt as in the seven-card games previously described, with a similar five betting rounds. However, the *lowest* exposed hand is first to act during each betting round. (An exception occurs on the first round in some casino games, in which a forced bet is required of the *high* card on board. Thereafter, of course, the low board is first to act and may bet or check.)

In our private game, we shall assume similar limits as specified for the previous ones. The ante is 25¢ per player. The limit is $1 (25¢ minimum) on the first three betting rounds and $2 on the last two. A maximum of three raises is allowed (except for the "right to bet" rule—page 9). There are no forced bets, and the low hand bets or checks first on all rounds.

Please recall from our discussion of Hi-Lo that more than one scale of values can be used in assessing a low hand. In Hi-Lo, we assumed that Ace,2,3,4,6 in different suits was a perfect low—simply because that seems to be the most prevalent scale used. In strict "Lowball" games, however, the more modern "California scale" is apparently more widely accepted. Thus, flushes and straights are ignored; Ace,2,3,4,5 is a perfect low. I even know "Dealer's-Choice" poker groups that routinely use the traditional scale in Hi-Lo games and the California scale in the straight Lowball games. In our discussions of poker for low only, we shall assume that the California scale is employed.

We shall assume an eight-player game, the normal complement at the usual table used in private games. In any event, any differences in proper strategy between an eight- and a seven-handed game are virtually imperceptible. The reason we initially assumed seven players in our previous games was to avoid, until clarification was convenient, any bewilderment that might be caused the reader who recognized that 52 cards will not provide eight full hands.

For practical purposes, even the clarification (pages 26-27) would be unnecessary for Razz: the deck simply will never run out, regardless of theoretical possibilities. The reason is that there are just a certain number of low-ranking cards. No matter how bad the players are, it is inconceivable that eight players could all receive cards at Razz that would give them justification to stay around long enough to exhaust the deck.

Strategy

To a substantial degree, various concepts of Seven Hi-Lo carry over to Razz. Naturally, however, only the low strategies apply, and some values are modified slightly—in one way because the winner takes the entire pot, and in another because no possibility exists for converting a busted low into a winner for high.

Razz is somewhat more of a gamble than Seven-Hi or Hi-Lo. The reason is that early values are more nebulous. While you must know and make the proper percentage plays in any of the forms, there is more danger of these going awry at low poker.

Note, for example, that at high poker, if you have trips after four cards, you will always have trips and may improve. At low poker, you may start with four excellent cards and end with a complete bust. Nevertheless, the better player will win the money in the long run. He simply must expect his swings of good and bad luck to be a bit wider than at other forms.

THE FIRST THREE CARDS

As in other Seven-Card Stud games, the play of the first three cards is the key to success. As in Seven Hi-Lo, the Ace-7 range contains the desirable cards, but the 8 plays a pivotal role, and higher cards receive more disdain than in Hi-Lo.

As you would probably expect, if you have three cards to a 7 low, you will be starting with the best hand around the board the substantial majority of the time. This hand or a better one is easily worth a raise in excellent position. In earlier position, merely call; you do not want to scare off the mediocre competition.

With three to an 8, you will have the best hand about half the time. It is difficult to conceive of a situation when such a hand should not be played. Perhaps a *rough* 8 (i.e., 8,7 and lower card) should be folded in late position if the 8 is the exposed card, some players with exposed low cards have called the opening bet, and a raise is made just to your right by a player showing a 7 or lower. The raiser probably has a better hand than you, and someone else may have too—despite the fact that with mostly low cards showing, *some* players very likely have high cards in the hole.

An 8 low on the first three cards seldom warrants raising. An occasional exception is with a very smooth 8 (say 8,5 and lower card) in late position when players ahead of you have called the opening bet with exposed cards of 8 or higher.

In your own case, you should practically never play the first three cards if your up-card is 9 or above. The only exception is with both hole cards in the Ace-7 range and with *every* opponent showing an up-card at least as high as yours—yes, *every one*.

Throughout this discussion, always remember that any card that gives you a pair is a "high" card, regardless of rank. The only thing that a pairing low card can do in your favor is to remove one card from the deck that might help your opponents—and just a single such card can make only minor difference. For the purpose of the strength of your own hand, a pairing card is worse than a K.

Except as recently described, any three-card hand of 9 or higher must be regarded as inferior. In theory, it would seem preferable almost never to play one. However, such tactics will soon mark you as so conservative that your opponents can easily "read" the hands you play. You will find yourself getting few calls on the excellent hands you make.

Also, a 9 with two other cards in the Ace-7 range is only a moderate underdog with four more cards to come to everyone. You are still shooting at a 7-low or better, and a smooth 9 itself will occasionally win a pot: you will be able to estimate its potential value from the exposed boards that develop.

Thus, with no raise ahead of me, I will normally play a three-card smooth 9 *provided the 9 is in the hole*. The hand is much more inferior if the 9 is up. Exposed, that high card will always be there for everyone to see. Thus, any kind of poker player at all will *know* that both hole cards are low.

You cannot reasonably expect a 10 to win; any higher card will virtually never do so. Still, largely for the advertising value of varying my play, I will sometimes stay with a 10 or higher, but I must be in late position with nothing but fairly high exposed cards behind me (9 or higher—or perhaps a single 8). The other two cards must be in the Ace-7 range—preferably the Ace-5 range to give me at least some chance at a "wheel," or perfect Ace,2,3,4,5. As before, the high card must be buried; if I continue to play but make a bust at the end, the hand may still have some bluffing potential if its weakness is concealed.

With these speculative hands containing a bad card in the hole, I will normally check if I am low on board and thus first to act. Then, after someone else opens, I will usually disregard the ploys just discussed and fold: I have already virtually announced my weakness with the previous check. (Just to mix things up a bit, I *may* open—or check and then call—with a very smooth 9, e.g., with two in the Ace-5 range.)

During early betting rounds of fixed-limit poker, if I call an initial bet, I am ordinarily prepared to invest further by calling a raise behind me. However, with a speculative hand, I do not feel at all committed to call a raise and re-raise all at once.

If the play of the first three cards is the key to success (and it is), a simultaneous necessity for mastery of the game is to begin to count low cards—and to continue to do so as long as you remain in the hand. As the deal proceeds, if you have seen several cards that would pair your good ones, your chances for improvement are obviously enhanced. On the other hand, the appearance of an abnormal number of low cards that you need could properly persuade you to abandon a hand that normally you would continue to play. You should always have at least a reasonable estimate of the ratio of helping cards to unwanted cards among those unseen.

Naturally, you ordinarily cannot be sure of the exact rank of your opponents' hole cards. However, you can generally assume some low cards among them, and the up-cards can often give you a reasonable inference as to how many. Further, say on the second round, a player stays with a 3 and K exposed; if he is a competent player, you can infer not only two small hole cards but also that neither is a 3.

At times you *can* infer the exact rank of an unseen card. Suppose an opponent has remained active to some point, then draws a 5, and folds the hand. You can be morally certain that he had another 5 in the hole. Such information can not only help in estimating your chances of improvement, but occasionally some key card can prove valuable in judging an opponent's hand.

For example, in the situation of the 5s just given, suppose another opponent catches a 5 on a late round and you also hold a 5. You now can be certain that the card has helped your opponent, because it could not possibly have paired him.

THE FOURTH CARD

A maxim for playing when the fourth card has been dealt might be written: Do not play with two cards higher than 8. Unless your opponents give you a free ride by checking all around, about the only exception would be the unlikely occurrence of *every* opponent showing two up-cards as high or higher than any of yours. Note that in such a situation, it will be your initial bet, and you should surely make one: if any player calls he will be incompetent,* but do not let him play free.

---

*Observe from prior discussion that only an inferior player will have called an opening bet on the *first* round with a high up-card.

About equally obvious, four cards to a 7 or better give an excellent hand. Raise in late position. Merely call in early position; avoid making it difficult for your opponents to call the opening bet. (If *you* have the opening bet, you should certainly make it.)

Four to a smooth 8 is also a good hand to be played. Only under unusual circumstances, however, would I raise with the hand. This would be when the first bettor and I both have an 8 (his other exposed card is slightly lower than mine), and players all with a high up-card are "sandwiched" between us and have already called.

Four to a rough 8 are more problematical. If both the 8 and 7 are exposed, a couple of lower boards could persuade me to fold, particularly if I am sandwiched between the opener and a later potential raiser.

On the other hand, if my 8 is buried, I might *raise* if I am first to the left of the opener, and more players are behind me all with one high up card. The reason is that I probably have the best hand *at the moment*. I *know* it is best except for the opener. Yet I do not have any great start. Thus, it may be well to drive out the players who could have three very good cards at which to draw—but the initial handicap of one bad card. My later problems (if any) may become more clear-cut if I can continue with my relatively borderline start against a single opponent.

If you have started the hand with a high card (naturally in the hole), three to a 7 or better on the fourth card will normally be worth continuing to play. With a high card, however, usually forget about three to an 8. If you have the handicap of an essentially useless card, you should otherwise be drawing to an excellent hand, not just a moderately good one. Remember that in giving the criteria for playing the first round with a high card, I specified that the other two be in the Ace-7 range. If the fourth card turns out to be an 8, it will of course be up. You should fold unless every active player also shows at least an 8—and you should probably fold even then if your three are to a *rough* 8.

Three low cards with the fourth (high) card *exposed* is a definitely inferior hand. True, it is as easy to help as if the card were hidden, but your hole cards will be almost an open book. (Not *quite* open, because their exact rank will usually remain unknown, but all competent opponents will easily and correctly infer that they are low.)

Despite the handicap, a high exposed card with three to a 7 can be worth playing if *only* the opening bettor shows two low cards. Even with players behind me, I do not fear a raise if they also have high cards. However, if another player between the opener and me has called with low cards, I infer a good hand. (Good or just fair, *two* players now have me at a disadvantage, as whatever weakness they may have is hidden.)

Sometimes that second player may raise. In this case, I am more likely to infer a mediocre hand than if he had just called (remember the tactic I suggested a few paragraphs back). But if he succeeds in driving me out, so be it; I do not want to call both a bet and raise and still risk a reraise by the opener.

While a low fourth card that pairs a hole card hurts the hand, further play is often warranted. The weakness is known only to you.

THE FIFTH CARD

Only rarely will your hand be "pat" or "made" (i.e., five to 8 or better) on the fifth card. When it is, you obviously should bet and raise strongly. Even with a rough 8, you have a reasonable chance to win unimproved, and either or both of two cards to come may give you even a better hand. I should caution, however, that if a reraise occurs behind you, you had better assume that this opponent has perfect hole cards. His hand may still be worth "chasing" with a call of the reraise, but you now know that you must improve to win.

The rule to remember with the fifth card is to play only if you need but one more card to make a good hand. The chances of drawing two excellent cards with only two more to come are just too slim to be worthwhile.

Again, by drawing to a "good" hand, I am normally thinking of an 8, but as before, you must consider the opposing boards. As noted with the fourth card, an 8 can be quite inferior between two opponents with better boards.

Four to a 9 are no good unless every opponent shows two cards as bad or worse.

THE SIXTH CARD

Play with six cards if one more good one will give you a reasonable chance to win. Remember now, however, that even a 7 may be a near-hopeless hand if better boards show and raising is occuring.

If you need a perfect draw to win, now is the time your observation of cards showing, previously folded, and inferred can serve you well. Do a reasonable number of cards you need remain in the deck?

It is well to remember that at this point you can be low on board and yet an opponent can be absolutely certain he will win—regardless of what the seventh cards may be. For example, a player may show a K (or a pair) but already have a wheel. A 5,6,7,8, will be a lower board with no chance whatever.

The preceding circumstance, however, is uncommon. If I am low on board, I will normally bet if I have already made a 7-low. I will normally check if I have an 8-low, although I will usually be prepared to call if someone else bets.

Similarly, I will check if my high card on board is an 8 or higher and I still must draw a card for a good hand. However, if my board is 7 or lower, I will practically always bet—even with two bad hole cards. This bet is a semi-bluff with two bad hole cards (say I have played with one high one, and the sixth card pairs the other one). Naturally, I hope to draw a perfect seventh card, in which case my bet will have built the pot. Failing this, however, I have set the stage for a real bluff on the last round.

In other words, if you are low on board, bet with an excellent hand or with a speculative hand that *appears* excellent. Check with a fair hand.

THE SEVENTH CARD

Little specific needs to be said about strategy on the last betting round. You naturally bet or raise with a probable winner. Call with a reasonable chance to win. Depending on the boards and the vigor of betting, consider the possibility now that a smooth 9 may win.

While exceptions occur, an 8 will normally warrant a call. However, do not initiate a bet with an 8-low except under the uncommon circumstance when you have a lock. Usually you will beat anyone who folds anyway; anyone who calls will probably have you beaten.

With three good cards and one high card exposed, sometimes bluff on a ruined hand against one or two players who have checked with mediocre boards. If you have an excellent low on board and have started the semi-bluff described on the sixth card, continue to bluff if you ruin your hand and only one opponent (rarely two) has stayed against you. True, you will usually be called. But if the opponent has also ruined his hand, he sometimes will fold. Pots are large enough that such a bluff needs to succeed only occasionally to be worthwhile in the long run. When the bluff fails, at least it provides the advertising to get calls on other occasions when you really do have the hand your board suggests. However, you should not try the bluff without some reasonable chance of success; with several opponents, there is little likelihood that *all* have busted.

Remember that all poker strategies have counterstrategies. Against a single opponent who may be trying a bluff as previously described, consider calling with a bad hand. While you will probably lose, a large pot can make the gamble worthwhile.

I should mention that at high-limit play (table stakes or pot limit) bluffs are more effective than in a fixed-limit game.

Razz—Casino Version

Razz as played in Nevada is usually for relatively high stakes, e.g., $15 and $30; $30 and $60. Recall from Chapter II the general structure of casino stud poker. With that background, the rules for a typical Razz game can be summarized.

Consider a $15 and $30 game. The ante may be $1 per player, with a forced bet of $5 by the *high* card on the first round (recall from Chapter II how suits are used to determine high and low when ranks are otherwise tied). The first raise (if any) may be $10 (no more and no less). Subsequent raises on the first round, and bets and raises on the second, are exactly $15. These are $30 on the last three rounds. A maximum of five raises may be permitted with three or more active players (no limit on number of raises, except for the stakes on the table, if only two players remain active).

Exact symmetry does not necessarily exist between the stakes for games of different limits. The ante for a 30-60 game, for example, may be $5 per player.

The house cut in these high-stake games tends to be quite reasonable. For example, a prominent casino that I know well cuts only $1 per hand—a very low percentage. In fact, with fewer than six players present, the cut is only 50¢ per hand.

STRATEGY AT CASINO RAZZ

As with Seven-Card Stud for High, your strategy at Razz in the casino game should be somewhat more conservative than with the $1 and $2 limits previously discussed. The reasons are the same: no sub-maximum bets, more raises allowed, forced bets, a house cut, tips to the dealer, commonly better-than-average players.

Most strategy variations involve the play of the first three cards. I would not play a 6,7,8; if you help, the hand you most reasonably expect to make will almost never beat anything but a 9. The tariff is just too high in relation to the overhead to make this mediocre start worthwhile.

Except in good position (no low cards behind me), I would not play any three-card rough 8 if the 8 is the up-card. A three-card smooth 9 (9 buried of course) should be played only in the good position just described—with no raise of the forced bet having been made. Even then, I would want a *very* smooth 9—two other cards to a wheel. The "advertising" play of a hole card higher than 9 should be made only with great discretion. (After all, a 9 has *some* chance to win on its merits; a 10 has virtually none.)

The other basic variation occurs with the fourth card. In the fixed-limit private game, recall that a high fourth card may *sometimes* be played; in the usual casino game, the hand should always be folded. (A low fourth card that pairs a hole card, however, may often be played, because the weakness of the hand is hidden.)

Chapter IV
SOME OTHER STUD
GAMES AND VARIANTS

The various forms of Seven-Card Stud just described were relatively recent innovations to enliven the more traditional form. The original and classical stud poker is the five-card* variety.

*Five-Card Stud**

This form of poker evidently emerged at about the time of the Civil War. It has perhaps the simplest structure of any of the well-established standard games. Yet after considerably more than a century, the substantial majority of poker devotees still do not know how to play it properly.

That is a remarkable commentary on such a basically uncomplicated game, but fortunately for the potential expert who is willing to *study* poker, it provides a true illustration of poker in general. From experience in dealer's-choice sessions, I have even observed that players who habitually opt in their turns to deal Five-Card Stud usually do not know the principles of good play.

By *simple structure* and *basically uncomplicated,* I do not mean that Five-Card Stud is in all senses easy to play well. It requires a considerable amount of analyzing and inferring, and card-watching is highly important. However, the game is the first stud variety discussed in most poker books and usually is rather thoroughly covered, practically everyone who has played much poker has had experience with it, and certain fundamental principles are quite easily learned.

---

*Although this book discusses high, low, and high-low poker, when the context does not otherwise clarify the matter, we are discussing games in which the high hand wins all.

RULES

After the ante, each player is initially dealt one hole card and one up card, and the first betting round occurs. As in Seven-Card stud (for high), the highest card acts first. If there is a tie for high, the hand nearest the dealer's left is first in most games. (However, if you are making the rules, I recommend the casino custom of letting suits of tied cards determine who is first. This is fairer.)

After the first betting round, another up card is dealt to each player, and another betting round occurs. Remember that the high hand may change from round to round; the first player to act changes accordingly.

Fourth cards are dealt up with another betting round, and then fifth cards up and a final betting round. (In a minority of games, the fifth card is dealt down instead of up.)

Usually, the limit increases when a pair shows or on the last or penultimate round. For our assumed game of eight players, the ante will be 25¢ per player, the limit will be $1 (25¢ minimum) until the last two rounds or until a pair shows, and it will rise to $2 at these times. Three raises per round are the maximum allowed.

In this game, the ante is sufficient in relation to the limits that no forced bet is needed. However, if a group so desired, they could require a small forced bet on the first round by the high card. Or by the *low* card!

STRATEGY (IN GENERAL)

Implied earlier but best illustrated by Five-Card Stud is one of the most fundamental and often quoted axioms of poker in general: *The best hand going in is usually the best hand coming out.* Some semantic debate could be offered to that principle, depending on how *usually* is interpreted. One thing, however, is certain. The best hand at the beginning has the best *chance* of eventually winning at the showdown.

This leads to a corollary axiom of Five-Card Stud: *Do not play unless you can beat the board.*

All right, sometimes you play if you *tie* the board. Or, you might play with moderately sub-par values if your opponents let you stay for some near-minimum opening bet. But otherwise it is difficult even to invent an exception to the rule other than sometimes after the fourth card—which will be discussed. And generally in our game we assume that opening bets are for the maximum.

Not every writer fully accepts the principle. Ordinarily, however, these have in mind a different game from the commonest serious private game with fixed limits like we are discussing.

I subscribe to the principle in our limit game almost without reservation during early betting rounds. (Occasional exceptions will be discussed for later betting rounds.) I know I *must* play numerous hands when I am second best—or not even that good—simply because I do not have X-ray eyes and cannot see my opponents' hole cards. I do not want to combine this speculative disadvantage with another one that I can *see:* the fact that I am beaten in sight. The "pot odds" will too rarely make playing under these circumstances worthwhile.

If generally following this strategy marks my play to the extent that some opponents can make good inferences about my hole card, so be it. Most opponents will not be sufficiently expert to take adequate advantage, and there are still techniques available for varying my play sufficiently to keep them off balance.

THE FIRST ROUND

On the first two cards, almost always play a pair "back to back." The exception is 8s or lower when another of your cards shows.

An Ace should nearly always be played. However, if another one shows, your other card should be 9 or higher (i.e., above average). If two (or all three) other Aces show, your other card must be a K, and no other K must show.

A K should ordinarily be played if no Ace shows. However, if another K shows, your other card must be at least a 10, and it must be unmatched elsewhere. Otherwise fold.

A Q is the *minimum* unpaired card that can be played on the first round, and if that is played, it *must* be accompanied by a J. Do not play that hand if you see an Ace or K elsewhere. Do not play if more than one up-card matches yours; do not play if even one matches your hole card.

Pay no attention whatever to two-card straights or flushes—including straight flushes. Such hands are merely bait for suckers.

Remember the folded cards whenever you stay. This should not be difficult. Although most of your opponents probably *should* fold, in the usual game most average players will see at least one more card. Many will fold only when they have two unattractive low cards.

Raising on the first round is seldon indicated. An otherwise legitimate raise gives too much of a clue to your hole card.

However, variation of tactics is highly important in Five-Card Stud. Some of this can begin on the first round under prescribed circumstances.

It is well to know that some opponent will have a pair back-to-back only about one-third of the time. If very few high cards show against you, an Ace and high card can usually be regarded as slightly above average.

With a small pair in very early position (first active player to the opener's left), a raise can be an excellent play. You probably have the best hand at the moment, but you would like to limit the competition that may draw out on you. If someone reraises, you will have some intelligent guesswork to do. You are probably beaten, but a good player might bluff. You might figure that a good player with a high pair might sandbag for a moment, hoping the pot will build more (depending on his position), or that he may later squeeze more out of you with a check-raise. But unless you have some good reason to suspect a bluff, it is better to say good-by to the pot at this time. If you try to draw out against a better hand, you will have to call maximum bets on every round, and that opponent has just as good a chance to improve as you do.

After a showdown has demonstrated that you will make the type of raise just discussed (once should be enough, perhaps twice against poor observers), do not make it again for a long time. Just call with the small pair. Sometimes in the same position with a small card up and Ace down, make a similar raise.

Fundamentally, this latter play is not sound. But with no other Ace showing, it is not too bad. And if you successfully lead everyone to think you have a small pair, you may set up a good bluffing situation later. Or if you luckily pair your Ace, you can be certain of calls from any pairs higher than the one they think you have. You are really making an "advertising" play—or semi-bluff. But like all such endeavors, it should be restricted to situations that give a reasonable possibility of paying off otherwise too.

Please note that advertising variations do not pay off unless you have potential customers. If you are in a dealer's choice session in which Five-Card Stud may only be dealt about half-a-dozen times during the evening, recurring situations cannot reasonably be expected. But if the game is fairly popular in your dealer's choice group and you play week after week, you must mix things up a bit—within acceptable limits.

The other sound raising situation with two cards is in last position holding a high pair. Say a K to your immediate left opens, three or four call with lower cards, and you hold *QQ*. You should sometimes raise. You are not now trying to drive out competition (though you would not be disappointed if the opener should fold). The opponents' money is now in the pot. You are simply making them pay more to try to draw out on your better hand.

What do *you* do if someone else raises on the first round? My advice is to believe he has a pair. Stay only if you have a higher pair.

True, he may have an Ace in the hole. But you will have to guess all the way, he *probably* has the pair, and you have far from any cinch anyway beginning, say, with 55, against *Ace*,8.

THE THIRD CARD (SECOND BETTING ROUND)

We begin our consideration of the second round with the

assumption that you could beat the board on the first round (or tie it with the proper high cards). You will continue to play now only if you continue to beat the board—and sometimes not then.

An Ace will beat your K,Q,J; fold the hand. An Ace,10 showing will beat your Ace,9,8: fold the hand. A pair will beat your lower pair: fold the hand. Never mind that you may have seen both cards that could give trips to your opponent; he already has his higher pair and you do not.

Other strategies, from this point until the finish of the hand, are based in part on your assessment of your opponents' hole cards. Your knowledge of their habits may modify your play somewhat, but unless you have such knowledge, it is better to assume that all have had at least some reasonable justification for playing.

If you have started with a small pair* backed up, the third card must help the hand for sound further play. By *help* I do not necessarily mean trips. These would be nice, but you ordinarily will not get them. An Ace or K is normally adequate help. Read further, however.

A high pair normally warrants further play, regardless of the other card. However, this leads both to a consideration of betting strategy and inferences about opponents' hole cards.

Suppose for example that a competent player catches an Ace on the third card, and his initial up-card was a J. If he called the opening bet, made by a player showing an Ace, you had better believe that opponent has either an Ace or a J in the hole. *Any* pair now lower than Qs is inferior and should be folded; Ks or Qs, however, are ordinarily worth a gamble.

In fact, if that player was in last position on the previous round and raised, you can almost read his hole card as a J. True, he might sometimes raise with an Ace in the hole as a semi-bluff to keep people guessing, but he would have been unlikely to do so with another Ace showing somewhere.

Proper betting and raising depend almost entirely on position. If you believe you have the best hand, you should do whatever figures to get the most money into the pot. Bet if you are high on board. Call in poor position; if you raise, you will drive out inferior opposition. Normally raise in good position. However, if you hold trips and someone has bet with a higher pair showing, restrain yourself from raising on the second round. You will virtually announce your holding. Trips are hard to get in Five-Card Stud, and you expect to win with them. Sandbag on this round to make the hand pay off well with an eventual big pot.

If you are high on board with a pair, you should nearly always bet.

*By *small,* I usually mean 8s or lower, with 9s or above meaning *high.* However, give the terms some leeway to mean 7s through 10s, depending on the preponderance of opponents' up-cards.

The exception occurs when you can read an opponent for a higher pair with reasonable certainty. Such a reading can be made on a competent opponent under circumstances similar to one discussed earlier. If he has called initially with a 7 against a couple of Ks around the board and now catches an Ace, you can be confident that he has either Aces or 7s. If you have stayed with *Ace,*6 and now make 6s, the pair is no good. Of course, such inferences cannot be made against poor players.

THE FOURTH CARD (THIRD BETTING ROUND)

In general, the principles discussed for the previous round continue on the third. Normally play if you can beat the board. However, good card watching on earlier rounds may induce you to fold. For example, if no pairs show but you are convinced that someone has played a medium-sized concealed pair to this point, you may hold two high cards and two low cards. If you have seen all but a couple of the cards you need to win, the gamble is not worthwhile. (Even if you help, the opponent can help too. Also, if other players are still active, they presumably have some reason to have stayed.)

However, even if you are convinced that hidden pairs are out against you, the pot odds will usually make it worthwhile to try to draw out with three or four higher cards. Sometimes you may now even chase an open pair if you have watched the folded cards carefully and know there is little or no chance that the opponent's hole card helps his hand.

Until this point, I have properly advised against paying any attention to possible straights and flushes. Now, however, you may have played high cards properly and just accidentally find yourself with four of a suit or perhaps K,Q,J,10. Unless an abnormal number of the cards you need have appeared, you have about one chance in five of making your hand on the fifth card. Almost always, the pot will be large enough to justify calling a bet, and even a raise. In fact, you also retain some chance of making a high pair that could win, particularly if no pairs are in sight.

Exceptions are obvious. For example, suppose you hold the K,Q,J,10 just mentioned but you have seen two or three of your 9s and a couple of Aces—and you are convinced that someone with an Ace has another one in the hole. About 30 to 35 cards remain unseen. You have only about one chance in 10 or 15 of making a winning hand. Thus, the pot must contain $20 to $30 to make it a good gamble to call a $2 bet.

Until now, I have said little specific about "pot odds," because the strategies I have recommended in our fixed-limit game have taken into consideration whether these odds would usually be worthwhile or not. Five-card Stud, however, provides a convenient opportunity to explore the concept more definitively.

If, with a single card to come, you have a chance to draw one that will make a hand you are reasonably certain will win, but have little or no chance of winning without that card, you must estimate your mathematical chance of drawing the right card. Then, you must estimate the amount of money in the pot and compare that with what it will cost to draw the card. Your chance of drawing the card should be at least close to the ratio of what you must risk to what is in the pot.

The odds of drawing to an inside straight provide an illustration. The usual futility of this play is legendary. However, the pot odds can sometimes make it worthwhile.

Suppose you have properly played a hand until the last round and find yourself with 10,J,K,Ace. A Q is needed for a high straight. Normally, you have only about one chance in 12 of drawing a Q. To call a $2 bet, about $24 should be in the pot.

However, suppose you have seen about 20 cards (including your own), and no Q has appeared. Now, you have about one chance in eight of filling; the pot would need to contain only $16 to make a $2 call a good gamble. Even if one Q has appeared, three remain and you should call if the pot is above $20; you have nearly one chance in 10 of filling, and may likely get a call on the final round to come if you do make the straight.

Note from the latter example that you may shade the pot odds slightly in favor of a marginal call in anticipation of the action on the last round if you catch. However, the potential value of this bird in the bush should not be over-estimated; the decision should be truly marginal. Also, you should not shade your requirements for favorable pot odds unless you are certain from the appearance of the board that you will win if you fill the hand. If someone holds trips, there is at least the small danger of his making a full house; one or two three-flushes on board present at least some possibility of a flush beating the filled straight.

I hope that no one will now say from the preceding discussion that John Archer wrote a book advising players to draw to inside straights. For illustration, I have constructed an unusual circumstance in which the strategy *can* be sound. However, consider a situation in which about 36 cards remain, you need precisely a Q, and you have already seen two. You have one chance in 18 of catching, about $18 is in the pot, and you must call a $2 bet to stay. Wouldn't it be stupid to give one-in-nine odds on a one-in-18 proposition!

THE FIFTH CARD (LAST BETTING ROUND)

After the last card is dealt, it is fairly common in Five-Card Stud for someone to have a cinch hand. If *you* have it, you should normally make the opponents call a maximum bet to see your hand. *Occasionally,* a smaller bet, say $1 instead of $2, may induce a speculative call when a maximum bet would have induced a fold, but this is ordinarily poor tactics. The whole thing is too unpredictable, and you may as well attempt to make as much money on the hand as possible. A *rare* situation could be imagined in which a check with the intention of a later raise might be effective. For practical purposes, however, this ploy is worth little notice because of a widely respected axiom: do not bet into a possible cinch. Note that if you do have a cinch winner, the *possibility* that you have it will be revealed by your board.

For example, if you have a pair of Aces (one in the hole) and no one else shows a pair, another Ace, or a possible straight or flush, you have a cinch. And everyone can see that you *might* have it. If you check, no one is likely to bet.

Note again the value of card watching—particularly in this poker form. Suppose you have low trips and an opponent shows a high pair. Normally you must be concerned that he may have high trips. But if you have seen both of the cards he needs, you are obviously aware that the best hand he can have is two pairs. You may bet or raise with confidence.

In this case, of course, you are not really betting into a possible cinch hand, although it may appear to be one to a less observant player. Otherwise, the axiom is one generally best observed, but there are exceptions.

Suppose you know your hole card gives you a winning hand against three or more opponents except for the possibility of a straight by one of them. Before becoming intimidated by the four-straight, try to make some inference about the hole card.

For example, the opponent may show 5,9,6,8, the cards having fallen in that order. A 7 would make a straight. But would the player have stayed with 7,5 in the first place?

Well, some people will stay with virtually any first two cards. But would even an incompetent have continued to play 7,5,9 in the hope of making *two* consecutive inside draws?

Against such a board, you should take a chance and "bet into a possible cinch"; you do not want to let the other players get away with a free ride against your probable winner. In fact, if the "possible straight" is held by a player of any competence, you can be *positive* that he has no straight, but rather a small pair or a high card in the hole.

Except for something like a pot-sized bet in a high-limit game, bluffing will usually fail. Nevertheless, when you have a reasonable bluffing hand on the fifth card in a fixed-limit game, the possible payoff can be sufficient that you should sometimes try. At least when you fail, you will help keep your opponents guessing on later hands.

Say you have played a K in the hole all the way, no Ace has shown, and you catch an ace on the last card. A bet *may* induce a cautious opponent with a small concealed pair to believe you have made a pair of Aces.

While these bluffs are in large measure "advertising" plays, they should not be made without at least an outside chance of success. Suppose, for example, that you show four clubs, the last one being the Q. A competent opponent, who knows you are competent, shows the Ace of clubs, and someone has folded the K along the way. You are never going to make that opponent believe you have a flush, simply because he will know you would not have played the J or lower club in the hole to this point. He will know your play has been based on either a pair or a very high card in the hole.

In an occasional variation of Five-Card Stud, the last card is dealt down like the first. This introduces somewhat more of a tendency for bluffing, but obviously many more good hands will be concealed than otherwise.

Against two or more opponents, it is well to assume that *someone* has at least a pair; an Ace high or a very low pair is unlikely to win if betting occurs—even though you have played properly to this point and can still beat what you can see. Unless there is raising, however, a fairly high pair should probably continue to be played. Against a single opponent who bets, suspect a bluff. With just a low pair, he probably would check; it is usually well to take a chance that he has not actually drawn the very good hand that he is attempting to represent.

THE CASINO GAME

Five-Card Stud is not very popular in Nevada, but a few games may be found. Usually these are for rather low stakes, and the action tends to be cautious; thus the percentage cut by the house is likely to be unacceptably high. For the latter reason, I do not generally recommend that you play.

If you do find a game with a sufficiently low cut to make the enterprise worthwhile, play like a robot according to previous instructions. Largely forget about any advertising value of bluffs or other variations in play; you are unlikely to compete against the same people enough to make these pay off. If you soon see that more than one or two opponents play essentially as you do, quit. You will not be able to beat even a modest house cut in this game unless nearly all opponents are fairly inept.

Antes tend to be low in casino Five-Card Stud, but there will usually be a forced bet on the first round. From then on, the betting will be structured along lines similar to those previously described for casino stud games. One Strip casino whose poker area used to offer Five-Card Stud exclusively posted a rule that no check-raising

was allowed. Such a rule is common in private games but unusual in
the casinos.

Five Card Stud for Low

This game is often appropriately called "Sudden Death." The
reason is that a single card can quickly turn an excellent hand into a
poor one. As in Lowball games in general, the element of luck plays
much more of a role than in Hi or Hi-Lo. Playing properly,
nevertheless, the good player still has the edge, and the game is
entirely acceptable.

Strategy is fairly simple. Play the first two cards with an 8 low or
better. Throughout the hand you must assume that every active
opponent has a reasonably low card in the hole, but it is not
necessary that you beat the board at this early stage. Do not play
with a 9 at this point (unless everyone else has a higher card). While a
9, 10, or even higher may eventually win, it makes little sense to
begin the hand with no chance of making anything better than that.

On the third card, continue to play if you still have an 8 low or
better. Also play with any higher hand that beats the board.

On the fourth card, you normally want to beat the board.
However, the pot can easily make it worthwhile to play with a 9 if
just one opponent shows a better board. The last card may ruin his
hand. In fact, the fourth card may *already* have paired him and he is
just bluffing along.

That leads to a corollary strategy. If you have an excellent low
board but your fourth card pairs your hole card, you should
consider a bluffing bet at this point against very high boards. You
may steal the pot at this point, and you can be confident that you will
not be raised. If your fifth card still gives you the lowest board, your
maximum bet then will put great pressure on your opponents.

Against a *single* opponent, it is normally worthwhile to call with
any hand not containing a pair.

On the fifth card, do not give up too quickly if you catch, say, a K
against a single opponent with a very low board. That fifth card (or
even the fourth) may have paired him. And if so, he will surely bet.
(Wouldn't you under similar circumstances?)

On the other hand, if you catch a K or Q and he catches a J, you
can be almost sure you are beaten. *No one* would play this game with
a J in the hole, and thus your only hope would be that he has been
bluffing all along with a paired fourth card—possible but ordinarily
too remote to be worth the gamble of a maximum call.

I offer these tips as a bonus: really good hands are uncommon in
this game. A 10 or better will usually win. But you must judge the
board and the opponents. Some people will play with a 10 in the hole
(don't do it). Some good players will play with a 9 in the hole
(borderline; I don't do it). Raising is uncommon, simply because the

low hand is first to act, and any potential raiser will be competing against a better board. Still, with an Ace in the hole and a very good hand, you should consider raising in excellent position on the third or fourth card if you are just slightly second best on board. Always bet if you are low on board and your hole card is satisfactory.

Five-Card Stud—Hi-Lo

Ordinarily, high-low games should be played from the outset with a hand giving a good prospect for low. Five-Card Stud Hi-Lo is a major exception. You should play for high or not at all. The reason is the "sudden death" feature just discussed with Five-Stud Lowball. A single card can ruin a previously excellent low hand. However, a pair will always retain its value for high. Even if extra cards do not help the hand, they cannot hurt it.

In the early and middle stages, play almost exactly as you would at Five-Stud Hi. About the only exception is when you have an Ace and low card, seeing other Aces should not compromise your play.

Near the end, if you happen to find yourself with a good low (say you have started with Ace,7 or so), that is all the better. Note that you have been playing with two-way possibilities all along.

Six-Card Stud

Six-Card Stud is dealt and bet like Five-Card Stud except that after the fifth card (fourth up-card) is dealt, another card is dealt down (to give a second hole card) and an extra betting round occurs. The limit normally increases during the last two rounds or whenever a pair shows. The game may be played high, low, or high-low.

SIX-CARD STUD FOR HIGH

Requirements for playing during early rounds are the same as for Five-Card Stud, with an uncommon exception to be noted momentarily. At the end, however, note that possible straights and flushes exposed become more dangerous because of the extra card. A medium-sized two pairs is the average winning hand. Nevertheless, I will usually risk a call with a pair of Aces or even Ks on the last round if no raising has occurred and I am not overly worried about a straight or flush behind me.

Contrary to common advice, I recommend that if you happen to find yourself holding a three-flush after three cards you should take another card, even when you would not do so in Five-Card Stud, *provided* several players are active and you have seen no more than one of your suit around the board.* Naturally, you will not play

---

*The advice is not quite as radical as it might seem, as you *will* have a high card or two to have been in this long.

further on this basis alone unless the fourth card helps the hand.

A casino variety of Six-Card Stud is played that starts like Seven-Card Stud: two hole cards and an up card are dealt before the first betting round, and all remaining cards are dealt up. Thus, only four betting rounds occur instead of five.

Most of these games are for low limits and thus too high a percentage house cut. Ordinarily, the Nevada casino games worth playing are the seven-card varieties (including Hold 'Em, to be discussed in the next chapter). If you find a six-card game with a satisfactory cut, play the first round only with a high pair, a three-flush or three straight, or Ace,K in the hole with no Ace or K in sight. Do not play a low pair. (Of course, if the low pair is in the hole and you are high on board, you will have a forced bet under commonest rules. However, do not call a raise; do not play the fourth round unless *both* of your up cards beat the board.)

After the fourth card, continue to play if you have a four-flush or four-straight. Otherwise play if you can beat the board (note the preceding exception) unless raising convinces you that someone has a better hand.

SIX-CARD STUD FOR LOW

The initial staying requirements at this game are the same as for the five-card variety: two to an 8 low. Thereafter, however, remember that opponents' hands are not as easily ruined as in "Sudden Death." Thus if your third or fourth card is bad (higher than 9, or a pairing card), do not stay unless *every* opponent also has a card at least as bad. You can play a bad fifth card in the hope that the sixth will give you a winner.

SIX-CARD STUD HI-LO

Play this game for low. You much want to start with an Ace because of its swing potential. An Ace and any card 8 or lower is satisfactory on the first round. Without an Ace you should have two low cards to a 6 or better. A pair of Aces is the best hand possible. No other pair is worth playing.

On subsequent rounds, merely watch the board and act accordingly. At about the fifth card, start thinking of the possibility of winning high if your start for low is ruined.

Note again the enormous potential of an Ace in this game. Occasionally (except at Simultaneous Declarations) it can even win high by its own weight (or more likely by its weight along with another high card). A pair of Aces has some chance of winning low (e.g., if everyone makes two pairs). And if everyone has two pairs, Aces up will also win high for the whole pot. (You are unlikely actually to have this result, however, except at Cards Speak.)

One-Two-Three-Four

A popular derivative of Stud Poker in the Middle West is often called "Push." "Push," however, is the name given in some books to a totally different game. Accordingly, I have titled this section with the less common nomenclature, "One-Two-Three-Four." The designation is appropriate for reasons to become evident. For convenience, however, I shall use the name "Push." Just remember that the game is not the "Push" of some other books.

All cards are dealt down in Push. The game may be played for high, low, or high-low. Five- six- and seven-card varieties are equally possible. As the model, I shall describe a seven-card game.

Each player's first four cards are dealt (down) before the first betting round. Then, another betting round occurs (for a total of four) as each of the last three cards is dealt.

Limits increase on each betting round by integers of one. For example consider our game with a $2 ante. The limit on the first betting round may be $1. Then, it will be $2 on the next round, $3 on the next and $4 on the last.*

No sub-maximum bets or raises are allowed. For example, on the round when the limit is $3, no one may bet or raise a lesser amount (note this similarity to most casino poker). As in our previous games, a limit of three raises per round is allowed.

No checking is permitted. At a player's turn to bet, he must either do so or fold his hand. If he folds, the turn to bet passes to the next player, clockwise.

Since all cards are dealt down, no up-cards are available to determine the player with the duty to act first. Therefore, on the first round, the first player to the dealer's left has this duty.

Note that in a dealer's choice session, such an arrangement would give the dealer far too much advantage if he could act last on every round. However, that problem is solved by having the turn to act first rotate with each betting round.

For example, designating players as A through H clockwise (see figure), suppose H deals and A is thus "under the gun."

A must bet or fold. Suppose he folds, B bets, and everyone calls. On the second round, C would be first to bet. Suppose he does so, D drops, and the others call. E would then be first on the third round. And so on. This betting arrangement makes the game essentially equitable for all players.

Push requires less mental alertness and judgment than the traditional games with open cards, because the deck cannot be

*Depending on the preference of the group, the bets might be half these with the same ante.

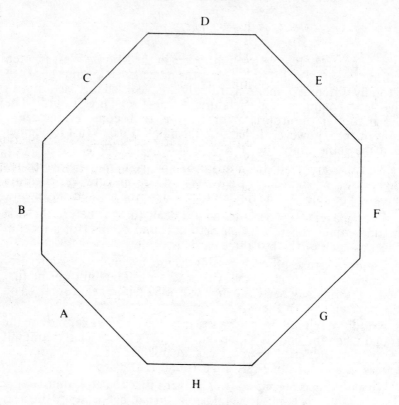

Eight-Member Poker Group

cased. If anything, however, it requires even more knowledge of fundamental hand values. It is a good, relatively easy game for the percentage player.

SEVEN-CARD PUSH FOR HIGH

If you have mastered Seven-Card Stud, its Push variation should give little trouble. A brief discussion, however, provides a good opportunity to review basics. Normally playable hands follow (shade the requirements downward slightly when only a single opponent remains active):

1. Play a small pair (8s or less) on the first four cards only if the hand also contains an Ace or a K,Q. Continue to play after five cards only if you make a high two pairs (9s up) or better.
2. With a high pair (9s or better) on the first four, take another card. Then, continue only under the conditions of *1* preceding.

(A pair of Aces without help may be played further if no more than two opponents remain, and no raising is occurring.)

3. With a three-straight or three-flush on four cards, draw another. Continue only if the fifth card continues the straight or flush or if conditions of *1* and *2* preceding are met.

4. As implied by *3* preceding, a four-straight or four-flush should be played all the way.

5. Trips should be played all the way.

6. Two small pairs on the first four cards present an interesting problem. If you stay all the way, your chance of filling is about one in four. If you could be *certain* of winning with the low full house (and you cannot) the pot still will not usually be sufficient to make your betting sound. Of course, the low two pairs *may* win without improvement. But the odds of this are rather low, and the pot will be small. While the decision is close, my advice is not to play this hand all the way. Remember, limits rise progressively, and you will see no up cards to permit reappraisals of your odds for improving. However, if no raise has occurred, I *would* buy a single further card. While the pot odds *at this point* will not appear sufficent for the bet (you have a 1/12 chance of improving with one card), if you do happen to make the full house early, you are in good shape from then on.

On the last betting round, be careful with two pairs or low trips; you will usually be beaten if raising is occurring. And with only two pairs, a raise could get me out *before* the last round.

With a probable winner (normally this is high trips or better), raise in good position—or in any position on the last round—unless other raisers persuade you otherwise. On the first round, a four-straight or four-flush is worth a raise in good position.

SEVEN-CARD PUSH FOR LOW

In this variation of Razz, play for a smooth 8. Until the sixth card, do not play with more than one bad card. On the sixth, you can draw a seventh even holding two bad cards. On the last betting round, consider the possibility of winning with a smooth 9 against a single opponent. A smooth 7 is a raising hand—except at the end with someone else raising. Little more needs to be said.

SEVEN-CARD PUSH HI-LO

Your previous knowledge of regular Seven Hi-Lo should equip you well for the Push variation. Simply play *slightly* more conservatively during early rounds, because you can see no cards but your own and cannot reappraise your odds for improvement or your opponents' hands.

In the beginning play for low unless you have a good chance at a straight or flush. By low at Cards Speak, I mean a 7. A smooth 8 may be worth a call if you happen to get it late, but do not begin the hand aiming at that holding. Trips (except for Aces) are tempting but nevertheless an inferior hand at Cards Speak. Play them only if they happen to come late. Trip Aces with an odd low card on the first four make an outstanding start. With any holding, however, trip Aces should be played all the way; even if unimproved, at least they are the *best* trips. (And if a pair ends up winning low as happens now and then, two of those trip Aces will be the lowest pair.)

With no boards in view, it makes little sense to play Hi-Lo Push in any way but Cards Speak. Nevertheless, some groups do play it with declarations. In this case, staying requirements may be relaxed slightly because of the possibility of stealing half the pot with a poor hand—particularly with Consecutive Declarations. Play for a smooth 8 if the hand contains an Ace. Any trips make a good start.

If you must declare before an opponent (or simultaneously), you can have no idea from *direct* evidence how he will declare. With a busted hand, however, when you have to guess, you can improve your chances through certain inferences.

A *good* opponent has probably played for low. True, he may have "accidentally" made a high hand, but it is better to guess that he ended with a low. An incompetent opponent, however, may very well have started with some mediocre high hand. Combine this fact with the possibility that he has converted an early low into an eventual high, and thus guess him for high. If you have no information from past experience about a player's habits, it is slightly superior to guess that he is high and thus to call low.

At Consecutive Declarations, this advice must be weighed against that given on pages 34-38.

A VARIATION

A variety of Seven-Card Push (for high, low, or high-low) can be played in which the initial betting round occurs on the first *three* cards. Thus, five betting rounds occur as in the regular Seven-Card Stud forms. According to the wishes of the group, the betting limit may not necessarily progress on *every* round; the last two, for example, might be for the same amount.

I am sure that no special discussion of strategy is needed for this variation. You can adapt the information given previously for the conventional Stud forms together with that given in the sections just preceding this one for the other Push forms.

Observe that the title *One-Two-Three-Four* would no longer be appropriate for this variation, which, in effect, is "One-Two-Three-Four-Five."

SIX-CARD PUSH

Three cards are dealt before the first betting round. Then three more are dealt with progressive betting as previously described for Seven-Card Push.

At Hi Push, start with a pair, a three-straight, or a three-flush. Try for two pairs or better. Trips or Aces up make a raising hand.

At Lo, play for an 8. At the end, try to win with a smooth 9 (or even a 10 against a single opponent).

At Hi-Lo, play early just about as you would at regular Stud. But since you get three cards initially, take another to a three-straight or flush. Thereafter, play for an 8 low or an improved chance at a straight or flush; play a pair of Aces all the way. If you are playing for a straight or flush and happen to make a *high* pair late, consider the possibility of winning high with that. But also consider the possibility that some conservative opponents will not play this game at all without an Ace!

FIVE-CARD PUSH

The first betting round starts with two cards. Subsequent rounds are as previously described.

At Hi, start with an Ace or a K,Q (K,J is borderline but probably all right). Play for a high pair or better. Ignore possible straights and flushes unless you happen to find yourself holding one on the fourth card. In that case, try to draw out. Do not raise until your hand is made.

At Lowball, start playing for a smooth 9, thereafter play a smooth 10, and at the end try to win with a smooth J. Against a single opponent, call with a very small pair (e.g., Aces, 2s, or 3s). He will likely bet even if he has ruined his hand.

Should you do the same thing under similar circumstances? Ordinarily yes. But judge your opponent, and his probable judgment of you. This is just one more reminder that poker is a "figuring" game, and every tactic has its countertactic.

At Hi-Lo, play for *high!* (Remember the exception: Five-Card Hi-Lo Stud is "Sudden Death" when you are aiming for a low hand.) Play any two cards with an Ace. Play a pair. Otherwise, play the first two only if both are face cards, and get out on the next round unless you have paired or caught another face card or an Ace.

Chapter V
THE GAME OF THE FUTURE

By the "game of the future," I mean "Hold 'Em," a recent Texas variation of Seven-Card Stud. It is a magnificent poker form. I call it the game of the future because practically all experienced players like it once they become familiar with it. One recommendation for the game comes from "Amarillo Slim" Preston,[10] a champion of the annual World's Series of Poker: "Hold 'Em ... is my game ... I'd rather play it than anything else."

Hold 'Em is played for high. While low and high-low innovations are possible, they destroy the subtlety of the game and are not very attractive to serious players. The dealer has enough of an advantage to make the ordinary form of the game quite unfair for dealer's-choice sessions; however, I shall eventually discuss an innovation I have invented that makes Hold 'Em more acceptable for Dealer's Choice. First, though, I shall present the game as conventionally played, in which it is the exclusive one played during a session—with the deal rotating.

In fact, a version as played in the Golden Nugget Casino in Las Vegas provides an excellent explanation of the game. The Golden Nugget for several years has been sort of a headquarters for Hold 'Em, although more recently the game has spread to numerous casinos. A wide variation is offered in ranges of limits, and slight variations in rules from one game to another. However, a typical $3 and $6 dollar game gives a good illustration, and the house cut is sufficiently reasonable to make the game acceptable to play.

As usual in Nevada casinos, a house dealer deals all cards. Players, however, clockwise in turn, are designated as putative dealers for purposes of determining the order of betting. This designation is accomplished by passing a buck—or "button" as it is commonly called. The button is a distinctive marker, about the size of a casino chip. The player with the button in front of him is putative dealer for a hand and last to act. Thus, the player to his immediate left is "under the gun" and first to act. On the next hand, the button is moved one place to the left, and the player under the gun on one hand becomes putative dealer on the next.

Hold 'Em is a "widow" game, and relatively few cards are used during a hand. Consequently, about as many players can participate as can get around a table. The typical casino table has places for eleven (plus the house dealer, who does not play). Some casinos have places for only ten players.

After an ante, each player is dealt two cards of his own, face down. These are the hole cards. A betting round occurs, and then three cards are turned face up in the middle. These are widow or community cards; they belong equally to each player and are used in conjunction with his hole cards. These initial three widow cards are often called the "flop" or the "turn."

After the flop, another betting round occurs. Then another widow card is turned up, with another betting round. Finally, a fifth widow card is turned, with the last betting round then occuring.

Hands are made up by the best five cards among the five widow cards and each remaining active player's two hole cards. High hand wins the pot. When a tie occurs, as occasionally happens, the pot is split.

In the $3 and $6 casino game that we shall use for our model, the ante is 25¢ per player. A limit of four raises per betting round is allowed. As usual in casino poker, the tablestakes rule applies. The dealer burns a card before dealing the flop, and before dealing each of the other two widow cards.*

The player under the gun has a $1 forced bet on the first round; i.e., after the hole cards are dealt. The first raise, if any, is for $2. Subsequent raises on this round are for $3. If no one after the forced bettor raises, then the forced bettor *himself* may raise $2 if he wishes. This provides an interesting feature in which a player may raise his own opening bet.

On the round after the flop, all bets and raises are for $3. The player under the gun remains first to act on this and subsequent rounds, but he may now check if he wishes.

On the last two betting rounds (i.e., those after the fourth and fifth widow cards are dealt), all bets and raises are for $6.

The winner of each hand customarily tips the dealer 25¢—the amount of the individual's ante.

It is not essential that rules provide for any forced bet on the first round. To my knowledge, no casino game permits checking at that time, but some have a bet-or-fold rule. Also, some games allow

---

*In private games, I *particularly* recommend this casino custom of burning cards when Hold 'Em is played. Note the enormous advantage anyone would have if he could recognize the back of a forthcoming widow card; he would always know that that card would be "his"— as well as everyone else's.

flexibility in betting limits, e.g., $1 to $5 on any round. With this rule in force, however, a player may not raise for less than a bet or raise made ahead of him.

Check-raise strategy is normally permitted, although you can occasionally find a casino that forbids it.

Some Preliminary Considerations

Before proceeding further with specific advice, it is well to consider some general measures for evaluating the strength of Hold 'Em hands. More than in practically any other game, it is difficult to set some scale of values to indicate strong hands and weak hands. Values vary enormously according to the composition of the widow. "Kickers" among the hole cards and "overlays" in the widow (terms to be explained) can play vital roles.

As one of the simplest examples, suppose 8,9,10,J,Q, a straight, appears in the widow, and no three cards are in the same suit. *Every* active player thus owns that straight (and no one can have a flush, full house, etc.). A K in the hole (the "kicker") thus becomes a magnificent card: if you have it, the 8 is ignored, and you have a K-high straight; Ace,K (*two* kickers) in the hole give a hand that cannot be beaten.

If you have Ace,J, the widow contains J,9,7,3,2, and another player has K,J, you both have a pair of Js, but your Ace kicker beats his K kicker.

The concept of overlays can be easiest illustrated by considering a medium-sized pair in the hole, say 9,9. If the flop brings 2,4,8 in odd suits, you still have a playable hand under most circumstances; while you cannot be sure, the chances are fair that you have the best hand at the moment. However, if the flop brings Ace,K,10, your hand is extraordinarily inferior: that flop contains three cards that overlay your 9s. With just a few active players, it is almost certain that some player (and probably more than one) has a higher pair. (Also, almost needless to say, anyone who happened to have started with J,Q already has a straight.)

If a pair appears in the widow, it is rather common for two players to end with identical two pairs. This will occur when both have a similar-ranking card to another one in the widow. If these two pairs beat the other hands, then a kicker *or* an overlay may determine the result. A high kicker in the hole may give one player the winning hand; however an overlay in the widow, higher than any kicker, may produce a tie. (I should caution now, however, that the appearance of a pair in the widow creates a strong danger of a full house somewhere.)

The appearance of a single card in the widow can suddenly alter the strength of a hand drastically. Thus, much of your playing strategy must be based on the possibility that a future widow card may bring improvement—to you or to your opponents.

This fact is emphasized by a nuance of Hold 'Em: immediately after the flop, it is better to have a split pair than a pair in the hole. Suppose you have J,J and the flop brings 3,7,Q. With two Js out and two cards to come, that is like having only four chances to improve with a card that doesn't help everyone else too. But if you have J,Q and the flop brings 3,7,J, producing the same basic hand, you now have four chances to make trips *plus* what amounts to six chances to pair your Q without necessarily improving an opponent's hand.

Please do not infer that I would rather not have a pair of Js than J,Q going in. I am merely pointing out that in the example given, the eventual combination produced by the latter sequence of events has worked out to produce a better hand than the former.

Strategy

BEFORE THE FLOP

In this game, the key to playing a hand comes after the flop—on the second betting round. Thus, I will play my hole cards on the first round with any *reasonable* start if this is not too expensive. And sometimes I will make things expensive for my opponents, to get more money into the pot and/or to deprive them of playing cheaply with just a "reasonable" start.

Usually or frequently playable hands on the first two cards include:

Any pair.

Any two to a flush that will also stretch into some straight possibility (e.g., 6,10, both spades). (Obviously, adjacent cards are better, e.g., 10,J, both in the same suit.)

Any two to a flush containing an Ace.

Ace plus any card 10 or higher.

Two adjacent cards to a straight (e.g., 10,J in different suits) or, less attractive, two near cards (e.g., 10,Q). With these combinations, however, exclude 2,3, 3,4, and 2,4—because of lack of versatility when the straight begins partially to fill on the low side.

Sometimes two assorted cards 9 or higher that fail to meet preceeding criteria.

I shall explain the last entry later. If we ignore it for a moment, hands that meet the other criteria as playable should be grouped into low and high categories.

The low category includes hands with one or both cards in the 2 through 8 range. The high category includes hands in the 9 through Ace range—i.e., in the stronger-ranking half of the deck. (An 8, of course, is an "average"-ranking card, but for practical purposes, I put it in the low category.)

Further, the top-ranking half of the high category should be sub-classified as the powerful category. This would include hands with both cards in the Q-K-Ace range. Note that in at least one way, any two such cards will always meet the playable criteria just given. True, K,Q in different suits lacks some of the versatility on the high side that is desirable for a beginning straight, but its high-card strength compensates for that flaw. (I will point out, however, that this particular combination is a bit less attractive than any of the other possible ones in the powerful category.)

While adjustments must be made with some circumstances to be mentioned, hands in the powerful category are generally raising (and reraising) hands. Other hands in the high category are playable, and they become raising hands in late position with no previous raises. Hands in the low category are playable if you can probably do so cheaply.

With those generalizations, pairs must be given special attention. A very high pair, i.e., Aces, Ks, or Qs, is powerful and warrants raising and reraising in any position. (Well, you wouldn't really reraise with Qs if you were fairly sure, from a previous raiser's habits and position, that he has a higher pair. But you can seldom make that inference with much confidence.) These high pairs probably have everyone beaten at the moment (you *know* Aces do), but they are hard to help. When they *are* helped in the widow, the cards that do so tend to frighten out weak hands. For both reasons, make people pay to draw or make them drop now and give you the small pot that exists.

In poor position, however, consider sandbagging other hands in the powerful (Q through Ace) category. You will have to help to realize the potential of your fine start, but you are a favorite to win if you do help. Thus, you don't mind having competitors, and may consider keeping your investment modest until you see what begins to develop. This can be especially worthwhile with highly versatile hands in the powerful range; e.g., those with cards in one suit that give you combined opportunities for flushes, straights, and high-card help. In late position, however, raise with these hands: the money of active players is already in the pot; make them pay more.

Lesser hands in the high categmry are speculative. While the pairs (9s, 10s, and Js) are hard to help without the opponents also helping, at least they are above average. And hands like 10,J and J,K have versatility. (They take on even an added dimension when in one suit.) With no raises, these hands are worth a call in any position, and *you* should often raise with them in late position.

Only with the highly versatile (one-suited) hands should you call near the left of an early raiser—where further raises behind you are a significant threat. Except with the pairs, however, you can call in late position, with little threat of a reraise.

The moderately high pairs require special handling; you should call a raise that was made early only if several players have called ahead of you. The reason involves the odds for helping. With someone raising, you have to assume that he has a high pair or a good draw for one. For the moment, at least, assume that you will need trips to win, and you have what amounts to about six chances in 50 of making them on the flop.

I would not insist that the pot offer eight-to-one odds at the moment; if you make your good draw, there should be some calls on later rounds. However, the value of that bird in the bush is reduced somewhat by the fact that the trips will not always hold up to win. So you want at least a substantial pot at the moment to draw to a pair.

If the raise is made *behind* you, with no reraise, you should ordinarily call it. Among other considerations, a late raise is not quite so intimidating as an early one. Also, the pot will have grown.

Every now and then, you will draw to a pair and just happen to find it fitting into a bobtail straight. But that is just an unexpected bonus when it happens.

With playable hands in the low category, you want to play as cheaply as possible with the best pot odds that are possible. In other words, you would like many other callers and no raisers. You wouldn't mind raises too badly if they drove no one out, but they will.

The reason for all this is that with a low hand, you are playing a long shot with the hope of an excellent flop. To make the gamble worthwhile, you need a good return when your investment succeeds.

Low hands are worth a minimum call in early position—on speculation that others will call. While there may be a raise, you can cope with that fact later; you haven't spent much thus far. (Remember, we are considering a $3-$6 game with a $1 force. In a bet-or-fold game, a hand that warrants a minimum "call" is equivalent to one that warrants a minimum opening bet.) You would not call a raise ahead of you, and in middle position, a low hand hardly would be worth a call if nearly everyone ahead of you has dropped: there would be little in the pot, and the potential raisers are behind you.

In *very* late position, a low playable hand may be worth a speculative call against few players.

While the situation rarely occurs, there is one time when you should raise with a weak hand. If you are "dealer" (have the button) and *no one* has called the forced opening bet, this is a good play. You may just win the ante right then, but if you do not, you will have the perfect one-on-one position thereafter.

I return now to the final entry in the list of playable two-card hands (page 91). If you will examine the first five entries, you will see that hands in the high range (9-Ace) that fail to meet the criteria are in the 9-K range (*some* remote straight possibility including two high cards), or precisely Ace,9 (no straight working, but containing the excellent Ace). Before the flop, these speculative hands should be played like those in the "low" category; they are calling hands in proper position.

I am sure you will realize that hands described in the many generalizations of this section vary in gradual degrees of potential strength. E.g., while for practical purposes you play a pair of Ks at the start almost precisely as you play a pair of Aces, the latter is obviously the better hand.

A very recent book by David Sklansky[11] provides a detailed rating scale on the strength of two-card hands, together with a comprehensive discussion of Hold 'Em strategy and related matters. Although the presentation is oriented precisely to the $10-$20 game as played at the Golden Nugget, its advice is clearly useful for Hold 'Em in general with intelligent adaptation.

AFTER THE FLOP (SECOND BETTING ROUND)

If there was a raise on the first round and the flop turns an Ace or K, I am now going to play with an almost unqualified assumption that the raiser has *at least* a very high pair in one way or another. If he doesn't and there are other players, then *someone* has such a hand. A Q is almost as much of a threat. If the flop fails to turn such a card, then I will simply bear in mind the fair possibility of a high pair when a raise occurred on the first round, but I will not be utterly intimidated.

Further advice now assumes that no raise occurred. If one did, modify the following in view of the preceding.

If you have played a low pair, you *must* make trips (or rarely a four-straight) to play further.

With other low hands, you almost have to make at least two split pairs or a bobtail. You would rather the bobtail be a straight than a flush, as it is less likely to be beaten if completed. But the four-flush is playable provided two of the cards are your hole cards; I will return to this matter momentarily.

Only rarely will some other type of low hand be playable. However, you might have something like 5,6 and the flop could bring 2,3,6. At least that low split pair is the highest in sight, and the inside-straight draw adds some value.

As we shall see later, once a flop makes a playable low hand, it usually makes one worth a bet or sometimes even a raise. True, your bobtails are still on the come, but the chance of filling is substantial.

An unimproved medium-high pair usually remains playable if the flop contains no more than one overlay, and if that is not an Ace. To call a raise, however, you should have the highest possible pair in sight. Also remember the caveat I gave about a raise that occurred before the flop.

Approximately the same principles apply to the play of a split pair after the flop, except that your kicker can make a difference in close decisions. Also, recall that a hand containing a split pair offers greater potential than a pair in the hole.

It is assumed that you had something of value when you stayed on the opening round in the first place. Now, after the flop, it is difficult to imagine a circumstance when you should not call on a split pair if it is the highest possible pair in sight—i.e., no overlays are in the widow.

Call with a high split pair (9s or better) if it is the second best possible (only one overlay). Call with even a lower split pair if it is the second best possible *and your kicker is higher than the overlay*.

Other normally playable hands include any two split pairs, any four-straight, and any four-flush with two of the flush as your hole cards. The latter point was alluded to earlier and requires special mention. If three cards to a flush appear *in the widow* and one of your hole cards is in the suit, its size is vitally important. If it is the Ace, you have a great start; if it is low, you have trash.

If you are playing a high hole pair and another pair hits the board, you have a usually playable hand. Until now, however, we have been mostly considering requirements for calling a second-round opening bet; calling raises involves much more discretion. Position, and the danger of raises behind you, must be considered.

Note that if no pair is in the widow, no one can yet hold a full house. But conversely, the appearance of a widow pair always signals danger of such a hand. The size of the pair influences the degree of the danger—or of course the danger of trips.

Suppose you have a pair of Aces, and a pair of 2s in the widow. While by no means impossible, the chance that someone has stayed with a 2 in the hole is relatively small, and you potentially have a good hand. But if that widow pair is Ks, your Aces up are in much danger of being beaten.

Three-flushes in the widow are a great threat to potential straights. In fact, I would not play a four-straight against such a widow; depending on the action, I might gamble along for a while if my straight happens already to be made. Three-straights in the widow are a considerable threat to two pairs, but not quite so dangerous at this point as three-flushes.

We should now consider when *you* should initiate the betting or raising, as opposed merely to checking or calling in your turn. You should certainly bet with trips—or raise if your position is good. You have a good hand already—with excellent chances for improvement. Whether to *re*raise with trips depends on their size and the threat offered by the widow.

If a straight, flush, or full house happens already to be made, *and the stronger part is in the hole,* consider sandbagging for one round.

Bet with two split pairs and an unthreatening widow. Usually raise if these two pairs are high and you see no overlay.

Bet (raise in poor position) with a high pair in the hole (no overlay) and a *low* pair in the widow. You probably have the high hand at the moment, but it is rather hard to help. Try to drive out the weaker competitors before they can improve their hands.

Bet, but do not raise, with a high split pair, a good kicker, and no other pair or overlay in the widow. Bet with concealed pairs of Aces, Ks, or Qs and trash in the widow. (Remember, you will already have raised with these pairs before the flop.)

As noted when we considered playable low hands, a bobtail is worth a speculative bet at this point if you have half of it in the hole and no pair is in the widow. In particular, with two spades in the widow and two *to the Ace* in your hand, you have an excellent start. With two cards to come, you have almost two chances in five of completing the flush, and you very likely will win if you do so. Therefore, start building the pot.

Note that if one of those two widow spades is the Ace, and one of yours is the K, then your holding is *almost* as good as the one just described. But not quite. The reason is that even if you do not complete the flush, there is still a chance that you may help your hole cards otherwise for a chance at winning. And for this purpose, an Ace has obviously better prospects than a K. Nevertheless, either hand would still be worth a speculative bet.

Four-straights, and four-flushes without the good kicker, are less attractive, but I still will usually bet them. Bear in mind that with any such speculative bet, there is at least some chance that the opponents will fold and give you the pot right then, which is something you wouldn't mind at all.

The Fourth Widow Card (Third Betting Round)

It is difficult to separate the discussions of the sixth and seventh cards (fourth and fifth widow cards), as so many of the same principles apply to both. Perhaps the greatest difference is that only rarely will anyone be absolutely certain of winning after six cards. On the other hand, cinch winners are common after seven.

On either round, remember that pairs in the widow are great threats to hands with less than full houses; they are even threats to *low* full houses. Three-straights and three-flushes threaten lesser hands. While a four-straight or four-flush in the widow does not absolutely assure that a completed hand has been made, you had certainly better believe it.

I would usually bet a "made" hand (straight or flush) even against a dangerous widow, but naturally I would feel safer in good position. Even then, there is always the possibility that someone who has checked is sandbagging. If someone else bets ahead of you, you are in danger without the best hand in sight. However, it is entirely possible that he is taking a chance with trips—or conceivably is bluffing. So no hard-and-fast advice is possible.

Just remember that if you call with a beaten hand on the sixth card, you will almost surely have to call again on the seventh, and the limit is higher on these last two rounds.

While sandbagging occasionally pays off, you should usually bet or raise if you are sure or reasonably sure you have the best hand at the moment. The problem with sandbagging at this point is that you can only rarely have a really powerful hand without a threatening widow that is likely to intimidate everyone else against betting. Two high split pairs should be bet with an indifferent widow. (By "high" I mean one of your pairs is the highest possible in sight.) With the same widow, a pair of Aces should be bet—or a pair of Ks with no Ace in the widow. Under none of these circumstances would I raise, however.

If you have bet a four-flush or four-straight on the fifth card but fail to fill on the sixth, it is usually not wise to bet again—although you should call unless you have good reason to believe you will be beaten even if you make your hand.

Suppose the sixth card produces three of a kind in the widow, and this does *not* give *you* a full house. What do you do? Well, let's consider why you are in the pot at this point in the first place when that could occur.

One possibility is that you took a chance against a widow pair on the flop and stayed with a four-straight or four-flush. Now, you have failed to fill. Your hand is very weak against such a widow. Get out fast.

The other possibility is that everyone checked after the flop and you are thus seeing the sixth card free. In this circumstance, the danger is much reduced that anyone has a full house. Whether your hand is good or bad depends on the size of your hole cards. With an Ace and another high card, I would bet! You have as good a chance of filling as anyone else, and if no one fills, you are likely to win with your hole-card kickers. (There is really a fair possibility that everyone will drop on the spot, thus giving you the pot without even waiting for the next card.)

THE SEVENTH CARD (LAST BETTING ROUND)

Little needs to be added about play of the last card. Most involves principles already discussed or that are obvious. However, certain problem hands may be appraised on the basis of the order in which the widow cards have fallen.

For example, suppose you have high trips, but three hearts in the widow cause you concern. Well, if two of them fell on the flop, you have reason for concern. However, if two of them came as the sixth and seventh cards, the danger is much reduced: just a moderately competent opponent would not have played after the first five cards with only a three-flush. I should caution that the possibility of a flush is not completely absent. An opponent who made two pairs or a four-straight on the flop may have just happened to have two hearts as his hole cards. However, if the five-card widow shows no serious threat except for the flush in these circumstances, the probabilities favor taking a small chance and betting high trips. If you are alert, numerous opportunities will present themselves for appraising the threat of the widow on the basis of what hole cards a reasonable opponent would have been likely to stay on.

As another example, suppose you have played a pair of Aces in the hole and the widow cards have fallen in precisely the following order:

The turn—   2C 8D KH
Sixth card—   3S
Seventh Card— AceC

Certainly, a possible straight is present in the widow. But what sensible player would have stayed with a 4,5 after that flop?

The size of pots are such in Hold 'Em that you must frequently risk a call on a fair hand even though the widow shows that you *may* be beaten. Usually, however, this is losing policy if the widow offers multiple threats. Suppose, for example, you hold 7C,JC, (a possibly playable hand at the beginning), and the widow contains:

8C 9D 10D AceC AceD

You had the luck to make a rather good straight early. But now you face a possible flush and possible full house. Also, someone could even have a higher straight than yours. You are probably beaten. Against more than a single opponent, you are almost surely beaten. After all, they stayed on something.

The Private Game

Until now, we have primarily considered Hold 'Em as it is played in casinos. A private game can be structured in the same way, or with moderate variations to suit the wishes of the group. The suggestion I would stress most is that if a fixed-limit game is played, there be a reasonable ratio between the limits and the ante.

In an eight-handed game, for example, if the total ante is $2 (25¢ per player), a $2 limit on the first two rounds and $4 on the last two would be reasonable. These would be roughly comparable to the casino game we have considered. Or, $1 and $2 would be more comparable to the other private games we have principally discussed in other chapters. By agreement, there could be a forced bet under the gun on the first round, a bet-or-fold rule, or the option of checking. The most standard rule is bet or fold. (I emphasize that this applies to the first round only; checking is routinely allowed on later rounds.)

For realistic purposes, these suggestions apply only to a poker session in which Hold 'Em is the only game played. The usual rules are unfair in a dealer's-choice session, because the dealer has too much advantage—and most private poker sessions involve at least a degree of dealer's choice.

I have invented a variation of rules that permits a dealer to choose Hold 'Em without creating too much of an unfair disadvantage to the player under the gun to his left and to others in early position. Assume an eight-handed dealer's choice session with a 25¢ ante (total $2). On the first round, the limit is $1, and the player to the dealer's left is first to act. He may bet or check, but if he bets, he must bet the full $1 limit. If he checks, the turn to act rotates clockwise in the usual fashion.

After the flop (second betting round), the *second* active player to the dealer's left acts first, and the limit is $2—no more and no less. Thus, the player under the gun on the first round achieves best position on the second.

On the third betting round, the *third* active player speaks first, with the limit $3. Note that I have specified *active* players. Thus, the rotating "under-the-gun" position will not necessarily involve the third person at the table each time; some players often will have folded, and the third active player may really be, say, the sixth—or even the dealer himself.

On the last betting round, the fourth active player speaks with a $4 limit. Depending on how many players have stayed, this could be the fourth player at the table, it could be the dealer, or it could be a player near the dealer's left again.

With this innovation, the dealer still has a bit of an advantage by my estimate, but not to a particularly unfair degree. His advantage is less than at some other games regarded as fully acceptable for Dealer's Choice.

Naturally, the limits I have used for the example can be varied according to the desires of the poker group. Whatever these may be, however, I strongly recommend structured betting (i.e., no less than the limit) and progressive increases in the limits from one betting round to another.

I constructed the example for convenience to provide round-dollar amounts and a *continuous* increase in limits. However, if a dealer's choice group adopts limits about like those I have described for most of our other games, more consistent limits for this one would be $1 before the flop, $1.50 just after the flop, and $2 on each of the last two rounds.

"Pineapple"

Hold 'Em was originally a Texas game, but a variant was introduced in Hawaii and is played at some of the lower-limit tables in the Golden Nugget in Las Vegas. Instead of two hole cards, each player is dealt three. The first betting round occurs as usual, but before the flop, every active player must discard one of his three. Play then proceeds as usual; anyone who fails to discard before the flop, and thus ridiculously sits there with three hole cards, has a "dead hand" and is disqualified from the competition—regardless of any contributions he has made to the pot.

A dealer at the Golden Nugget told me that a woman from Hawaii explained this variant to the casino management a few years ago, they liked it, and adopted it under the name of "Pineapple"—in honor of the excellent fruit that is grown in our 50th state. As I mentioned, however, the casino version is mostly confined to the lower-limit games; the traditional form of Hold 'Em is generally played in the higher-limit games.

Pineapple has a feature that commends the game to the typical private poker group in which the table accommodates only eight players, and where a seat or two may be empty. This is really a rather small number for regular Hold 'Em. But with a choice of two among three hole cards to play, more players will be able to see the flop, and the action may be about the same as if a couple of more players were present.

Playing strategy after the flop is about the same as at regular Hold 'Em. Just remember that you will usually have more active opponents than if the same number of players were at the table in the traditional game.

As you might suspect, some discarding problems present themselves from time to time when you must choose between two possible playable hands. Remember, you must discard one of your three *before* the flop.

With a choice of playing a fairly high pair or a two-card straight or flush, I would hold the pair. However, hands with multiple possibilities are another matter. Holding, say, 10C,10D,AD, I would throw the 10C. While the chance for a straight is remote, the flush possibility is there, and a single Ace in the hole is a potentially powerful card.

With 9D,10C,AceD, I would again throw the 10C and play for the flush instead of the straight—largely because of that lovely Ace kicker. I must admit, however, that a disagreeable feature of Pineapple is that I sometimes have holdings from which I simply do not know what two cards among three would be best to keep.

The choice seems very close with, say, 10C,10D,JD. I handle this particular dilemma as follows: if most of my opponents remain active, I discard the 10C; if most have dropped, I hold on to the pair.

Of course, I take consolation from the fact that my opponents will have similar problems.

Chapter VI
DRAW POKER

In the original form of poker, which I would assume no one plays today, each player was simply dealt five cards face down, a single betting round occurred, and then a showdown determined the winner if anyone called the opening bet.* Such a game was obviously dull. The first innovation was to introduce a "draw" feature, which created a poker form that is still very popular today.

After an ante and a deal of five cards, one at a time, clockwise, to each player, a betting round occurs. Then, each player, again clockwise in turn, may throw away as many cards from his hand as he chooses and have the dealer replace them with the same number of cards from the top of the deck. After all active players have drawn their cards (if any) in an effort to improve their hands, another and final betting round occurs before the showdown.

Note that with only two betting rounds, a higher limit will be required at Draw Poker if the action is to be comparable to Stud. In a dealer's-choice session, it is generally desirable to keep the action in the various games reasonably consistent. Thus, if we continue to assume the Stud limits of previous chapters in our hypothetical game (ante 25¢ per person, $1 limit on early rounds, and $2 limit on late rounds), these limits should be doubled, or approximately so, if the dealer chooses a Draw-type game. Accordingly, with a 50¢ ante per person, the limit before the draw might be raised to $2, and after the draw to $4.

Remember that I suggested earlier the convenience in a private session of having the dealer make the total ante, and in the game we assumed, this was $2. If you are using this method, and the dealer, at his turn, is anteing $2 on each Stud game, it would be unthinkable to ask him to increase this to $4 if he chose Draw. This would virtually have the effect of banning Draw games; who would choose to ante $4 if he could choose a different game for $2?

This problem is easily circumvented. If each dealer is anteing $2 in

---

*Well, I once played a "pass-and-out" version of this, but let's ignore the matter. Just note the *enormous* advantage to the dealer if everyone ahead of him must make either a maximum bet or fold.

his turn, this would continue to be the ante of the Draw dealer. However, when Draw is chosen, *each* player, *including* the dealer, would add another 25¢ to the ante.

The dealer has an advantage at Draw Poker that is absent (or nearly so) at the Stud games we have considered until now. This advantage accrues from the fact that the dealer is last to act on the first betting round and thus always has best position before the draw. (Also, while less important, there is sometimes an advantage in knowing how many cards the opponents have drawn before making your own decision on how many cards to draw. This rather seldom makes a difference at Draw for high, but it does so more frequently at the low and high-low forms.)

Nevertheless, the dealer's advantage is not so great as to make Draw Poker unacceptable to most dealer's-choice poker groups—provided suitable rules for opening the betting are in force.

Draw Poker for High

As implied a moment ago, Draw may be played for high, low, or high-low. We shall first consider the traditional and probably still most common form: High Draw. Limits as just discussed will be assumed. A three-raise limit per round will be in force except that the right-to-bet rule applies (see page 9).

A variety of rules are possible for opening the betting. We shall first assume the simplest and probably commonest method for private, dealer's-choice sessions. Each player, in his turn beginning at the dealer's left, may check or open the betting for any amount up to the $2 limit (minimum 25¢ in our game). Once an opening bet is made, all subsequent players must, of course, call or pass—or they may raise if they choose. A player who has checked may call the opening bet (and any raises) when the turn reverts to him. Under standard rules of poker, which we assume for our game, he may also raise if he wishes.

If no one opens, a redeal is made—normally by the same dealer. If Draw is the only game being played, the deal may rotate after a passed-out hand, but this is unfair in a dealer's-choice session; it deprives the next dealer of the privilege of choosing his own game. Many poker groups add a second ante to the first (e.g., an extra 25¢ per player), but this is a matter of option.* When such a custom is followed, the limits may also be raised—say to $3 and $6 in the game we are assuming.

---

*If the custom is being followed in which the dealer, in his turn, makes a larger ante each time, then he certainly must not be required to repeat his large ante—only the small one like everyone else.

STRATEGY ON THE FIRST ROUND

When to Open.—In our fixed-limit game ($4 total ante, $2 initial limit), if you decide to open, you should almost invariably do so for the limit. Whether it is to your advantage to open depends in great part on position in relation to the dealer.

At place 1 ("under the gun") in an eight-handed game, or even at place 2, I would not open with less than a pair of Aces. Ks are adequate at places 3 and 4. (Remember, all players ahead of you have checked, thus indicating no great strength.)* At places 5 and 6, I would open with Qs, and at place 7 or as dealer, with Js.

In the type of game we are discussing, it is quite risky to open with two very low pairs in early position. While any two pairs are probably the best hand at the moment, they are far from any cinch of being so, and they are hard to improve. These two facts combine to make it unwise to open with less than about Qs up in first or second position. I would take a chance with Js up in about third or fourth position, and open on any two pairs in fairly late position.

Almost needless to say, trips and pat hands clearly dictate that you should open. The exception might be if you decide to sandbag in very early position. That play, however, obviously involves the risk of having the hand passed out. In a fixed-limit game, it is seldom worthwhile unless the game is full of loose players who will open on about anything. And if they will open on little, they will call on little. Thus, sandbagging an otherwise opening hand is best reserved for high-limit games in which, when successful, the maneuver pays off well.

One of my favorite plays in poker is to open in Draw on absolutely nothing—with the intention of playing the hand pat and continuing the bluff after the other players have drawn. Unless you try this too frequently, it will succeed more often than it fails, and it is quite profitable in the long run. I offer this further advice, however: if you begin this bluff but your opening bet is raised, give up right then. Your chances for eventual success are greatly reduced, and it will be too expensive to continue the bluff.

It is unwise to open on a four-straight or four-flush. You have less than one chance in five of filling. While calls and betting after the draw *may* bring the amount you can win high enough to make the gamble worthwhile, there is no assurance of this, and no complete assurance of winning if you *do* fill. True, there is some possibility that no one will call and thus you will steal the ante, but the overall prospects for opening with four-straights and four-flushes are not good.

Some poker experts will disagree with me, but in our fixed limit game, I usually *will* open with a four-card straight flush. I recognize

*Naturally, someone *may* be sandbagging, but usually this will not be the case.

that the strategy is not too easy to defend mathematically (less than one chance in three of filling in one of the variety of ways possible). Usually, however, I will coax enough out of my opponents to offer adequate odds, and usually I will win when I fill. The decision is admittedly close, but sometimes I will "buy" the pot (win without a call—before or *after* the draw).

When to Stay, When to Raise—As a rule of thumb, consider a pair of Ks as the minimum playable hand when someone else has opened. Modify this slightly according to position. If a reasonably good player has opened under the gun, you need Aces or better to call. If you have checked with a pair of Qs in poor position and the dealer (in last position) opens, you should probably call.

Very near the opener's left, just call with trips or better. You want to make it easy for other players to call and thus to build the pot you expect to win. In later position, raise with these good hands.

Two pairs continue to require delicate handling when someone has opened. Qs up or better normally are playable. With a lower two pairs, everything depends on the action ahead of you. If you are the first active player to the opener's left, raise! You probably have the best hand at the moment, but you have only one chance in 12 of helping; you want to drive out the potential callers with single pairs that are relatively easy to help. If one player has called between you and the opener, just call with a small two pairs and await developments. If there have been *two* callers between you and the opener, give up! Throw in the hand; you are now a distinct underdog.

"Pot odds" are important in calling with four-straights and four-flushes, but I distinctly disagree with anyone who advises that the pot *at the moment* must offer odds like five to one in a fixed-limit game. Immediately to the opener's left in early position, I will call with the expectation that there will probably be other callers.* Fairly near his right, I want at least one caller ahead of me. But only *immediately* to his right, with no chance of a caller behind me, will I insist on two callers ahead of me if I have a draw to a four-straight. And with the slightly better overall prospects offered by a four-flush, one previous caller would be enough even in this circumstance. Remember: there will be another betting round. (With a four-card straight flush, even one requiring an inside draw, I will call under any circumstance.)

The calling of raises requires judgment and obviously a good hand. If a good player, whom I *know* to be a good player, raises immediately to the opener's left, then I will assume he has two pairs (see previous discussion) and will call with approximately Aces up or better. The reason I do not say Qs up is that I must call two bets at once, and I must remember that the *opener* has something. I want

---

*In this discussion, I am assuming that the opening bet is $2 with a $4 total ante.

my chances to be rather good to have him beaten now and to beat any two pairs he may catch if he calls and draws.

Except under these special conditions, I am going to assume that any raiser has at least trips. Often, he will have a pat hand, but as a rule of thumb, I will put him with fairly high trips and call a raise ahead of me only if I have three Qs or better. I admit that it is tempting to call with even a low three of a kind, but a full house (or four of a kind) is hard to make. I must feel that I have a fair chance to win without improvement. If the raise is *behind* me, and I can call the extra bet fairly cheaply with no chance of further raising, I will shade my requirements downward a bit to about three 8s or 9s; note that the pot will now be rather large.

I will seldom call a raise to draw to a low straight. To draw to a flush or high straight, the pot must offer favorable odds *at* the moment. In other words, to draw to a flush, the pot must be five times what I must put in—six times the amount for a straight.

This is in contrast to the shaded requirements I previously recommended for calling merely an opening bet. I know that I have a fair chance of being beaten even if I fill my hand. This fact offsets that prospective extra money that I hope to get from the second betting round if I win.

Note that the requirements for drawing to the flush or straight will not often be met if the raise is ahead of you, but rather often will be if it is behind you.

I regard the pot requirements for calling a raise to draw to a straight-flush as about three-to-one—or slightly less if it is a *high* one.

In the usual Draw Poker game, a reraise nearly always indicates a pat hand. I will reraise only in good position with an Ace-high straight, a flush, or better. (In poor position, I will sandbag these hands). My calling requirements of a reraise are about the same, although if a raise and reraise are both *ahead* of me, I want at least an Ace- or K-high flush.

I would make a third raise only with a full house, and I would assume that any other player who does so has a full house. I say I would *assume* it, but with an Ace-high flush, I might still take a gambling chance and call, because of the size of the pot.

These generalizations must be adjusted moderately by your knowledge of the quality and habits of your opponents, but they are reasonable under usual conditions. You can find very dubious advice in certain books on poker, including some that are rather good in many respects, about raising on high pairs, reraising on trips, and so forth. If you make plays like that, your game is appropriate for little more than penny-ante sessions with the family around the dining room table. In serious poker, you must assume that raises are made with good hands, and reraises are made with excellent hands. And for success, you want to be one degree more conservative than your opponents.

Usually! But that brings us back to the previously discussed matter of opening on nothing with the intention of running a pat-hand bluff. You may sometimes raise under similar circumstances.

Suppose you are in excellent position (dealer), someone has opened in fair position, and one player has called. Now and then, consider raising with nothing in your hand.

Admittedly, this is more risky than the pat-hand opening bluff. For one thing, it is more expensive. Also, the fact that someone has opened, and someone else has called, indicates that there are hands out against you with at least some values.

Still, unless tried too often, the maneuver should succeed about half the time, and that is enough to make it profitable. And when it fails, it has provided some advertising value to help you get calls when you really do have a pat hand. Thus, the money you lose will probably come back later.

THE DRAW

Recall that after the initial betting, each active player, beginning with the opening bettor and proceeding in clockwise rotation, has the option of discarding any number of cards and having the dealer replace them with an equal number of cards from the top of the deck.

Frequently in an eight-handed game (rarely in a seven-handed game), the deck will be exhausted before everyone can complete his draw. Note that eight five-card initial hands will use 40 of the 51 available cards (51 instead of 52, because the last card is never dealt). If 11 cards are drawn and the player(s) in late position still need more, the discards are shuffled and cut, and the draw(s) are completed from these.

A player who must draw from the discards should be careful *not* to put his own discards among these. He is not required to run the risk of getting back one or more of the useless cards he held previously.

Unless your hand is pat, you should know that the best mathematical odds for improvement are to discard the maximum number of unpaired cards; i.e., draw three to a pair, two to trips, and obviously one to two pairs (or to a four-flush or four-straight). However, an element of deception is frequently important in the draw; also, you occasionally have a choice in precisely which of two hands you may try to make.

The simplest illustration of deception on the draw involves those rare circumstances when you are dealt a pat four of a kind. Do you draw one card in an effort to lead your opponents to believe you started with two pairs, or are trying to make a straight, or do you play pat, suggesting that you probably hold a straight? The answer depends on your action before the draw. If no raising has occurred, e.g., you have opened or have made just a sandbagging call, then you should draw one. If you have raised, you should usually play pat.

I say *usually* because in certain circumstances you might have made a single raise in late position, and a one-card draw may still deceive your opponents into thinking you have a high two pairs or trips with a kicker. That possibility will depend on how well your opponents know your habits, and you must judge this matter for yourself. But I repeat, if you have raised, normal better strategy is to play four of a kind pat.

Opportunities for the preceding strategy are rare, simply because a pat four-of-a-kind is rare. Three of a kind, however, are frequent, and a deceptive draw is usually indicated. In other words, normally hold a kicker and draw one.

This tactic requires understanding, and bear in mind that once again I have said *usually*. Mathematically it is better to draw two to trips: the chances for a full house are identical, but you have twice as good a chance for four of a kind, and thus a moderately better chance for *some* improvement. In any event, however, the chances for any improvement are small (about one in 10 or 12), and if possible you do not want to disclose your fine three of a kind. But suppose you have already advertised a good hand with a raise: in this case, give yourself the greatest chance of improvement by drawing two. The only other time that theoretically you might draw two would be with the hope that your opponents will figure you for a pair and a kicker, but that is too remote a consideration for practical application.

And *should* you ever draw two to a pair—holding a kicker? Remember, drawing three gives the best chance for overall improvement. Well, there are times when you can be fairly certain that you need a *specific* hand to win—say Aces up. Now and then, occasions occur when you can virtually know from an opponent's habits that he has two pairs. (The circumstances are too involved to warrant discussion at this point; they are brought out piecemeal elsewhere.) In this case, drawing two cards to an Ace and a pair can be mathematically the better play.

In a different uncommon circumstance, you may *infer* that mathematical odds favor keeping a high (K or Q) kicker to a pair of Aces. Suppose someone has opened in early position, someone else has called near his left, and both draw three cards ahead of you. They both obviously have pairs, and the chances are great that one holds the other two Aces. If so, you cannot make trip Aces, but Aces up will probably win. By holding the high kicker, you are giving yourself a better chance for a *high* Aces up, plus retaining the possibility, when no one improves, that your high kicker will be just the card you need to win against the other pair of Aces.

Under nearly all conditions, however, draw three to a pair— forget about kickers. (Bear in mind, though, that *many* unsound players *do* routinely hold Ace kickers; it is important to know the habits of your opponents.)

The preceding introduces the occasional question in choosing between which of two possible hands to try to make on the draw. Again, let's start with the simplest example, where no real problem is involved. Sometimes you have the opportunity to draw to either a straight or a flush. Say you hold KD,QD,JD,10C,2D. While you have a choice to make, the choice is obvious. Not only is the flush a better hand than the straight, but it is slightly easier to fill; you clearly should discard the 10.

On the other hand you will frequently have a choice between drawing to a pair or to a straight flush. The pair is about twice as easy to help, but is much less likely to help *as much* as hitting a straight or flush. One rule of thumb is to ask which hand, the pair or the "bobtail," kept you in the pot in the first place. If a high pair was sufficient for you to call or open, it should probably be played— unless you are persuaded by something about an opponent's draw, action before the draw, or both that he has trips or better. With a low pair, the bobtail was almost surely the only reason you stayed (and this can occassionally be true with a high pair): throw away one of the cards of the pair.

Rarely, you may have a normally playable high pair but the chance to draw to a straight flush. E.g., you may have KS and KH but also Q,J,10—all hearts. I can hardly think of a situation in which it could be better tactics to draw to the Ks. Any of 15 cards will give you a powerful hand, and you have at least a prayer for a magnificent straight-flush. Throw away the K of spades. In fact, I would virtually always draw to an *inside* straight flush in these circumstances, say KS,KH,QH,10H,9H.

Previously, we considered pat-hand bluffs and deceptive draws, the most common of the latter being to hold a kicker to three of a kind. A related tactic, recommended by some authors, is occassionally to play pat with trips or a high two pairs.

In my opinion, this ploy is just too cute for practical use. For it to be worthwhile, you must make the following assumptions:

1. You have the best hand before the draw.
2. No one will draw out against you.
3. Someone with moderate values will suspect (from previous habits) a pat-hand bluff—and will call when he would not have called against a one-card draw.

All that is quite an order. True, after you have shown your hand, some advertising assets will result. But I do not like giving up that one chance in 12 of making a great hand—just in case I may need it to win a big pot.

BETTING AFER THE DRAW

The opener is first to act after the draw. As usual, the remaining players who have called then act in turn clockwise. Recall that the limit increases on this second and final betting round (to $4 in the hypothetical game we assume for our example).

Whether to check, bet, call, raise, or drop with a particular hand naturally depends on your estimate of your opponents' strength on the basis of the number of cards drawn and the possibility that they may have helped. So many variables are involved that only a small amount of specific advice is possible; your judgment is required and is based on position, the opponents' prior action during the hand, and your knowledge of their habits.

While the dealer has an overall advantage in Draw, it is modified by the fact that on the second betting round, the worst position is assumed by whoever happened to open. Best position then obviously accrues to the active player nearest his right. That fact provided part of the reasoning for the recommendations in the earlier section on opening.

It is rarely wise to initiate the betting with less than Aces up. With such a hand, a bet is usually worthwhile against three-card draws.

A two-card draw by an opponent must strongly alert you to trips. You should assume he has trips unless: he is known strongly to favor holding kickers; *and* his action before the draw convinces you that he did not start with trips.

If you have opened with, say, trip Aces, have been raised before the draw, and the raising opponent draws a card or more, consider sandbagging after drawing your one card (you would almost routinely have held a kicker). You expect the opponent to bet, and then you can come back with a raise.*

Almost an axiom of Draw Poker for high is never to bet into a one-card draw (unless you have a pat hand or have drawn the equivalent of one). While such a bet is certainly dangerous, the strategy should not be followed *too* religiously. Sometimes you can judge fairly accurately, from the opponent's habits, that he has two pairs—sometimes that he has trips. If you are reasonably sure that you can beat the hand to which he has drawn, it is well to bet on the assumption that he has failed to fill with the draw.

Similarly suppose you hold something like trip Aces, an opponent behind you has drawn one card, and say about two other opponents have drawn two or three each. It is frequently well just to hope that the one-card draw failed to fill the hand instead of checking and thus sacrificing your opportunity to get calls from fair hands around the board.

---

*If you happen to be in one of those games in which check-raising is forbidden, simply make a minimum (25¢) bet *before you even look at the card* you draw. This is virtually the equivalent of checking, but preserves your right to raise.

Raising is strictly a matter of judgment. For example, if someone behind the opener has bet into *my* one-card draw I would not raise without at least a *very* high straight—and even then I would recognize that I am taking a chance on being beaten by something like a flush or full house.

Draw is very much of a bluffing game. A "busted" flush or straight, for example, after a one-card draw, has powerful bluffing potential. Of course, other players know this, and a bluff will usually fail, but it needs to succeed only a reasonable part of the time to be profitable.

Except for the added danger that someone has helped his hand, it is not much harder to bluff two opponents than one, simply because each opponent knows that you have made your bet with the realization that either might have improved. Also, a single opponent often seems to consider it a matter of pride not to fold a fair hand; but with two, number one will realize that number two behind him may have a better hand, and number two in turn may take solace from the hint that number one has not really felt disgraced by folding his hand.

The best time to bluff after missing a draw to a bobtail is against three-card draw(s), as you know the opposition has at least not started with much. A favorite position of mine is second, when the opener has drawn three cards and checked, and one other player is behind me and has also drawn three. Also consider this when that number three player has drawn one! Assuming your opponents fail to make good hands, the chance for a bluff to succeed often improves with the degree of its boldness.

However, a bluff against *too* many opponents is extremely risky. Not only is the danger increased that *someone* will suspect you, but there is a progressive danger that a really good hand will be drawn somewhere.

As I often have said before, every poker strategy has its counterpart. If someone draws a card and bets against your fair hand, you must simply try to make an intelligent guess as to his true values.

Finally, suppose you are third to act, the first player has bet, and the second has called. Regardless of whether you suspect a bluff, you can be certain that the player who has called without raising is *not* bluffing. It may be difficult to assess his actual values, but he surely has *something* worthwhile, as he knows you are still behind him. Thus, you will usually waste your money if you call on just a hope and a prayer; you need at least some kind of substantial values.

THE SHOWDOWN

After the betting is completed, the high hand wins. (Very rarely a tie occurs, and the pot is split.)

If everyone has checked, then all players who stayed for the draw remain active and compare their hands. If a bet is made and no one calls, then the bettor wins and need not show his hand. Otherwise, any player, active or inactive, has a right to see all hands that have remained to the showdown.

Other Forms of High Draw

Many varieties of opening requirements exist for Draw Poker. I shall describe some of these now. For a number of reasons, introduction of a few others is deferred until a later chapter.

JACKS OR BETTER

Often called "Jackpots" or "Jacks to Open," the name of this game essentially describes it. To open the betting, a player must have a pair of Jacks or a hand that will beat a pair of Jacks. Otherwise, the game is played essentially like the regular Draw Poker just described.

For the expert, playing requirements are almost the same as those described earlier. Just remember that no one can open with a small pair or a bobtail.

Only rarely would the expert do this anyway. Thus, "Jacks" is not quite so desirable a game, as it has the effect of *forcing* the inferior players to play a better brand of poker. Also, a pat-hand bluff is impossible as opener, as eventually you must prove that you had Jacks or better—whether anyone calls or not.*

Similarly, if the opener drops out before the showdown, he is required to show his "openers"—although he does not necessarily have to show his whole hand unless he opened on a straight or flush.

Remember that occasionally you may have begun a hand with a high pair but have an option of discarding one of the pair in order to draw to a bobtail. When the opener decides this is his better strategy, he should put the discard somewhere out in front with a chip or coin on it. This is called "splitting the openers." When the hand is over, or the opening bettor folds, the discard is matched with the similar card in the hand to demonstrate that openers were held.

STRAIGHT DRAW ("BET OR QUIT")

The two Draw games previously described are called "pass-and-back-in" games; i.e., a player can check and then call an opening bet. In Straight Draw, if a player in his turn on the opening round fails to

---

*Well, not actually *impossible:* you could open with a high pair and play the hand pat; but I doubt the wisdom of sacrificing your chances for improvement with such a play.

open, he must throw away his hand. This is a "pass-and-out" game.

These rules give the dealer even more of an advantage than the games just discussed—so much so that Straight Draw is not really suitable for Dealer's Choice.

If you must open with a substantial bet, requirements in early position are about the same as previously discussed. You need a very high pair or a reasonably high two pairs or better. However, after a few players have dropped ahead of you, opening requirements decline sharply. With only four players remaining behind you, you should open on Js. With three, open on 9s. With two, open on any pair above 4s or 5s. With only the dealer remaining, open on an Ace or any two face cards. Note that if no one opens, the dealer simply takes the ante.

I would also open with a four-flush or very high four-straight in any position. The earlier your position, the better is the chance of getting enough calls to make the pot odds worthwhile; the later your position, the better is your chance of stealing the ante without a call.

The preceding is just a rough estimate of opening strategy, because proper play varies greatly with the size of the ante and the betting limits. Under the rules for the dealer's-choice game we have been considering, a low, 25¢ bet is permitted, and people in early position may complicate the game by a minimum opening—and there may be similar minimum calls. In this case, the first substantial raise really amounts to the true opening bet; but players in late position will need more than a small pair to make such a raise. Those early minimum bets may have been made with middling pairs, or as sandbagging maneuvers.

In any event, I do not recommend that pass-and-out Draw games be permitted in dealer's-choice sessions. Thus, I shall not analyze this game in further detail.

BLIND OPENINGS (AND RAISES)

Some Draw games *require* some minimum opening bet by the man under the gun. (This would be 25¢ under the betting structure we have assumed.) Some others require such an opening bet *plus* a similar raise by the second player. (This latter is called a "blind-and-straddle" game—the second player being the "straddle.") Thus, these early forced bettors are really just making a routine addition to the ante, and the game is totally unsuitable for Dealer's Choice.* For fairness, a blind-opening or blind-and-straddle game must be the only one played during a session—or at least for one complete series of deals around the table.

---

*In fact, a game can be so structured that the blind-and-straddle bets are the *only* antes, so we are really getting far away (temporarily) from the type of poker we are primarily considering.

Note that for practical purposes, the player to the immediate left of the blind bettor(s) is really the "opener." Calling and raising strategy varies greatly with the particular rules and limits in force. Since these games are only played in rather limited circles, I shall not attempt to analyze them in detail. I merely include them to make you aware of their existence.

PROGRESSIVE OPENERS

Sooner or later, you will run into a dealer's-choice game in which someone will deal a variation of Jackpots in which, after a passed-out hand, opening requirements are increased to Qs on the next hand. If that is passed out, Ks are next required. Then Aces. Ordinarily, if all this goes so far that the fourth hand is passed, the requirements revert to Js.

Some players seem to think this novelty adds "excitement." Actually, it just introduces dullness: too much time is spent dealing instead of playing poker.

If someone imposes this game on you, your calling requirements obviously increase with the requirements for opening. If the requirements should happen to progress to Aces, you need something better than Aces to call, and a small two pairs are quite unattractive.

JACKS AND BACK

A variation of Jackpots is sometimes dealt in which, after a deal is passed out, the hands are retained and played under the rules of Lowball Draw—the subject of the following section. Little analysis is needed at the moment. With an uncommon exception, I believe you should play the initial (high) interval just as you would the regular Jackpots recently described. That exception comes with a *very* low straight.

For example, Ace,2,3,4,5, while a good hand in High Draw, is an unbeatable hand at Lowball (California scale). Thus, you should pass this hand and hope the entire deal is passed out for high. Note that in poor position, even if the hand is opened for high, you will have sandbagged without the danger of losing the chance to play the hand.

I would similarly pass a 6-high straight, which could become a 6 for low in Lowball. With more borderline choices, I shall leave you on your own—after you have read the following section.

Lowball

Lowball, or Draw Poker in which the low hand wins, is structured like the regular draw previously discussed. We shall assume the same limits as before for our hypothetical Draw game. After the ante, each player receives five cards, and an initial betting round allows checking or an opening bet in turn, with calling or raising as in regular Draw. After the draw, the final betting round and showdown (if any) occur.*

While there is inconsistency in the scale for low values in high-low games, there is little disagreement in games played strictly for low: practically all groups count the Ace low and disregard straights and flushes. Thus, the lowest possible hand is Ace,2,3,4,5. A "flush" is simply five cards of different ranks; the fact that they all happen to be of the same suit is immaterial.

A simplistic introduction to hand values at Lowball might be to advise you to play for a smooth 8. This is approximately the average winning hand. A 7 or better is a superior hand, and a 9 has a reasonable chance.

However, position is especially important at Lowball, and the potential value of a hand can change greatly depending on this factor. In fact, there are circumstances in which, with the same 8-low hand, best play might call for checking, opening, calling, raising, or folding.

You should be aware that if Lowball is frequently played in your dealer's-choice group (or if you are in a session of Lowball only), your capital must be somewhat greater for a high probability of success than at traditional Draw Poker. For one thing, more raising and bluffing occur. Also, luck plays a greater factor in the short run. This is largely because you must play many more hands on almost pure speculation than at High Draw.

In other words, with the great majority of High Draw hands, you go in with certain irreducible values: when you draw to a high pair, two pairs, or three of a kind, you are assured that you are *not* going to come out with anything less. At Lowball, however, you may draw to a magnificent hand like 2,3,4,5—a potentially perfect or otherwise excellent hand. If you are so unlucky as to draw a card that gives you a pair, a very common occurrence, your potentially fine hand is suddenly very poor.

Strategy Before the Draw—I am confident that from previous discussions you now will understand "good" and "poor" position to involve two concepts. Your position is poor if your are near the dealer's left, and it tends to be poor if you are near the opener's left. It is good if several players have checked ahead of you or if the opener

---

*In some games, the betting differs from High Draw on the second round in that the first active player to the dealer's left bets or checks first, regardless of who has opened. In fact, this variation probably should be regarded as the "standard" rule for Lowball. Also, the game may be played "pass and out" on the first round. However, I shall analyze the game primarily as it is usually played in private, dealer's-choice sessions: the opener acts first after the draw; a player may check and back in before the draw.

is near your left and no one has raised.

In very bad position, it is unwise to open with less (or perhaps I should say *more*) than a pat 7 or a draw to a 6. If you open with a draw to a 6, the hand should preferably be one with about a 9, which will give you a later option of drawing or playing pat—depending on the action and number of opponents. Even with a good pat hand, you should consider sandbagging in our "pass-and-back-in" game. True, you would find it disagreeable to check a "wheel" and have the hand passed out. However, if no one opens in later position (when opening requirements are looser), no one would likely have called your opening bet anyway. Thus you would win only the ante, whereas at other times the play would help you win a really large pot.

A decision to sandbag depends much on the quality of the opposition. If players frequently make unsound calls with hands they would not open, then sandbagging is less likely to work to your advantage.

In excellent position, open with a rough 8. In any fair or better position, open if you have a one-card draw to a 7—particularly a smooth 7. (Obviously you would open with a pat 7, and it is almost equally indicated to open with a smooth 8.)

If someone opens "under the gun," you must suspect an excellent hand unless you know that opponent to be a careless player. In the latter case, or if you are to the immediate left of an opener in medium position, sometimes raise with a rough 8 or 9,7,. . . This is a "semi-bluff." You want to drive out the competition that might call a mere opening bet, and you hope to win against the opener with your pat hand—or perhaps with a one-card draw if *he* plays pat.

Lowball is a complicated game, and I can give only a few general principles. I must leave your action in specific situations to your judgment in view of the knowledge you must have acquired from previous discussions. Usually, however, I would raise with a hand if I have a one-card draw to a 6 or less. Occasionally, of course, you will run up against a pat 5. But this is a gambling game.

Another general principle is this: Do not play a hand in which you intend to *draw* to anything higher than a 7—or sometimes a very smooth 8. (Thus, you can see that you should never play a rough 9, i.e., 9,8,7,X,X.)

Do not play a hand to which you must draw two cards. The chances of making a playable hand (which may be beaten even if playable) are about one in ten. With any kind of reasonable limits and normal betting, I would have to contrive an example that would make such a draw sound. (I might mention that you *will* run into many players who do draw two cards in Lowball. They will be losers. They will occasionally frustrate you by making an excellent hand to beat you, but they will return your money many times over on other hands. You want this type of gambler as an opponent.)

With an outstanding pat hand, a wheel-5 or a 6, your betting strategy should be obvious. You want as much money in the pot as possible. Thus, you raise, reraise, or merely call depending on position. When several potential callers are behind you, you do not want to drive them out with aggressive betting.

One of the many oddities of Lowball is that the more the active players in a hand, the more difficult it becomes to improve on the draw. The reason is that when several people have playable hands, they *must* have many of the low cards you would need for improvement. Thus, the phenomenon is not really "odd" at all. The compensating feature is that when you *do* draw a perfect card against high odds, the pot will be large by virtue of the many players who have contributed to it.

The other item of general advice I can offer at Lowball is not to open or call in poor position unless you are prepared to call a raise.

The Draw—The only problem presented by drawing at Lowball is whether to play a fair hand pat or whether to draw a card in an effort to make an excellent hand. Usually this will involve a very smooth 9. With more than two opponents, discard the 9 and draw—unless *everyone* has foolishly drawn two cards ahead of you. With one or two opponents, it is usually better to play the 9 *unless someone has played pat ahead of you.* Against a single opponent who draws a card, it is well to play a smooth 10 rather than to draw to the better hand.

Note that much more often at Lowball that at High Draw, your drawing strategy can be altered by what someone does ahead of you. This fact reemphasizes some of the information presented in the previous section: position can make a vital difference not only in how you play a hand, but in whether you play one at all.

After the Draw. — Betting, calling, and raising after the draw involve many variables of judgment and psychology. As rules of thumb, however, a 7 is a betting or raising hand, and an 8 is a calling hand. A 6 is a hand for reraising all the way (assuming a three-raise limit). Admittedly, it will occasionally lose to a 5 (or a smoother 6), but that is one of the elements of luck. For overall success, you simply must play your excellent hands to the hilt.

Adjustments to the rules of thumb are made in view of the large element of bluffing that exists in Lowball. Because raising is common in this game, pots are often large. Thus, particularly in good position, you must often call with a mediocre hand just on hope—simply because even a slight chance that your opponent is bluffing will make the pot odds worthwhile. Similarly, *you* must bluff at times with only a small chance of success, because those few occasions when the strategy works will reward you highly.

Bluffing strategy can be fairly easily illustrated by a rather common situation when you have opened, drawn a card, and paired your hand. Against one opponent who has also drawn, you should bet! You are hoping that he has drawn a very high card, or has made some very low pair himself, and will fold to give you the pot.

This strategy can occasionally be tried against two opponents if one of them has foolishly drawn two cards. And note the advertising value of the play when it fails; it will help get calls on other hands when you make a good draw. However, the play will succeed too rarely to be worthwhile against more than one sound draw; the chances are too small that everyone will bust.

A similar strategy occasionally works against an opener who has drawn and checked, but you must know the opponent. If he is a good player, he probably has made a mediocre hand (he, too, would have bet with a true bust), and he may suspect your bluff.

This leads to an inference to be made from the previous discussion. You do not bluff with a hand that may win on its own merits. For example, suppose you draw to four very low cards and catch something like a 10 or J. This is certainly no desirable hand. But it still has a fair chance to win on a showdown against a hand that was not pat. The important point is this: an opponent who calls will almost surely beat you; and anyone who folds against a "bluff" would have lost to your hand anyway.

Thus, under all but circumstances too exceptional to discuss, you initiate the betting only with good hands or with hands that are hopeless for any purpose besides bluffing.

LOWBALL WITH THE "BUG" (OR "JOKER")

I have deferred any discussion of "wild cards" until now as a matter of convenience. Some wild-card games will be presented later, but we have thus far considered mostly a variety of games for a dealer's-choice session in which wild cards are not used. I am sure you know, however, that standard decks of playing cards come with an extra card labeled a "Joker." In many sessions limited strictly to Lowball, this card is used and is "wild." That is, its holder may regard it as of any rank to produce the best hand.

Thus, Joker,2,3,4,5 is a 5-low hand, becuase the Joker is counted as an Ace. On the other hand, in Ace,4,5,6,Joker, the Joker would be considered a 2. Similarly, with Ace,2,3,7,Joker, it would be a 4.

When the Joker is used in Lowball, it is usually called the "Bug." (I contend that "Joker" is better terminology, because when this extra card is used in high poker, the term "Bug" has a different meaning. Discussion of this matter, however, will be postponed.)

Use of the Bug in Lowball does not change the game as much as you might think. It really does not lower the average winning hand greatly.

It *does* considerably increase the number of outstanding hands, e.g., 5s and 6s low. However, these hands are still in the substantial minority. The number of 8s and 9s low are increased only slightly, as are the number of playable hands overall.

When you hold the Bug, your playing requirements should remain about what they have been in my previous recommendations. Just remember that your chances of improvement with a one-card draw are slightly better, because there are only 12 cards in the undealt deck that can pair you as opposed to 16 when the wild card is not held. (In other words, you can't pair the Bug.) Also, at the showdown, the Bug will sometimes determine the winner when hands are otherwise very close, because it will always serve as a "perfect" card in the hand.

Possession of the Bug gives you the consolation of knowing that no one else has it. Obviously, you will usually not have it. I still recommend that you play *almost* as before, but with mediocre hands and borderline decisions, be just slightly more conservative than otherwise.

HI-LO DRAW

As the name implies, the structure of this game is just like High Draw or Lowball, but the highest and lowest hands split the pot. We shall assume the same limits as before in our dealer's-choice Draw games. The California scale of values will be assumed, although playing requirements are essentially the same as if straights and flushes are considered high only. Note, however, that with the latter rules, swing hands are virtually impossible. The only exception would be at Cards Speak (or with a very brave declaration) in which a pair of Aces might win both high and low when all other players catch a pair.

Hi-Lo Draw is best played with simultaneous declarations. Consecutive declarations really make no sense at any high-low game in which all hands are closed and thus no clues can be obtained from open cards as to which way a player is going. Still, this distinction escapes many people, and the game is frequently played with consecutive declarations. If you must play in such a session, simply employ the strategy of jockeying for position in the declaration similar to that discussed for previous high-low games. (Recall that the last bettor on the final round declares first; if everyone checks on the final round, the opener declares first.)

Cards Speak is all right for Hi-Lo Draw, but it deprives the expert of opportunities for deceptiveness when he has a very high hand. The reason is that when you play pat or draw one card, your opponents will probably guess you for a low hand. And any time you have played the opening round, you always *will* either play pat or draw one card!

Remember that in this game you are competing for only half the pot, and you cannot know whether you are competing against high hands or low hands. Thus, to have a reasonable play, you must have more than just a good chance of winning in whichever way you go;

you must have an excellent chance. This means that you need better values in one direction or another than you would need in a one-winner game.

Except with an unusual positional advantage to be discussed, the lowest strictly high hand worth playing is Aces up. Trips are definitely playable, but you should draw only one card for purposes of deception.

A one-card draw to a 7 low is playable. The best draw to a four-card hand is to a very low straight or flush; you have a chance to win either or both ways. The highest four-card flush worth a draw is to an 8; an 8-high four-straight is borderline.

A pat smooth 8 is playable for low in excellent position. In mediocre position, it should be played only if the lower cards will give you an option of drawing to a flush or straight (e.g., 2,3,4,5,8); you will decide on drawing or playing pat by the action of the opponent(s) who must draw ahead of you—and the number of opponents who stay in behind you.

Occasionally, you can relax your calling requirements slightly in excellent position against only two opponents with no raise ahead of you and no raise possible or likely behind you. A pat rough 8, Ks or Qs up, or a pair of Aces might be played. But you are definitely gambling. If, after the draw, your hand does not improve, you had better get out if the opener bets and the caller ahead of you raises.

If you play a pair of Aces in this circumstance, you should still just draw one card! You must not recklessly announce to your opponents that you are drawing to a mere pair and thus are obviously trying for high.

Rarely, you will find yourself to the immediate right of the opener when no one else has called. In this case, you can call on anything, hoping to outguess the opener on the declaration. Of course, you are gambling that the opener does not make a two-way hand, but this danger is partly counter-balanced by the possibility that he may ruin his hand and *you* may luckily win the whole pot. This positional advantage is particularly good if you are the dealer and your opponent has thus opened under the gun and must draw first. In any event, you will draw no more than one card.

In Simultaneous Declarations, if the opponent plays pat, it is slightly better to guess him for a low hand than a high one, and thus you declare high. If he draws one card, you should declare high if you make any kind of pair and low otherwise (hoping that he either paired or had a high hand all along). If he foolishly draws three, he virtually announces that he is playing high with a pair. If he draws two, he is a poor player; while he may be so bad as to draw two to a low in a high-low game, your normal better guess is to assume he has (or will have drawn) some kind of high hand.

In Consecutive Declarations (a game I do not prefer for Hi-Lo Draw but one that nevertheless is played), you should merely call opposite to the opener if you have a poor hand. However, these one-on-one situations are not common in Hi-Lo Draw, and they are particularly rare at Consecutive Declarations: there is a strong tendency for players in good, even though not quite perfect, position to call on poor values in the hope of getting a positional advantage at the declaration.

In perfect position against two opponents in which you suspect that this tactic is being used, *you* should call on nothing, intending to declare opposite to the opener; if you make *anything* on the draw, you plan to assume that the opener has what he represents and hope that your poor hand will still beat the other caller's even poorer hand. The pot odds will usually make this effort to steal half the money worthwhile. However, you must beware of being caught between two raisers after the draw. Your only hope then will be to suspect bluffing or hope that both opponents are going in the same direction; when you are wrong, things can get expensive.

Thus, as you can see, so many variations of conditions can occur at Hi-Lo that it would be impractical to try to discuss them all. You must use judgment according to the situation. I do recommend this: if you have drawn against two opponents and ruined your hand in Consecutive Declarations, you should bet if no one else has done so (i.e., you were the opener or everyone else has checked). Then, when you declare first, there is an excellent chance the opponents will believe you and declare the other way.

By this time, your poker education should be sufficient that no long discussion is required about betting after the draw. With excellent hands, bet and raise. With fair hands call, unless the pressure of raises becomes too great with several players still competing. Depending on the number of players and type of declarations, sometimes try to steal half the pot with a poor hand. Note that at Cards Speak, a poor hand is *very* poor against more than a single opponent; at Cards Speak, there is no way for a hand to win at the showdown except on its own merits.

Chapter VII
SOME VARIATIONS

I would hesitate to guess at how many variations of poker are played—much less at the number possible. Several forms not yet discussed have achieved a degree of status as fairly standard forms. I shall attempt a description and partial analysis of a representative sample of these, plus a few less common games that I have played that illustrate certain broad principles that may help you as you run into the nearly infinite possible varieties.

The Wild-Card Concept

The principle of the "wild card" was introduced in the presentation of Lowball, in which the Joker, or "Bug," may count as a card of any rank, and thus is used by its holder to represent whatever card will improve the hand the most. Such cards are rarely used in high-low games. However, they were once used commonly in High Poker, and are still used to some extent.

HIGH POKER WITH THE BUG

When the Joker is used in High Poker, it is usually regarded as a wild card only to help complete straights and flushes (and straight-flushes, of course). Otherwise, it simply counts as a fifth Ace. When used in this way, the term "Bug" is rather generally regarded as the proper term. Lacking a complete poker vocabulary, many players often explain, "The Joker's wild in Aces, straights, and flushes."

I do not particularly like to see the Bug used, because it produces the incongruous result of rendering the highest pair (Aces) the easiest pair to get. In playing Draw, you must become slightly more conservative in valuing the strength of pairs, two pairs, and trips if you do not hold Aces. A pair of Aces, on the other hand, becomes more powerful than ever before the draw, because it is easier to help.

Note further that a flush is slightly easier to make with the Bug in the deck, and straights are much more common. A three-card straight open on both ends with the Bug working can be completed with any of 16 cards—odds of about one in three. (Also, note that just catching an Ace will sometimes produce a winning hand when the straight is missed.) An "inside straight" with the Bug gives one chance in four (12 cards among 48) of completion.

Simple possession of the Bug enhances your hand somewhat by the mere consolation that no one else can hold it. However, I do not recommend that you relax your standards too much by possession of the Bug. You must still appraise your chances of improvement and gauge the possible strength of your opponents' hands as always.

I have even known players who, with an otherwise worthless hand, would actually call an opening bet and draw four cards to the Bug. That is sheer foolishness. (Well, I did it one time and made four Aces! But that was long ago, and I was very young and inexperienced and drinking a bit too much at the time. On this occasion I must advise you: Do as I say, not as I did. *I* certainly would not try such a thing today.)

One of my most interesting poker experiences involved a Jacks-or-Better game when I opened with 9C,10H,JH,QH, Bug. After the raising before the draw was completed (which included a sandbag raise), I was convinced that my straight could not win. I announced that I was splitting openers, discarded the 9 of clubs (with a chip on it for future reference), and drew the K of hearts—a royal flush!

The original straight certainly would not have won: the showdown revealed two pat full houses and a pat flush. When I exposed the discarded 9 and began raking in the pot, someone cheerfully proclaimed, "Hey, you didn't have openers." The shock of my opponents was increased when I pointed out that I had opened with a straight and had broken it up.

The trouble with this story is that I rather doubt that the pot odds really justified my calling all those raises before the draw (again, this was long ago, and I was far less experienced than now). However, with the Bug working, I did have four cards in the deck that would fill some kind of straight flush, and from my memory of the limits, pot, and sequence of betting, the play wasn't *too* bad. I knew that I would win an exceptional pot if I hit, in view of the anticipated betting after the draw. I did. (I still wonder what I might have done if I had merely drawn a flush. I know that if I had stayed all the way on that, I would have been third or fourth best at the showdown.)

The implications of the Bug in Stud Poker can be readily appreciated. Its greatest intimidating influence is when it is up and some type of straight possibility is developing. Otherwise, I would not alter my playing strategy greatly merely because a Bug is in the deck, although Aces in the opponents' boards become slightly more ominous simply because there are five in the deck.

THE JOKER

In one form of High poker, the Joker is completely wild; it may count as any card its holder chooses (except as a second card exactly like another in its holder's hand). It has been years since I have even seen a game of Joker Poker, and consider it fortunate that this poker form is no longer popular. One might think that the wild card would lead to more action, but it has the opposite effect.

At Stud Poker in particular, the appearance of the Joker on the board greatly intimidates all other players, and properly so. It automatically gives the holder a pair, plus an excellent chance for trips, often a straight, or better. A very good hand is needed to compete against a holder of that card.

The Joker does not quite destroy a Draw game as much as a Stud game. However, if you play with it in the deck, you must bear in mind that trips will be considerably more common than otherwise. The card naturally has the same effect as a Bug in producing straights (considerably more) and flushes (a few more), but full houses are also considerably more common. In addition, while four of a kind are still an uncommon hand, they are not the extreme rarity as at regular Draw.

(I should mention that my disdain for the Joker in high poker does not particularly apply to Lowball Draw, where the card is commonly used and incongruously called "The Bug." To a degree, however, I am departing again from my main thesis—a dealer's choice session that includes high-low games. In that case, a standard 52-card deck is practically universal, and properly so.)

It is well to note now that in wild-card games, five-of-a-kind is possible and beats a straight flush. A slight incongruity is present in this rule, because ordinarily a wild card cannot count as a card identical to another in the hand. Yet there are only four suits: if a hand contains a natural four-of-a-kind plus a wild card, counting the hand as five-of-a-kind implies two cards somewhere of both the same suit and rank. Well, maybe in this case there is a "fifth suit." In any event, the rule is as stated unless altered by some "local option."

DEUCES WILD

This is a form of Draw Poker in which the name of the game tells the story. All deuces are used as wild cards. Serious poker players tend to disdain the game, although there is nothing wrong with it if your group happens to like it.

But if you play it, you must know how. The most important thing to remember is that the strength of your hand varies not only by its rank on the poker scale but by the number of wild cards that help make it up: the more 2s you hold, the fewer your opponents can hold. The converse is obvious: a strong hand made up entirely of natural cards loses some of its value because the wild cards are available to the opponents.

Also, Deuces Wild illustrates well an incongruity of certain wild card games: an outstanding hand can be easier to catch than just a reasonably good hand. For example, there are more possibilities for four-of-a-kind than for full houses and flushes combined. And trips are much more common than two pairs.

The latter fact sets the strategy for this game. Absolutely forget about playing any two pairs. This is a very inferior hand. No natural pair should be played, and the only time I would play *any* kind of pair would be with 2,Ace in perfect position with no raises. Also, four-straights and four-flushes are not worth playing. Straights and flushes are desirable to have once you get them, but in this game, they are not worth trying to catch on speculation when you must spend money to do so.

Despite the large number of high-ranking hands that occur, trip Aces are still probable winners and are worth a raise before the draw. I would raise with trip Ks only if they were made of 2,K,K. Natural trip Qs and Js are worth a call, but trip 10s and 9s should contain a 2. Lower trips are not playable if someone else has opened.

Two 2s make a raising hand. You are assured of *some* kind of trips on the draw, have a reasonable chance for something better, and very importantly, the danger of good hands being drawn against you is substantially reduced, because you have half of the wild cards.

Always raise with a pat straight before the draw. You want to act last after the draw. Thus, in poor or fair position, you are trying to drive out potential callers behind you; in excellent position, the advantage will accrue to you naturally.

Flushes and full houses are clearly raising hands, but unless the flush is a low one, you might want to sandbag in poor position in relation to the opener. On those rare occasions when you hold three 2s, play according to position to get as much money into the pot as possible.

The oddities of this game have led me to discuss calling and raising before the matter of opening. In poor position, I would open with trip Ks or better, in good position with trip Js or better, and in perfect position (dealer) with any trips. Remember: everyone else has checked, advertising weakness.

Drawing (carding) can sometimes depend on the action of players ahead of you. With a low straight, you must assume that a player who plays pat ahead of you has at least a high straight. Occasionally you may have something like 5H,6H,7H,8C,2. In that case, discard the 8 of clubs and try for the straight flush—or at least a high flush. If you miss, so be it; it would likely have become expensive to call with a probable loser anyway. However, if everyone ahead of you has drawn, hang on to the straight and then decide what to do according to how they bet.

Ordinarily, deceptive draws are not worthwhile at Deuces Wild. Normally draw to your best hand. With 2,2, I would throw away everything else unless I held an Ace. With trips, always draw two: because of the wild cards working, you simply give up too much additional opportunity for improvement by holding a kicker. (But by "trips," I do not mean three 2s. Ordinarily draw one card to this exceptional hand. You *know* you are going to have at least four-of-a-kind, and with only a single additional wild card out, you will rarely be beaten. Do not let your opponents think you have trips, and do not announce a pat hand. An exception will occur if you are sure your opponents know you so well that they will realize you would never play in this game with two-pairs or a bobtail.)

Little needs be said about betting after the draw. The calling and betting by the opponents may convince you that a straight or perhaps a low flush cannot win, and if so, save your money. A full house just about has to be played all the way with a three-raise limit, but it is not necessarily a great hand. Remember that in this game, four-of-a-kind, while not exactly common, is no rarity.

However, do not let me intimidate you too much by these caveats. Three Aces still make an excellent hand before the draw, and will win about half the pots at the showdown. Just watch the carding and betting, and play good poker. By this time, I am confident you are capable of using judgment in appraising the nuances.

ONE-EYED JACKS

I throw in this wild-card Draw game, once fairly popular, because its features fall between Joker Poker and Deuces Wild. If you will examine a standard deck of cards you will see that two of the Js (the S and H) are in profile, while the D and C are full face. The JS and JH thus are "one eyed" and are used as wild cards.

Trips of any rank make a good hand provided one among the trips is a wild card. With natural trips, nothing below Qs can be considered a good hand—unless you are in fine position and no one has opened.

DOCTOR PEPPER

It is difficult for me to believe that I ever played this game in serious poker. But in my early youth, the nickle, dime, and maybe quarter bets that we made amounted to real money. I include the game because it has become sort of a classic in the many innovations that have been introduced into poker—and because it illustrates the absurdity to which the wild-card concept can be carried.

This is a Draw game in which all 10s, 2s, and 4s are wild. The notion for all this, and the name of the game, were derived from an old advertising format for the popular soft drink that originated in my wife's home town of Waco, Texas.

In this game, a straight flush is just a fairly good hand! You need five of a kind for a really excellent chance to win, and a low-ranking hand of this type is often beaten by a higher one.

Four Aces may not be playable, and any lesser four of a kind must be played with great caution—depending on position, the draws, and the betting.

The clue for any kind of strategy involves the hands to play before the draw. Two wild cards give you a reasonably good chance, and are better than natural trips (although *high* ones of this type are playable). Three wild cards before the draw are great.

A Stud form of Dr. Pepper can be played. But let's just forget it.

If you are ever in a dealer's-choice session in which *anything* is allowed, and Dr. Pepper irritates you as much as it would me, I suggest you announce a game in which every card in the deck is wild. That should break things up in a hurry. (But no, to be serious, I could not advise you to give up your dealer's advantage, when it is your turn, merely to make the point of dealing every player five Aces.)

SPIT IN THE OCEAN

This is one of the classic wild-card games that involves features of Draw and widow poker. Each player is dealt four cards (down), and a common card is turned up in the center. This center (widow) card *and all like it* are wild. Thus, everyone has at least one wild card—the one in the widow. As in wild-card games in general, the value of your hand increases not only by its rank but by the number of wild cards it contains, because holding a wild card deprives your opponents of the opportunity to hold it.

As in other Draw games, a betting round occurs after the deal. Then, each player may discard as many of his cards as he wishes and have them replaced by the same number from the deck. After the draw, another betting round occurs, the opener acting first.

Forget about straights and flushes in this game. They may be the best hand going in, but they have little chance of winning after the draw. You normally play for four of a kind. While a straight flush is an excellent hand, improvement of a four-card straight flush is too difficult to make such a hand playable before the draw—particularly since it could lose to five of a kind, which is not exceptionally rare.

The typical playable hand before the draw is trips (which include the wild card in the widow). You want four (or five) of a kind, but if you happen to catch an odd pair, you have a fighting chance with your full house and can use judgment according to the opponents' carding and betting. With *low* trips, raise in poor position in an effort to reduce competition.

Problem hands are those with a single wild card in your hand (matching the widow) and nothing else worthwhile, and those with two natural pairs in your hand. Play these hands in good position if it is not expensive. The only further comment involves the two pairs: the widow gives you a full house. Depending on the carding before you (remember, you will only be playing in good position), you will have an option of playing pat or discarding your lower pair to draw to a better hand.

On the rare occasion when you hold two wild cards, you naturally have a guarantee of four of a kind (you may "accidentally" make a straight-flush), and the absence of wild cards will make it unlikely that anyone else will get an exceptionally good hand. Play this hand cozily, and get as much into the pot as possible.

BASEBALL

I do not want to belabor the subject of wild-card games (you should understand the general concept by now), but a couple of Stud varieties should be thrown in, and Baseball is a classic, although rather gimmicky. It is usually played with the Seven-Card format.

The 9s and 3s are wild, but a *3* has a special role when it is dealt *up.* Its holder must either match the pot with an equal sum of money or fold his hand.

This latter feature can create a problem if two players receive 3s on the same round. Is each required to match only the pot at its size at the beginning of the round, or (assuming that the first player to the dealer's left matches it instead of folding) does the second player have to match it at the inflated size in his turn? It has been so many years since I have played Baseball that I simply cannot remember what rule we used, but if your group plays this game, you had better decide on the matter in advance.

The 4 also plays a special role in Baseball. It is not wild, but whenever a player receives one *up,* he is entitled to an extra hole card, dealt immediately. Thus, it is not at all uncommon for a player to end with a hand of more than seven cards. If you have more than six players in the game, you need some type of pre-arranged rule for procedure in case the deck runs out.

You aim for a high four of a kind in this game, and only a straight flush or five of a kind can be considered outstanding. On the first round, any hand with a wild card is normally playable. Otherwise, I would play with nothing less than a pair of Aces or a three-card straight flush. On the second round, stay only if you can anticipate the possibility of a still-playable hand on the third.

The key to playing strategy comes on that third round (with five cards); you must have at least three Aces or four to a straight flush (an exception would be two wild cards *in the hole,* some kind of fairly high trips, and no great strength showing around the board). Since a wild card is such a fine thing to have, you should normally match a small pot when you catch a 3 early and your hand is playable by previous criteria (but in borderline decisions, don't). On late rounds, however (third and fourth), match a large pot only if that 3 makes you a good hand—either four of a kind or a four-card straight flush without too many of the cards in sight that you need.

LOW HOLE-CARD WILD

One more example of a Seven-Card Stud game should be sufficient to give you a fair grasp of this general variety of games, and this one is really wild. Every player will have at least one wild card because, as the name of the game indicates, each player's lowest card in the hole, and every card of the same rank, is wild in his own hand. But note that unless you have a 2 in the hole, you cannot be certain until the last card is dealt what that wild card will be. (An Ace counts strictly as high for purposes of the wild-card feature.)

At the beginning, three assorted high cards should not be played. Otherwise, the variables are so great that detailed analysis is better left to your judgment than to try to cover everything here for this uncommonly played game. A very low card in the hole (or a very low pair!) is good simply because it lessens doubt as you go along on whether the final hole card may change the value of your hand. (A 2 eliminates all doubt.) It is true that the seventh card could turn out to be a better wild card than you started with, but you can seldom remain in a hand that long entirely on such hope. And note that if that seventh card undercuts your previously low hole card, your values can be reduced.

The key to strategy comes on the fourth card. You should continue to play only if you make natural trips, pair your low hole card, or see a good chance for a straight flush developing. With these requirements in mind, you can see that your play of the *third* card must provide a *reasonable* prospect that the fourth will be playable.

It is important to watch the board carefully both for developing strength and cards you need. If no pairs show and betting is modest, a high full house can become a very good hand at the end—provided you had reason to stay in to that point and just happen to catch such a hand. Even a straight or flush could win under similar circumstances, but do not play for such hands; you must have had something far better in reasonable view to have stayed. Remember: Each player has at least one wild card, and he *can* have four. Thus, while four-of-a-kind is normally a probable winner, only a straight flush or five-of-a-kind can be considered an outstanding hand. And again, I remind you to watch the board and take note of the betting: winning hands vary greatly in this nutty game.

KANKAKEE

I promised just "one more." I shall essentially keep my promise by mentioning this one only in passing.

Kankakee is a small city just a few miles down the road from where I have written most of this book. Several authors describe a poker game by the same name, and I feel compelled to include it for sentimental reasons. It is Seven-Card Stud with the Joker as a common (widow) card belonging to all hands. I won't try to analyze it. I have never played it and hope I never do.

Some Other Widow Games

The concept of Widow poker was introduced with the discussion of Hold 'Em (Chapter V) and continued with Spit in the Ocean and Kankakee when the widow and wild-card concepts were combined. Recall that in Widow poker, one or more common cards are turned up in the middle and belong equally to all players.

Hold 'Em is probably the only current widow game frequently played in really big-money sessions.* However, a great deal of serious poker is played for pots around the $25 to $50 range—a bit less or somewhat more—that most players do not consider frivolous. Many dealer's-choice sessions are played with stakes approximately like those we are typically considering ($2 total ante and about a $2 limit on individual bets) in which a wide variety of widow games are employed. Most of these games today are usually played high-low.

I shall not attempt to describe all such poker forms. I shall present just enough to give you the flavor of the high-low widow concept. This will include a rather standard classic to set the stage, then the most complicated form that I have played, and finally a game of rather average perplexity—the three of which should give you a fair understanding of the general problems to be encountered with this family of games.

CINCINNATI

Most descriptions of this game, which goes under a variety of names, present it as a High game. However, the only way I have ever played it is Hi-Lo; if you run into it, I suspect that you will have the same experience.

Each player is dealt five cards face down. A five-card widow hand is also dealt face down, and a betting round occurs. Then, the top

---

*By *widow game,* I do not really include those Seven-Card Stud forms in which a common card is used when the deck runs out (pages 54-55). These games are definitely played for high stakes.

widow card is turned up, and another betting round occurs. Then the second widow card, and so on—until the five widow cards are exposed and a betting round has taken place after each. Finally, the high-low declarations are made (unless you play Cards Speak), and the showdown occurs.

A player may use any five of the combined ten cards from his own hand and the widow for either high or low, and he can use different combinations to call both high and low. Thus, swing hands are common in Cincinnati. Remember, however, that if you call both ways, you lose the whole pot if you are beaten *or tied* in either direction. And with ten cards from which to choose, winning hands generally run very high and very low.

For descriptive purpose, I shall assume our eight-player game with a $2 total ante. I consider reasonable limits to be those that start rather low and increase to $2 (remember, there are *six* betting rounds in this game). The fairest way to play the game in Dealer's Choice is reminiscent of the rotating "under-the-gun" role that was devised for the "One, Two, Three, Four" game described on pages 83-84. Let the first player bet 50¢ (bet or fold). On the second round, same thing by the second active player. Then $1 by the third active player. $1.50 on the fourth round. Then $2 on each of the last two rounds, still with the obligation to bet or fold rotating.*

As in all games with multiple widow cards, you often cannot have a very confident appraisal of the relative value of your hand until late in the game, because a single widow card can alter either your hand or those of your opponents so much. You set certain standards at the beginning, and prepare yourself to alter these with the development of the widow. Only uncommonly will you make a perfect low or a high full house very early, and nothing else can be considered an excellent hand. In fact, four-of-a-kind is not uncommon at the end, and it is not especially rare for a perfect low to be tied.

Playable hands at the beginning are those that offer reasonable prospects for the hands just mentioned, i.e., wheels, high full houses, or both. (Well, I wouldn't *throw away* a *pat* middle-sized full house. It isn't really a bad hand, and you retain an outside chance of making four-of-a-kind. But I would be prepared to get a sort of sick feeling if a high pair later turned up in the widow.)

Hands to be played at the beginning include:

Very high trips. By this I mean Aces or Ks, with Qs borderline. With lower trips, you need your other cards to be in the wheel range (Ace through 5 or 6, depending on the low scale used) because when your trips are eventually overlayed by a

---

*Please do not assume that this betting structure is necessarily "standard." I like it, but you may find a game with an unchanging limit, some other type of increasing limits, checking allowed, the privilege of betting less than the limit, and so forth.

higher card in the widow, they no longer look so good.

Three cards to a wheel.

Two pairs, *both* very high (Qs or better) or both in the wheel range. With these combinations and in poor position, do not call a raise unless one of the pairs is Aces or (with the low two pairs) the fifth card is in the wheel range.

A high pair with two cards in the wheel range. Note that Ace, Ace,5,X,X meet these criteria. But again, this hand should not be played if raising and position indicate that you must pay unduly to see the first widow card.

Two middle-sized pairs, say 8s and 9s, or anything close to them, are pure trash in this game. You have no hope for low, must improve to have a chance for high, and can easily lose if you do improve.

Completely forget straights. Flushes are not worthwhile unless they come incidentally when you are playing for low. A high four-card straight-flush is really not a playable hand, because you have only about one chance in 4½ of completing it with five cards, and you are competing for only half the pot.*

When the widow cards start being exposed, you must constantly reevaluate your hand—not only by whether the cards help you, but by whether they may help your opponents. I must emphasize this principle, because it is important in all widow games, and has distinctive features in Hi-Lo.

Suppose you have started with 2,3,4,X,X, and the first widow card is a J. You haven't helped, but no one else has helped for low. On the other hand, if the card had been a 2, your cards would no longer be playable; the 2 probably helped some opponent(s), while not increasing your values in any worthwhile way. Even with *four* cards to a wheel, say Ace,2,3,5,X, a pairing low card should cause you to pause. I do not mean that the hand would no longer be playable on the second round, but its potential would be much reduced. A 6, however, would be great. While you *begin* a hand with a reasonable hope for a perfect low, a 6,5 low cannot be disdained.

Similarly, suppose you are playing a pair of Qs (naturally with other cards to make the hand worthwhile). A Q in the widow not only helps you, but certifies that no one else can have two hidden Qs. However, a K or Ace, overlaying your Qs, is a dangerous card.

When you are playing for high, a pair in the widow that overlays your full house is a terrible sight. I cannot advise you automatically to assume you are beaten, but you must play very cautiously

*The reason I qualified this sentence with the word "really" is the precise structure of the Cincinnati game I am now describing—i.e., the one in which limits start quite low and progress. If I can see the first two widow cards rather cheaply and know I can bet considerably more later, I might try this long shot early in the game. But please read between the lines in all this and use judgment according to pot odds. As Cincinnati is usually played, without such a wide variation in progressive betting limits, four to a straight flush are a good hand only if you are also playing for a low hand.

according to the betting, size of the pot, and position. In a close decision (well, it will always be close in the circumstances described), consider whether you have any reasonable chance for winning low instead of high.

You do not play for flushes in Cincinnati (I am speaking of the game, not the nice city by the same name). However, a flush cannot be ignored if you just happen to find you have one at the end. If headed by an Ace, it can be worth playing against limited competition when no pair shows in the widow. With declarations, however, do not risk a two-way call if you have a probable low winner plus an incidental flush. At Cards Speak, on the other hand, raise freely: that flush may just "happen" to get you the whole pot— or at least the half you had no good reason to expect to win.

The time to call both ways in Hi-Lo without *excellent* hands in both directions is when you have fair hands both ways, the betting is modest (or you suspect a bluff), and you simply have no clue as to what your opponent(s)' values may be. Let's assume you have a fairly smooth 7 (Ace,2,3,5,7,X,X) in Cincinnati, the widow is imponderable but contains no pair, you have an Ace-high flush, and must declare first (or simultaneously). This is the time to declare both ways.

FIVE AND FIVE

This is an interesting variation of Cincinnati, and I present it as an illustration of the innovativeness available to those who like variety in their Dealer's-Choice poker. If you are a traditionalist, you may become outraged by the format, but to be a versatile poker player, you need the ability to cope with the strange forms you may encounter. Analysis of this game should help.

We shall assume the same betting structure as just described for Cincinnati. As in that game, each player receives five hole-cards. The widow, however, contains five *sets* of two cards each. These two-card sets are turned up with each betting round.

The great difference from Cincinnati is that the usable hands must consist of only *one* of the widow sets plus three, *and exactly three,* cards among the hole cards. Since the game is Hi-Lo, three different cards among the hole cards and two different widow sets may be used for calling high and low.

Too complicated? It really shouldn't be if I illustrate with an example:

Say you hold—
     AceC, 3C, 5C, KC, KH
The widow contains—

1	2	3	4	5
2C	4H	2S	QC	10H
KD	2H	6C	KS	10C

Although you have two Ks, and 2Ks are in the widow, you do *not* have four of a kind, because the two Ks in the widow are not in the same set. Also, while clubs are scattered all through the widow, you do not have a flush, because you must use only *exactly* three cards in your hand plus *one* two-card set in the widow in whatever direction you are going. Your best high hand is a 5-high straight, a very inferior holding in that direction: note the pair in set 5 that could give someone a full house (or even four of a kind), the two hearts in set 2 that could make a flush, a higher straight than yours (or conceivably a straight flush), and the possible straight in set 3 (unplayable for high by the player who might have it, because of the combined threats of sets 2 and 5).

However, you have a perfect low by the California scale (see set 2) or a quite good low by the "6-4" scale (set 3 gives you a 6,5 . . .).

Consider another example; your hand is—

Ace,2,3,K,K

The widow (no single-suited sets)—

1	2	3	4	5
4	5	Q	K	K
10	10	J	Q	Ace

Your best low is a 10—ordinarily not much. But *no one* can beat your low: it is a "perfect" 10, and no opponent can have anything better, as he must play three and only three cards in his hand in any direction.

You also have a magnificent high hand. Set 5 reveals that you have Ks full.

Although no cinch, this is a fine swing hand. Careful analysis will show that Aces full against you are impossible, since anyone with the available pair of Aces cannot have a K. And he cannot have Aces full in any other way: he can only use three cards in his hand. The only way you can be beaten high is with four 4s, 5, or Js. But you can be *tied* for *low* by anyone who also has Ace,2,3. . . . So use your judgment, against very strong betting, in deciding whether to call high, low, or both ways. Some clues may be gained by just *when* an opponent begins suddenly to start raising. Consider his position, the order in which the widow sets have fallen, and whether you appraise him as a sandbagger or a compulsive bettor with any good hand.

Several hundred practice deals have shown me that a rough 6 or smooth 7 is about the average low winner in Five and Five. A flush is about the average high winner. However, these averages are almost meaningless in actual play: you must begin with a hand of playable values (get out otherwise) and then reappraise your hand according to the way the widow develops.

While a hidden full house (or rarely four of a kind) is always possible, a flush is a rather good hand provided no pair appears in the widow. In the latter case, a full house somewhere is very likely.

Whatever hand you may be playing for high, it is well to bear in mind that a high pair appearing *early* in the widow is more dangerous than one appearing in the last set or two. The reason is that most people, while they may stay for a cheap round or two, will not have stayed until the end purely on the basis of a high card plus a pair of some sort. Nevertheless, it is entirely possible that someone playing sound values could just happen to have such other cards incidentally. Also, remember that some people will play on practically anything.

Whenever you make a flush, the two-card set that completes it will always create the possibility that an opponent may make a flush in the same suit simultaneously. Thus, if yours is made up partly by the Ace in the hole, you are assured that your flush will beat his (unless the cards reveal the remote possibility of a straight flush). Somewhat as with pairs, a flush that appears late is a bit less dangerous than one that appears early. It is not at all uncommon, however, for someone to be playing other sound values and just happen to have three cards in a suit.

A straight has a fair chance of winning high if no pairs or flushes appear in the widow. You will make these hands only incidentally, however, in the process of playing other values.

Three of a kind will sometimes win high when there is only a very nondescript widow.

The only really good hands going in are three low cards to a 5 (three to a 6 with the 6-4 perfect scale) or high trips. With the former of these hands, odd high pairs are valuable bonuses, and three-card flushes are valuable with either.

Three low to a six (California scale) and low trips are gambling hands. I regard them as definitely playable if they contain one of the bonus features just mentioned. Also, an Ace among three to a very smooth 6 makes a reasonably good hand. The great problem with low trips is that making four of a kind is a longshot, they are very unlikely to win without some improvement, and when a higher pair overlays the trips to complete a full house, that pair can easily give someone else a higher full house.

In a game with progressive limits that begin rather low and end rather high, and you are in position to see the first two widow sets cheaply, I consider it reasonable speculation to do so merely with a high pair, particularly with some other high cards in the hand. While unlikely, you may be so fortunate as to catch a full house early, and it will be concealed. You then have an excellent chance to win a large half-pot, as you will do much raising at the opportune times. On the far more common occasions when you fail to help, your investment will have been just a small one. I should emphasize that this is sound speculation only with some type of betting similar to that I described for a variety of Cincinnati on pages 129-132. Also, do not be tempted to stay around if you merely make trips; you were trying for a full house.

As in other high-low games with a widow, the important thing to remember when playing for low is that widow cards that pair your low cards are probably helping other hands while doing yours no good. Thus, such cards greatly diminish your values. On the other hand, low widow sets that fit well among your three low cards help you *greatly,* because there is an excellent chance that they are pairing other hands.

Also remember in Five and Five that *no one* can have a lower hand than is made possible by the lowest widow set—because only three hole cards can be used.

Among the peculiarities of this game is that being dealt four of a kind in your hand is not nearly as good as trips: you not only do not have four of a kind, but you have no chance of *making* four of a kind; the card you would need to make the hand is wasted. Similarly, a four-flush in your hand is not quite as good as a three-flush; one of your cards is gone. Also note that a "pat full house" is not a full house at all, but merely trips. That extra pair is practically useless baggage. (Only in *very* freakish circumstances will a widow set help it any useful way.)

Many games with features somewhat similar to Five and Five can be found in other books. However, I am limiting my presentation of widow games to just a few for two reasons: I refuse to describe *and analyze* any game that I have not actually played; and if you understand the principles of Cincinnati, the nuances of Five and Five, and the special features of the simpler Criss-Cross to follow, you should be able to hold your own in the many comparable poker forms you may encounter.

CRISS-CROSS

Many major and minor variations of this game have been described. I shall present it as played by a group I am in. It is a high-low widow game with six betting rounds. We use a type of progressive limits with turn to act first rotating, similar to that described on page 130 for Cincinnati. As in Cincinnati, there is a five-card widow. However, each player receives only *four* hole cards, and the widow has different characteristics from that in Cincinnati plus more restricted uses. The widow is dealt down as in the figure on page 136.

There is a betting round before each card is turned and after the last one. The cards are turned in the order noted in the diagram. Or, they may be turned counterclockwise, but the middle card is always turned last.

Unlike in Cincinnati, not all five widow cards may be used for a high or low hand, but only three in a row. Thus the four hole cards may be combined with widow cards 1,5,3 or 2,5,4, but not, say, with 1,2,3 or 2,3,4. You may also use three in one row for a high hand and

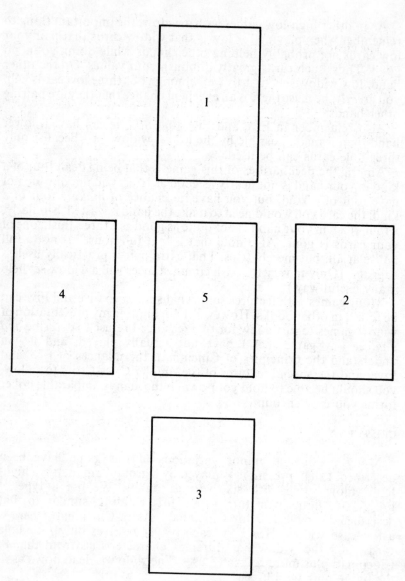

Widow in Criss-Cross

three in the other row for a low hand. Thus, if you stay all the way, you really have *two* seven-card hands from which to pick your best high and low. (Note that there is no restriction or requirement as to how many or how few of your hole cards you may play, as in Five and Five, although obviously you must use at least two to make up a five-card hand.) You will undoubtedly notice some similarities between this game and Seven-Card Stud.

The clearly outstanding start in Criss-Cross is four low hole cards, i.e., four to a 7 or better (or, obviously, four of a kind if you should ever be so lucky). Otherwise, playable hands at the start include three to a 7 low, a three-flush, a three-straight, or trips.

When you play three low cards, three-straights, and three flushes, you see two widow cards and then get out unless you have helped toward your low, straight, or flush. You normally plan to play four low cards or trips all the way. The problems occur when a widow pair overlays your trips (this may give someone else a higher full house than yours), or when too many widow cards pair your low ones. This latter problem is particularly acute in the more common circumstance when you started with only three to a low and have continued to play because of improvement with widow cards 1 or 2.

If you play three-straights and three-flushes, you obviously play *four* cards to such hands, and tentatively plan to play them all the way. You modify these plans with the realization that flush possibilities in the widow threaten straights, and pairs are potential full houses.

While hidden full houses are not rare, a flush will usually win high unless the widow contains a pair. And remember that a "pair" is not a pair unless the two cards are in the same row. If you have made your flush "accidentally," i.e., most of it is in a row in the widow, be *very* aware that an opponent may have a flush in the same suit. In that case, the high flush card in the hole will determine the winner.

A straight is a good hand if the widow contains no pair, not much threat of a flush, and no great threat of a higher straight. If a three-straight appears in the widow, one factor to consider is the likelihood of someone playing all the way on the precise cards he would need to complete it.

Trips will sometimes win high if the widow is trashy.

For low you ordinarily aim for a 7, but an abnormally high widow can easily lead you to adjust your values, just as a very low one can convince you that a 7 will be beaten.

Some Stud Variations

BIG SQUEEZE

This game is something of a hybrid between Six- and Seven-Card Stud, played high-low. One card is dealt down and one up to each player. Eventually, four cards are up and then a final card is dealt down—naturally with a betting round on each up card and another at the end.* Then, in clockwise rotation beginning at the dealer's left,

---

*Alternatively, some groups deal the last card up; thus, there is only one hole card per hand.

each active player has the option of throwing away one of his cards and drawing another—up or down according to the card he threw away. If he draws this card, he must "buy" it by adding some specified sum to the pot—say $1 in our $1-$2 game. After the buys, a final betting round occurs.

Position is important in this game, because the last man to "buy" can frequently base his decision on his opponent(s)' previous "buy(s)." Thus, the dealer has an advantage.

For example, imagine the following two boards:

A: 4,3,7,4
B: Ace,3,5,Q

Now, suppose B has 6,J in the hole. If he were forced to buy first, he would surely have to discard a high card and try for a good low. He could not know whether A were playing for high or low. However, if A buys first, discards his 3, and draws a 7, B would *know* that his low, poor as it ordinarily would be, is a certain winner for half the pot without buying a card.

While this is a simplified example, and usually there will be more than two contestants, it is often that the last player to act can gain either certain knowledge or make good inferences about his opponents' hands from a combination of their boards and their buys. The knowledge may persuade the player not only whether to buy, but which type of hand to try for. For example, he may have the option of trying for a difficult flush (several needed cards have shown) or a fairly good low. But an opponent's prior action may be convincing that even a perfect low card would not be enough; thus, the flush try would be the only reasonable recourse.

In a different circumstance, you may have low trips plus three odd low cards. All the boards may appear high enough to convince you that trips cannot win. You may find your prospects much better for throwing away one of the trips and trying to buy a helping card for low than for trying a difficult draw for a small full house.

It should be noted that whenever you have a reasonable option of drawing a card either up or down, always take it down. For example, suppose your board is Ace,2,3,K and you have 6,Q in the hole. You will naturally try a draw for low. For practical purposes, your Q can hardly be much better than the K. Therefore, discard the Q in order that your substitute card will be concealed.

Playable hands at the beginning are two low cards to a 7 or a pair of 7s or below. In good position, the requirement can be relaxed to two low cards to a smooth 8. Play after the third card if you hold two cards for low (or happen to have caught trips). After the fourth card, pay attention to the board, but normally play three to a low hand or any four-flush or four-straight. Borderline hands are two pairs, three-flushes, and three-straights that retain some chance for low. These are playable if inexpensive and position is good, but you will play them further only if you improve the high or continue with some prospects for low.

It is highly important in this game to watch the board for cards you need and for developing strength. Ordinarily, however, whenever you find yourself with a four-flush, a four-straight, or four toward a good low, you plan to play all the way to the buy.

LITTLE SQUEEZE

This game is Five-Card Stud Hi-Lo with a substitution (a "buy") at the end. Thus, the game is a hybrid between Five- and Six-Card Stud Hi-Lo. Usually, the first and fifth cards are dealt down (although the fifth may be dealt up).

While the dealer has some advantage in Big Squeeze just described, he has much more of one in Little Squeeze.* It is fairly common, at the time of the buys, for the last player to act to be able to see that an ordinarily poor low hand cannot be beaten. For example, he may have an absolute bust, but be against two opponents who have bought first and who both show pairs. In my opinion, the game should not even be allowed in a dealer's-choice session, but you may not be able to make the rules.

Playing requirements may be stated fairly simply. As in regular Five Stud Hi-Lo, you begin playing for high (i.e., a hand with an Ace or a pair) and watch the board for developments. In Little Squeeze, however, two low cards (to a 7) are playable in late buying position—even two to an 8 by the dealer. In intermediate (fair) position with the California scale, potential low flushes and straights are playable at the beginning; you will continue if the hand goes on to give promise for high, low, or both.

TAKE IT OR LEAVE IT

When I have played this game, it usually has been called "Monte," and it has numerous other names. *Monte,* however, is historically associated with the name of a totally different game. Thus, I shall use the most descriptive term for this form of option poker.

Take It or Leave It is played much like Seven Stud Hi-Lo.** However, after the initial round of betting (two hole cards and one up card), the next card off the deck (dealt up) may be refused by the player who would ordinarily receive it automatically. If he refuses the card, he *must* take the next card off the deck. Then, the second player has the option of taking that initial up card, and so on. Once an option card is taken, the next card off the deck becomes an option card (for the next player to act) and continues to be one until someone takes it in his turn.

---

*He has a *formidable* advantage if the game is played with five cards up.

**A variety can also be played like Five- or Six-Card.

An option card is buried among the discards only when *every* player has refused it, and thus the player who had the chance for it first would have it for his choice a second time. In that circumstance, a different card is turned up. Thus, one option card is always available until every active player has completed his seven-card hand.

Betting rounds occur as in regular Seven-Card Stud. When the dealer is the one who takes the option card, the next one is not turned up until the betting round is finished. The eventual difference between the form of the hands and the traditional type is that the seventh card is up; the option feature dictates this.

Because of the option feature, hands tend to run better than in regular Seven Hi-Lo. Nevertheless, I regard playing requirements at the beginning to be about the same. After that, watch the board and take note of the optional plays. If a player voluntarily takes a very high card, you can be sure he is going for high. Taking a low card usually *suggests* a low hand, but only occasionally can you be certain; unless the board tells you otherwise, he may be making low trips or helping a straight or flush.

A frequent tactic in this game is to take a card that does not help your hand just to deprive a player to your left of having it. This maneuver is most frequently advantageous when both of you are playing for high and the card would obviously help him. On the other hand, if you have an excellent low, you would usually *want* to leave a card that would help someone going high; he may well help you build the pot with raises. Of course, the tactic may sometimes backfire. His improved high hand plus your low may combine to frighten everyone else out. It is not often, however, that you can predict such developments with confidence.

HIGH SPADE

This game is also called *Chicago,* but curiously, in the circles in the Chicago area in which I have played, that designation has not been used. The game is dealt like Seven-Card Stud, but the pot is split between the highest hand and the hand with the highest spade *in the hole.* One hand can, of course, be both high and contain the high spade to take the whole pot.

I do not care for High Spade because it involves too much luck. Obviously, a player who happens to catch the Ace of spades on his first two cards is assured of half the pot. If you are that lucky individual, your only "strategy" is to play with a view to getting as much money into the pot as possible. You should surely sandbag on the first round, and maybe longer depending on the action, position, and strength that seems to be developing. You hope for several players to remain in with high hands toward the end.

The K of spades in the hole is playable, because it becomes the master card if the Ace appears somewhere as an up card (or remains among the undealt cards at the end). However, if someone showing no particular high strength begins to bet aggressively, you should be much aware that he may have the Ace unless you see it. Note also that the Q becomes the equivalent of the K if you see either the K or Ace; it becomes the master spade if you see both. However, I would not play from the beginning on the strength of the Q alone. You need something with it to give you some values toward high. And in that case, you must start helping or see the Ace and K appear to hang around long.

Unless you have a very high spade in the hole, you must have considerably more toward high than at usual Seven-Card Stud, as you are competing for only half the pot. (Forget about making a freak draw of the highest outstanding spade on the last hole card; that is just a pleasant bonus when it happens to occur.) At the beginning you need at least a pair of Aces to play. A three-flush or straight is playable, but only for one round unless you help in some way, or unless perfect position shows that you can draw the fifth card cheaply.

PINOCHLE POKER

A variation of High Spade introduces an additional minor element of luck. If a player happens to catch the Q of spades *and* J of diamonds, *both* in the hole, he automatically wins the entire pot at the showdown. Yes, even against a royal flush and Ace of spades in the hole.

The precise "pinochle" combination occurs so rarely that you should play the game almost exactly as you would High Spade. However, if neither of the pinochle cards is in sight, and someone without high values bets furiously on the last round, you must consider the possibility that he holds the hand.

My particular dislike for this game involves partly a matter of prejudice. On the very first hand of it that I ever played, I had the Ace of spades in the hole from the beginning, two or three good highs developed, and the pot became huge. Not only did I have the AceS concealed, but the K never appeared. Yet an opponent unsoundly called all those raises purely on the basis of the QS in the hole. Wouldn't you know it? He drew the JD for his final hole card!

A Few Miscellaneous Games

ANACONDA

Anaconda is also (descriptively) called "Pass the Trash," "Pass the Garbage," and a few terms not appropriate in polite company. The game is usually played high-low. Each player receives seven cards, all down, at the beginning. After a betting round, each player passes three of his cards (all still down) to the opponent on his left; similarly, he receives three cards from the opponent on his right.* Alternatively, the passes can be counterclockwise, according to mutual agreement, announcement by the dealer, or whatever.

After the pass, another betting round occurs, and each player discards two cards and arranges his other five for a "roll-back" sequence. I.e., each player will turn up his top card from the stack of five. Another betting round occurs. (From this point on, the high card usually designates the first player to act, as in Stud.) Then the second cards are "rolled"—with a betting round. And so on until every active player has exposed four cards and a betting round has occurred after each. Then, the final (hole) cards are exposed and the winner(s) determined. (Thus, Anaconda is automatically played Cards Speak; declarations would make no sense in this game.)

Please note that once the roll-back has begun, the cards in a hand cannot be *re*-arranged. In addition, you can readily see that Anaconda cannot be played with more than seven players; since everyone receives seven cards *at the beginning*, the deck does not contain enough for eight players.

With a three-card pass and five betting rounds to come, it is tempting to stay on the first round with just about anything. I advise against this; you are not likely to get a really excellent hand just from a lucky pass, and a mediocre hand can get you into trouble.

Strong hands are high full houses and 6 lows. The 7 low is in the marginal area. Regard a rough 7 with disdain. But a smooth 7 is a quite good hand with the traditional (6-4) scale; there can be no 5 lows, and a 6 will have to contain some element of smoothness to avoid being a straight. With the California scale, a smooth 7 is just fairly good.

For high, a middling or low full house is not really a *bad* hand, but it is nothing to get excited about. At the showdown, two or more full houses are not uncommon in this game.

In my opinion, the key to *clearly* playable hands before the pass depends on whether there is a reasonably good chance that *one* card among the three will give you a playable hand. Further, if that one card will produce only a fairly good hand, then you would like to have *some* chance, as an alternative, of obtaining an excellent hand in the other direction.

Four to a smooth 7 are playable.

High trips (Js or better) are playable.

Low trips (7s or lower**) are playable *if* the fourth card is in

---

*Note this outrageous feature: If you are dealt a straight flush, you cannot keep it, as you must pass three cards, leaving you with only four of your original ones. You also cannot hang on to, say, a pat full house or a perfect low.

**Make that 6s with the California scale.

the winning low range.

Two high pairs are playable (both in the Js through Aces range).

Two low pairs are playable (both in the Aces through 6s or 7s range).

A four-card straight flush is playable.

Note that with only one exception in the preceding recommendations, any of four or more single cards will give you either a very good high or low—or at least a fair high while you have drawn with some chance for a good low. The trouble with middle-sized trips is that you have nothing for low, you will not make any outstanding full house, and the chance for four of a kind is remote. Two pairs that fail to give some chance for an "accidental" low should provide a reasonably *good* chance for a *high* full house (and Qs and 5s give only half the chance that Qs and Ks give).

I have not said that these borderline hands are clearly *un*playable. Are you in good position where you can probably play them cheaply? Does the limit increase with late betting rounds, thus increasing the potential profits from a successful early gamble? What is the quality of the opposition?

I merely note that after the pass, you must often speculate for a while with some moderate hands, but it is far better at least to be *seeking* something better when you go in.

Four-straights and four-flushes are not playable—unless, of course, they just happen to be there when you play for low. (And notice that with the 6-4 scale, a 2,3,4,5 should not be played; you would have to catch precisely a 7 to have anything worthwhile, and even that could lose.) I recommended playing for a straight flush, even though only two cards are available to fill it, mostly because it is such a magnificent high when you make it, but with the California scale it could also win low (when everyone else has a high hand), and a simple flush or broken hand has *some* chance (to be noted).

If you have a playable hand after the pass, arranging the hands for the roll-back is very important—and you must notice how the other hands are rolled back. A high card (other than an Ace) announces a high hand. But with a low hand, no one can know you do not have a low full house (or four of a kind) until the third roll.

So many subtleties can be involved in the roll-back that it would become just too intricate to try to discuss everything—in fact impossible even to begin. The main principle, however, is ordinarily to keep people guessing. For example, with something like Ks full over 2s, you normally should roll 2,K,2,K. A player with something like Qs full cannot know until the showdown whether you have Ks or 2s full.

On the other hand, suppose you have 2s full over 3s. You will never drive out a high full house. So perhaps you should hope that no one has one and show your *low* opponents early that you have a high hand, thus encouraging them to stay in against each other. This is probably better than trying to drive out the lows by turning a 2,3; your only hope would be to beat higher full houses with a lower one, and one way or another, you will probably fail.

Much bluffing is possible on the roll-back. Trips are normally a poor hand. But if high ones are rolled immediately, much pressure will be put on low full houses. Simply because of this, sometimes roll trips first when you *do* have a high full house; you may be suspected of bluffing and get a call from a mediocre high. In other words, vary your play if Anaconda is dealt often in your group.

Against limited opposition, (e.g., two opponents) do not give up too quickly if you bust a low hand. You may see fairly early during the rolls that something like a 10 is unbeatable. Also, while you would not have gone in trying for a mediocre low, if you see that only a single opponent is representing a low hand, consider the possibility that he, too, has a worse bust than you and that he is bluffing. This is a complicated game with wide-ranging possibilities.

Similarly, while a flush is not much of a hand, if you accidentally catch one and can play cheaply, you may find at the third roll card that it is unbeatable for high.

Important things to remember always are the cards you pass and those you receive on the pass. If your left-hand opponent plays all the way without revealing a card you passed, you will know that his hole card is one of them—and usually you will know *which* one if the matter is important. Similarly, if you have an option, roll the card(s) you are passed instead of one of your originals—unless for some reason you *want* your right-hand opponent to know your hole card.

Some extraordinary swing hands should be borne in mind in Anaconda (remember, it is played Cards Speak). Ace,Ace,Ace,2,2 is not only the highest full house, but also the lowest! A straight flush (California scale) will win low against any hand with so much as a pair.

JACKS TO OPEN, TRIPS TO WIN

This is a Draw variety with features so eccentric that I reserved it for the "Miscellaneous" chapter; it just doesn't belong in a chapter devoted to traditional Draw poker. The title is descriptive but fails to tell the whole story.

A deal of this game begins like any hand of Jackpots. As the name suggests, however, no one can win the pot with less than three of a kind. Thus, if no one has such a good hand (despite whatever betting that may have occurred), the money simply stays in the pot for another deal. Same thing after the next deal. The only way the pot can be won with less than trips is to bet and have no callers (and remember, you must have a pair of Js or better to open).

The thing the name of the game does not reveal sets the tone for "... Trips to Win": once you fold a hand, you are out of the pot forever—no matter how many deals are required to produce a winner. And clearly, the more players who drop make it less likely that one of the few who stay will obtain the criteria for a winning hand on a given deal.

Trips to Win is disliked by good players simply because they will play early only with sound values, and thus will often find themselves taking a nap while other people compete endlessly in an effort to get a good hand to win a steadily enlarging pot.

If the game is imposed on you, do not play the first hand without trips or a reasonable draw to a straight or flush. However, if you draw to bobtails early and miss, you may find the pot building to the point that it is worthwhile to stay with almost anything.

In the latter circumstance, normally do not draw to two pairs: discard and draw to your higher pair. The exception is when you are convinced, from someone else's draw or pat hand, that you *must* make a full house to win. Never open with less than trips—unless you plan to run a bluff or can split openers and draw to a bobtail. If you bluff, you obviously hold a kicker to your pair (or play J,J pat?). The trouble with opening with a high pair in the hope of drawing trips is that you let people draw to bobtails when they could not open.

The larger the pot becomes, the more difficult it becomes to bluff successfully. But note that in this game, you can be caught bluffing and still not lose! In the absence of a *successful* bluff, it takes trips or better to *win*.

FOUR FOR THREE (A FORM OF MONTE)

The term *Monte* (or Mont*y*?) covers a wide variety of three-card games with winning hands based on a modified poker scale. E.g., three of a kind rank highest, pairs next,* and high-card hands next. Ace,2,3 is a perfect low, Ace,2,4 next best, and so on. In this presentation, I shall concentrate on a high-low modification called "Four for Three."

Four cards are dealt down to each active player, one at a time, with a betting round on each. With each card, the turn to act first rotates clockwise, and the limit increases with each round. The "pass-and-out" rule is used. After the final round, the high-low declarations are made. The three best cards in the hands are used to make up the winning combinations. The four-card feature permits swing hands. E.g., Ace,Ace,2,3 is a perfect low and a very strong

---

*In a variation of this scale, three-card flushes and straights can be allowed to rank between trips and pairs. As I have played the game, however, flushes and straights have no meaning.

high, since Aces count high or low.

On the opening round you should play only a low card. An Ace is obviously the key card. However, play anything up to a 4. A 5 is also playable if you can do so cheaply.

An Ace is normally played to the last card. If the hand fails to develop low, you have increasing possibilities for making a high pair. Otherwise, play the second round only if you make a pair or help low—neither card above a 5.

The third round should normally be played with a pair, an Ace, or still two toward low. However, if two people are raising, beware of a rough 5 unless it is completely made (e.g., 2,4,5, thus giving you a draw toward a still better low).

On the fourth card, trips are an excellent hand. A high pair will usually win (although you do not go in at the beginning merely playing for a high pair—these hands come as incidental bonuses as hands develop).

With a busted low do not give up too quickly on the last round. Under commonest circumstances, three and exactly three players will be in at this point. While 6s and 7s are not desirable hands, they still will take low money fairly often against even worse busts. A pair of 2s is an underdog for high, yet it is not uncommon for no one else to have a pair; simply an Ace,K will take some half-pots merely on high-card strength. This game is always played with declarations (or at least I have never seen it played Cards Speak). With limited opposition, a large pot may make a complete bust worth a gamble in an effort to "steal" half; the other hands may be in the different direction—or perhaps even worse than yours in the same direction.

A Final Word

A question can be raised of whether Four-for-Three, or the numerous varieties of Monte that I elected not to describe, should even be called "Poker." While values are based on the poker scale, recall that *poker* hands are made up of *five*-card combinations. Thus, having come to the point of describing a form of "non-poker" in a poker book, I believe it is time to close.

With a few acknowledged exceptions, I have confined myself to games that I not only have analyzed but have personally played—at least with a structure reasonably similar to that described if not always precisely the same. And I have not included every last one of these. While I have not come near to describing all existing varieties of this card game, I have presented enough to allow you to make adaptations that should be appropriate to most different but related forms.

I doubt that the completely definitive book on poker will ever be written: just too many variables are possible. You will find much good additional advice on the game among books given in my list of references, some of which (12-16) I have not yet cited specifically. If you sometimes find one author recommending a certain strategy and another apparently contradicting him, do not automatically infer that one is necessarily right and the other wrong: they may have been assuming different conditions of play.

I shall conclude with the wish that your poker career may be successful.

GLOSSARY

Act: whatever a player does in his turn. This may be to bet, call, check, fold, pass, raise, or reraise—or to declare in high-low poker. (These terms are explained in their own places in this glossary.)

Action: the wagering.

Active Player: one who has not abandoned his hand, and thus remains in the competition for the pot.

All In: see "In for the Pot."

Anaconda: a complicated game in which each player is dealt seven cards, passes three to an adjacent opponent (and receives three likewise), and then arranges his best five for a roll-back sequence (qv).

Ante: the beginning of a pot before a deal commences. Also used as a verb for the act of contributing to the pot before the deal.

Backed up: see "Back to Back."

Back to Back: in stud, an initial up card pairs an initial hole card.

Baseball: a stud form in which the 3s, 4s, and 9s have special (and different) functions.

Beat the Board: have a better hand than any shown by the open cards of the opponents.

Bet: a wager placed in the pot at a player's turn. Opponents must at least call (qv) this bet to retain any chance to win the pot (see "In for the Pot" for a partial exception). The term may be used generically, but its technical role is to designate the first wager made during a betting round.

Betting Interval: see "Betting Round."

Betting Round: a period during which each active player may make a wager or sometimes more than one.

Big Squeeze: High-Low Six-Card Stud with a "Buy" (qv).

Blind Bet: one made without looking at the hand. Also see "Forced Bet" for a variation of a blind bet that is not optional and that has nothing to do with whether the bettor has looked at his cards.

Blind Opening: a forced bet (qv) by the player under the gun (qv). (The term can be used also for an opening bet made voluntarily by a player who does not first look at his cards.)

Bluff: a bet or raise made with a poor hand in an effort to intimidate opponents into abandoning their hands and thus their chance to win with better hands.

Board: the open card(s) of any or all active players.

Bobtail: a four-flush or four-straight.

"Both Ways": in Consecutive Declarations, an oral announcement that a player is competing for the entire pot.

Buck: see "Button."

Bug: the Joker when used only as a fifth Ace or as a wild card to compete a straight or flush. In low poker, the term is often used to apply to a completely wild Joker.

Burn Card: one that is discarded from the top of the deck.

Bust: a speculative hand that has been drawn to unsuccessfully.

Busted Hand: see "Bust."

Button: a marker that designates the putative dealer in a casino game in which a house dealer actually distributes the cards.

Buy: under the rules of some games, to substitute a new card for one in the hand by adding a predesignated sum to the pot. Also used to designate simply drawing cards. Also sometimes used in the sense of "Buy-In" (qv). Also see "Buy the Pot" and "Steal the Pot."

Buy-In: the amount of chips or money that a player invests in a session. Sometimes the term applies to some mandatory amount that a player must have at the beginning of play.

Buy the Pot: to bluff successfully. Also see "Steal the Pot."

California Scale: a method of ranking hands in low and high-low poker in which straights and flushes are disregarded for the purpose of low. Thus, Ace,2,3,4,5 is the best low hand possible, even if all cards are in one suit.

Call: add a sum to the pot equal to that placed by the previous active player on a particular betting round. The term is also used to refer to any "Act" (qv). It is also used synonymously with *declare* or *declaration* in high-low poker.

Carding: discarding. See "Discard," second definition.

Card Mechanic: a cheating dealer.

Card Room: in a casino, this term less often pertains to a "room" as to an area designated for poker—plus sometimes other card games (e.g., Pan—a variation of Rummy not described in this book).

Cards Speak: a form of high-low in which no declarations are made; the winners are determined by a simple showdown. The term is also used in any poker form in the sense that the best exposed hand(s) at the showdown win— regardless of whether the owner(s) may have previously misread the hand(s).

Cards Speak for Themselves: see "Cards Speak."

Case Card: the last one of a rank after the other three have been seen.

Case the Deck: remember cards that are played for the purpose of appraising the potential for improving hands on future draws.

Casino: a public place or large private club designed mostly or exclusively for gambling.

Chase: to play an inferior hand with the hope of "Drawing Out" (qv).

Check: decline to initiate the betting in one's turn, while retaining the right to call subsequent bets if any are made. A word with the same spelling is also an out-of-vogue term for "Chip" (qv).

Check-Raise: a tactic in which a player checks and then raises after an opponent has bet. This maneuver is outlawed under some rules and resented by some players, but it is legal and acceptable under standard rules of poker.

Cheque: see "Chip."

Chicago: see "High Spade."

Chip: a token bought for money in a game, and redeemable for money.

Chips Declare: see "Simultaneous Declarations." Under commonest rules, players hide (or pretend to hide) chips in their closed fists. The fists are opened simultaneously. An empty fist indicates a declaration for low; one chip for high; two chips for both ways and the entire pot.

Cinch: a hand that cannot be beaten.

Cincinnati: a form in which each player receives five hole cards, and a five-card widow is dealt.

Closed Poker: any form in which all cards are dealt face down and remain so until the showdown.

Common Card: a widow card (qv). Also a term to designate an up card in stud that belongs to all players; it is dealt under some rules when the dealer realizes that the remaining deck does not contain enough cards to provide every active player his full allotment.

Consecutive Declarations: a form of high-low in which players announce in turn whether they are competing for high, low, or both.

Criss-Cross: a widow game with four hole cards and five common cards whose uses have certain restrictions.

Cut: a sum taken from the pot—either for profit in a casino game or to pay expenses in a private game. Also, the final act of the shuffle, in which the lower part of the deck is moved to the top. This latter maneuver is a long-established technique in card playing that reduces the danger of cheating.

Dead: said of a rank when all four of the cards have been dealt from the deck.

Dead Hand: one that must be abandoned because of an irregularity.

Deal: distributing cards to the players. Also used to designate the turn to act as dealer (i.e., "It's John's deal"). Also used to designate the period for the play of a hand from the shuffle to the winning of the pot.

Dealer: the person who distributes the cards to the players.

Dealer's Choice: a poker session in which each player, at his turn to deal, names the game to be played. In many groups, the options are limited to certain games.

Deck: a pack of cards—usually 52 in poker, sometimes 53 with the use of a Joker.

Declaration: in high-low, a statement or other indication that a player is competing for high, low, or both.

Declarations Poker: any form of high-low in which a declaration (qv) by each active player is required.

Declare: in high-low, the act of indicating the direction(s) in which a player is competing.

Deuces Wild: Draw Poker in which all 2s are wild cards.

Discard: a card removed from a hand and not used further by its original holder. Also one removed from the top of the deck and thus not dealt. The term is also used verbally to indicate the preceding acts.

Doctor Pepper: Seven-Card Stud with the 10s, 2s, and 4s wild.

"Down": synonymous with "Low" (qv).

Down Card: see "Hole Card."

Down the River: Seven-Card Stud for high. Occasionally the term is also applied to the high-low form.

Draw: receive cards to further or complete a hand. Also used synonymously with "Draw Poker" (qv).

Draw Out: receive card(s) that convert a previously inferior hand into a winning hand.

Draw Poker: closed poker in which players may discard and receive replacement cards.

Drop: see "Fold."

Elder (or Eldest) Hand: the first one required to act.

Exposed Card: see "Open Card." The term also applies to a card accidentally turned up.

Face Card: a King(K), Queen(Q), or Jack(J).

Fill: receive a card that converts a speculative hand into a good one, e.g., a straight, flush, or full house.

Five and Five: a variation of Cincinnati (qv) in which the widow contains five two-card sets, and only three cards among a player's hole cards may be used to compete in a particular direction for high or low.

Five-Card Stud: one card (the first, i.e., the hole card) to each hand is dealt down and the other four up. Played high, this was the original form of stud poker. Now, it is also played low or high-low. Occasionally, the fifth card, in addition to the first, is dealt down.

Five of a Kind: five cards of the same rank—possible in poker only if containing at least one wild card.

Five-Stud: an abbreviation sometimes used in the text for Five-Card Stud (qv).

Fixed Limit: the betting is restricted to exact sums or ranges, often depending on the betting round or the board, but not influenced by the size of the pot.

Floor Man: a supervisor of games in a casino. Obviously, there may also be Floor Women. Also see "Pit Boss."

Flop: the first three widow cards in Hold 'Em. These are turned all at once.

Flush: five cards in the same suit.

Fold: decline to call (or sometimes to make) a bet, and thus abandon a hand and the chance to win the pot. The term is equivalent to *pass* in most contexts, but not quite in all.

Forced Bet: a specified amount that a player, under certain rules, *must* place in the pot—regardless of the quality of his hand.

Four-Flush: four cards in one suit, requiring that a fifth be drawn to complete the flush.

Four for Three: a form of Monte (qv) in which each player receives four cards and may play any three for high or low.

Four of a kind: four cards of the same rank.

Four-Straight: four cards in sequence, requiring that a fifth be drawn to complete the straight.

Free Ride: the opportunity to play a poor hand further because all players have checked.

Full House: five cards consisting of three of one rank and two of another.

Hand: all cards held by a player. Also, the five-card combination among these (if more than five) used in an effort to win. The term is also used in the same sense as the second definition given for "Deal" (qv).

Hi: a phonetic abbreviation often used in the text as a substitute for high poker.

"High": in Consecutive Declarations, an oral announcement that a player is competing for high. Also a term denoting the winning high hand.

High-Card Hand: one without a pair, but which can compete for the pot merely on the rank of the highest card.

High-Limit Poker: see "Pot Limit" and "Table Stakes Limit." Basically, the term is used to distinguish games with these limits from those with a "Fixed Limit" (qv), rather than to apply to the actual sums at stake.

High-Low Poker: a form in which the pot is split between the player with the highest hand and the one with the lowest.

High on Board: in stud, the highest partially exposed hand.

High Poker: the form in which the highest-ranking hand wins the entire pot.

High Spade: a variation of Seven-Card Stud in which the highest-ranking spade in the hole splits the pot with the highest ranking hand otherwise. Also called "Chicago."

Hi-Lo: a phonetic abbreviation often used in the text as a substitute for high-low poker.

Hit: same as "Buy" (first definition, qv).

Hold 'Em: a form in which each player receives two hole cards, and a five-card widow is eventually dealt.

Hold Me: see "Hold 'Em."

Hold Me Darling: see "Hold 'Em."

Hole Card: a card dealt down and thus seen only by its holder in stud and related poker forms.

House: a casino (qv).

Improve: receive cards that make a better hand.

In for the Pot: a circumstance under the "Table-Stakes" rule (qv) in which a player competes for only part of the pot after depleting his funds on the table.

Inside Straight: four cards to a five-card sequence, requiring that an interior card be drawn to complete a straight.

Jackpots: see "Jacks or Better."

Jacks: see "Jacks or Better."

Jacks and Back: a variation of "Jacks or Better" (qv) in which, after an opening round is passed out, the hands are retained and played under the rules of Lowball.

Jacks or Better: a draw game in which the opener must have a pair of Js or some hand that will beat a pair of Js.

Jacks to Open: see "Jacks or Better."

Jacks to Open, Trips to Win: a draw variety, played like Jacks or Better, except that no player may win at a showdown without trips or better. A player who folds on a deal is eliminated from the competition until the pot is eventually won on that or a subsequent deal.

Joker: a 53rd card sometimes added to the deck and serving as a wild card or as a Bug.

Joker Poker: Draw for high in which a 53rd card is completely wild.

Kankakee: Seven-Card Stud with the Joker a common wild card in every hand.

Kibitzer: a nonplaying spectator.

Kick: raise.

Kicker: an unmatched card held for deception, the possibility if improvement, or the chance of providing the winning hand on high-card strength.

Kill a Raise: when permitted by the rules, to make a minimum bet, raise, or reraise in order to reduce the possible number of allowable higher raises.

Light: owing money to the pot.

Limit: the maximum amount that may be bet at a particular time. (There can also be a minimum amount that may be bet.) The term is also applied to the maximum number of raises that may be made during a betting round.

Little Squeeze: High-Low Five-Card Stud with a "Buy" (qv).

Lo: a phonetic abbreviation often used in the text as a substitute for low poker.

Lock: a cinch (qv).

Long Shot: a wager made with only a small chance of winning. (A gamble of this type may be sound or unsound, depending on the amount to be won if the effort is successful.)

Loose Player: one who competes in many pots and wagers often. The term usually connotes recklessness and marks a player as inferior, but depending on the game and circumstances, this is not invariably so. See also "Tight Player."

"Low": in Consecutive Declarations, an oral announcement that a player is competing for low. Also a term denoting the winning low hand.

Lowball: Draw Poker in which the low hand wins. Also frequently used adjectivally with non-draw forms in which the low hand wins.

Low Hole Card Wild: Seven-Card Stud in which each player's lowest hole card, and all like it in his own hand, are wild cards.

Low on Board: in stud, the lowest partially exposed hand.

Low Poker: the form in which the lowest-ranking hand wins the entire pot.

Made Hand: see "Pat Hand."

Man in the Middle: in high-low, a player with a mediocre or speculative hand who (to stay) must call repeated raises by two opponents with apparently good hands.

Mechanic: see "Card Mechanic."

Misdeal: an irregularity that requires a new shuffle and deal. Some players claim that "There are no misdeals in poker"; thus, mistakes are resolved by arbitration. Instead, I recommend consultation of *Official Rules of Card Games.*[7]

Misrepresentation: involves a hand in high-low that, from the open cards, appears strong in one direction but whose true strength is in the opposite direction. The term also applies in any form of poker to a hand that appears strong but really is not.

Monte: any of many varieties of three-card "poker." Also sometimes used synonymously with "Take It or Leave It" (qv).

Monty: see "Monte."

Nevada Gaming Commission: the regulatory agency that oversees casino gambling in Nevada.

Nevada State Gaming Control Board: the enforcement arm of the Nevada Gaming Commission (qv).

Nuts: see "Cinch."

One-Eyed Jacks: a draw form in which the JS and JH (i.e., the two Js in profile instead of full-face) are wild cards.

On the Come: betting with a hand that must improve on the draw(s) for any notable chance to be best.

Open: make the first bet on the first betting round.

Open Card: one dealt face up in stud or widow games.

Opener: the Player who "Opens" (qv).

Openers: in some draw games, the cards that make up the minimum (or better) requirement for making the first bet on the initial betting round.

Open Poker: a game in which some cards are dealt face up.

Option Poker: a form in which a player may accept a known card to a hand, or refuse it in favor of an unknown card (see "Take It or Leave It" for an example).

Over Card: see "Overlay."

Overcutting: in a casino, this term applies to a "Cut" (qv) of more than the announced, customary, or legal amount.

Overhead: the cost of playing in a poker game beyond wagers made voluntarily. For example, the ante is overhead expense, but under certain circumstances, the term may involve other expenses.

Overlay: an open card that may help an opponent's hole card(s) sufficiently to beat a player's own hand.

Pair: two cards of the same rank.

Pass: decline to call (or sometimes to make) a bet, and thus abandon a hand and the chance to win the pot (i.e., "fold"). In some contexts, the term is also used in the sense of "Check" (qv).

Pass and Back In: a game in which a player may check but retain the right to call subsequent bets if any are made.

Pass and Out: a game that does not permit checking. At a player's turn, he must either bet or fold. In most but not all forms, the rule applies only on the first betting round.

Passed-Out Hand: a situation in draw in which no one opens, and thus a full complement of hands is redealt—often after an extra ante.

Pass the Garbage: see "Anaconda."

Pass the Trash: see "Anaconda."

Pat Hand: in draw poker, one to which no cards are taken beyond the original five. Loosely in other forms, a good hand obtained with the early cards.

Penny-Ante Poker: except as obvious, this term is often applied to any session in which the stakes are trivial.

Perfect Low: in low or high-low poker, the best possible low hand under the rules of the game being played.

Pineapple: a variation of Hold 'Em (qv) in which each player receives a third hole card but must discard one before the flop.

Pinochle Poker: played like High Spade (qv) except that QS,JD in the hole wins the entire pot—all other hands notwithstanding.

Pip Card: one with "spots," as distinguished from a "Face Card" (qv).

Pit: an area in a casino where a particular type of game is played.

Pit Boss: a "Floor Man (or Woman)" (qv), but ordinarily a supervisor of lower rank than the manager of a casino or of a shift.

Play: in addition to the obvious sense, this term is often used synonymously with "Act" (qv).

Playing Light: see "Light."

Ploy: any stratagem or artifice used to take advantage of the opponents.

Poker Pit: the area in a casino where poker is played.

Poker Room: in a casino, not usually a "room" in the usual sense. See "Poker Pit."

Position: the seating relationship of a player to an opponent who "Acts" (qv). In some poker forms, the term also applies to the seating in relationship to the dealer.

Pot: the accumulation of all money (or chips) to be won on a deal.

Pot Limit: any bet or raise may be for as much but no more money than is in the pot when the wager is made.

Pot Odds: a consideration of whether the money in the pot justifies playing further with a speculative hand.

Progressive Openers: a draw form in which the requirements for opening become more stringent after hands are passed out.

Railbird: a "Kibitzer" (qv) in a casino.

Raise: an additional wager added to the pot by a player calling a bet.

Rake: see "Cut" (first definition).

Razz: Seven-Card Stud for low.

Read: to make accurate inferences about an opponent's hand based on such clues as his habits and mannerisms.

Representation: the play of a hand in a manner to suggest values in the high or low direction, whether or not this comprises the true strength of the total hand.

Reraise: an additional wager after calling any previous bet plus raise(s).

Right to Bet: a rule that permits any active player to raise *once* during a betting round, even though the maximum number of normally allowable raises has been made ahead of him.

Roll-Back: each player stacks five cards face down, and the cards are turned up, one at a time, with a betting round on each turn. (See Anaconda for a poker form involving this feature.)

Rough: a relatively unfavorable low hand, because the second and possibly third, etc. lower cards are in sequence with higher ones. E.g., 7,6,5,4,2 is a *very* "rough 7"; 7,4,3,2,Ace is exceptionally "smooth" (qv)—or a "perfect 7."

Round: see "Betting Round." The term may also apply to a series of rotating deals in which the turn reverts to the original dealer.

Royal Flush: Ace,K,Q,J,10 in one suit. The best possible natural high poker hand; beaten only by five of a kind when wild cards are used. (By local option, some rules make this or any straight flush higher than five of a kind.)

Sandbag: to check with a strong hand, hoping that an opponent will bet, thus providing an opportunity for a reraise. (Also see "Check-Raise" and "Slow Play.")

Semi-Bluff: a bet or raise made with a speculative hand while awaiting developments. If all opponents pass, the bettor is pleased, as he wins the pot. If opponents call, the bettor tentatively plans a true bluff later if he fails to fill the hand—all the time hoping he does fill to provide a hand that will win on its true strength.

Seven-Card Lowball: see Razz.

Seven-Card Stud: three cards to each hand are dealt down and four up. May be played high (often called "Down the River"), low (often called "Razz"), or high-low.

Seven-Hi: an abbreviation used in the text for Seven-Card Stud—High only.

Seven Hi-Lo: an abbreviation used in the text for High-Low Seven-Card Stud.

Shill: a casino employee who plays for the house—whether to start a game, keep it intact, or simply to win money for the employer.

Short Buy: in a casino, a second or later "Buy-In" (qv) for less than the mandatory amount for beginning to play.

Showdown: comparison of the hands of active players to determine the winner(s).

Showdown Poker: a simple form of the game in which the five-card hands are dealt after the ante, and then the best hand wins without further betting. (Variations are possible in which a betting round occurs after a closed deal, but no draws are allowed. This is sometimes called "Straight Poker.")

Shuffle: mix the cards together randomly before dealing.

Simultaneous Declarations: a high-low form in which all active players announce at the same time by prearranged signal whether they are competing for high, low, or both. Also see "Chips Declare."

Six-Card Stud: two cards to each hand are dealt down and four up. May be played high, low, or high-low.

Six-Four (or "Sixty-Four") Scale: a method (frequently designated "the traditional scale" in the text) of ranking hands in high-low poker (and rarely strictly low poker) by allowing straights and flushes to count only as they would in high poker. Thus, 6,4,3,2,Ace (not all in one suit) is the best low hand possible.

Slow Play: similar to "Sandbagging" (qv), except that checking or failing to raise with a good hand is designed to keep players in competition—as contrasted with planning the "Check-Raise" tactic (qv).

Smooth: a relatively favorable low hand, because the second ranking card is well below the highest. E.g., 7,5 . . . is a "smooth 7"; 7,4 . . . is even smoother. Compare this with "Rough."

Speak: see "Act."

Spit in the Ocean: a draw variation in which each player receives four cards, a one-card widow is turned up, and the widow card and all of the same rank are wild.

Split: division of a pot between winners.

Split Openers: to discard part of a draw-poker hand that qualified it for an opening bet, in order to try for something better. The relevant card(s) must be isolated, face down, to prove later that the bettor actually had the "Openers" (qv).

Splitting by Agreement: in high-low, when only two active players remain, they may save time by agreeing to split the pot before the last cards are dealt. Unethical under standard rules, the custom is acceptable at high-low—provided no predetermined (and illegal) partnership agreement exists.

Stand: decline to draw cards. I.e., play a hand "Pat" (qv).

Stay: see "Call."

Steal the Pot (or half the pot): to win with a poor hand because of lack of competition—either with a bluff or an uncontested declaration.

Straddle: a mandatory raise made under circumstances similar to a "Blind Opening" (qv).

Straight: five cards in sequential rank.

Straight Draw Poker: a form of draw with a "Pass-and-Out" feature (qv).

Straight Flush: five cards in sequential rank, all in the same suit.

Straight Poker: see "Showdown Poker"—the parenthetic definition.

Stud Poker: a form in which part of each player's hand is dealt up and part down (as "hole card(s)").

Substitution Poker: see "Big Squeeze" and "Little Squeeze" for examples.

Sudden Death: Five-Card Stud (qv) played for low.

Swing: in high-low, to win or attempt to win in both directions.

Swing Card: in high-low, one that improves the hand in both directions.

Swing Hand: one used to "Swing" (qv).

Table Stakes: a rule that a player must use only the money he has on the table for wagering on a particular deal (qv; second definition). See also "Table Stakes Limit."

Table Stakes Limit: regardless of the size of the pot, a player may bet, raise, or re-raise for up to any amount he has on the table at the beginning of a deal (qv, second definition).

Take It or Leave It: High-Low Stud in which option cards are dealt. A player in his turn may accept the option card (dealt up) or take the next card off the deck. (Sometimes, this variation is incongruously called "Monte"—a term better reserved for a totally different game.)

Tell: a mannerism or habit by a player that tends to reveal the strength of his hand.

Three of a Kind: three cards of one rank.

Tight Player: one who competes in relatively few pots and who tends to wager conservatively. The term usually connotes a superior player who competes only with sound values, but carried too far (especially the conservative wagering aspect), the trait can become a disadvantage. See also "Loose Player."

Toss: see "Fold."

Trap: to check with the intent of raising after a bet is made (see "Check-Raise"), or to "Slow Play" (qv).

Trips: three of a kind.

Trips to Win: see "Jacks to Open, Trips to Win."

Turn: see "Flop."

Two Pairs: a hand containing two cards of one rank and two others of another rank.

Two-Way Winner: in high-low, a hand that contains the best values in both directions.

Underdog: a player with little chance of winning, or one whose chances are insufficient to justify continuing to compete for the pot. (The two definitions do not necessarily denote the same thing.)

Under the Gun: in draw or Hold 'Em, the player immediately to the left of the dealer.

"Up": synonymous with "High" (qv). Also, in speaking of two pairs, a term like "Aces up" indicates two Aces and a lower pair; similarly, "10s up" means that a pair of 10s is the higher of two pairs in a hand.

Up Card: see "Open Card."

Wheel: in low or high-low, the lowest hand possible.

Widow: card(s) dealt up and belonging equally to all active players.

Widow Card: any one that helps constitute a "Widow" (qv).

Wild Card: one that may be designated as of any rank and suit.

X: a symbol used in the text for a card immaterial to the strength of a hand under discussion.

REFERENCES

1. Morehead, A.H., *The Complete Guide to Winning Poker.* New York: Simon and Schuster, 1967.
2. Livingston, A.D. *Poker Strategy and Winning Play.* Philadelphia and New York: J.B. Lippincott, 1971.
3. Jacoby, O. *Oswald Jacoby on Poker.* Garden City, New York: Doubleday, 1947.
4. Zadeh, N. *Winning Poker Systems.* Englewood Cliffs, New Jersey: Prentice-Hall, 1974.
5. Morehead, A.H. (ed). *Poker.* Cincinnati: United States Playing Card Company, 1950.
6. Archer, J. *The Archer Method of Winning at 21.* No. Hollywood: Wilshire Book Company, 1978.
7. Morehead, A.H. (ed). *Official Rules of Card Games,* Ed. 55. Racine, Wisconsin: Whitman, 1968.
8. Silberstang, E. *Playboy's Book of Games.* Chicago: Playboy Press, 1972.
9. Scarne, J. *Scarne on Cards.* New York: Crown Publishers, 1949.
10. Preston, "A.S." with Cox, B.G. *Play Poker to Win.* New York: Grosset & Dunlap, 1973.
11. Sklansky, D. *Hold 'Em Poker.* Las Vegas: Gambler's Book Club, 1976.
12. Roddy, I. *Friday Night Poker.* New York: Simon and Schuster, 1961.
13. Rubens, J. *Win at Poker.* New York: Funk & Wagnalls, 1968.
14. Steig, I. *Common Sense in Poker.* New York: Cornerstone Library, 1963.
15. Thackery, T. *Dealer's Choice.* Chicago: Henry Regnery, 1971.
16. Yardley, H.O. *The Education of a Poker Player.* New York: Simon and Schuster, 1957.

MELVIN POWERS SELF-IMPROVEMENT LIBRARY

ASTROLOGY

____ASTROLOGY: HOW TO CHART YOUR HOROSCOPE *Max Heindel* 3.00
____ASTROLOGY: YOUR PERSONAL SUN-SIGN GUIDE *Beatrice Ryder* 3.00
____ASTROLOGY FOR EVERYDAY LIVING *Janet Harris* 2.00
____ASTROLOGY MADE EASY *Astarte* 3.00
____ASTROLOGY MADE PRACTICAL *Alexandra Kayhle* 3.00
____ASTROLOGY, ROMANCE, YOU AND THE STARS *Anthony Norvell* 4.00
____MY WORLD OF ASTROLOGY *Sydney Omarr* 5.00
____THOUGHT DIAL *Sydney Omarr* 3.00
____WHAT THE STARS REVEAL ABOUT THE MEN IN YOUR LIFE *Thelma White* 3.00
____ZODIAC REVEALED *Rupert Gleadow* 2.00

BRIDGE

____BRIDGE BIDDING MADE EASY *Edwin B. Kantar* 5.00
____BRIDGE CONVENTIONS *Edwin B. Kantar* 5.00
____BRIDGE HUMOR *Edwin B. Kantar* 3.00
____COMPETITIVE BIDDING IN MODERN BRIDGE *Edgar Kaplan* 4.00
____DEFENSIVE BRIDGE PLAY COMPLETE *Edwin B. Kantar* 10.00
____HOW TO IMPROVE YOUR BRIDGE *Alfred Sheinwold* 2.00
____INTRODUCTION TO DEFENDER'S PLAY *Edwin B. Kantar* 3.00
____SHORT CUT TO WINNING BRIDGE *Alfred Sheinwold* 3.00
____TEST YOUR BRIDGE PLAY *Edwin B. Kantar* 3.00
____WINNING DECLARER PLAY *Dorothy Hayden Truscott* 4.00

BUSINESS, STUDY & REFERENCE

____CONVERSATION MADE EASY *Elliot Russell* 2.00
____EXAM SECRET *Dennis B. Jackson* 2.00
____FIX-IT BOOK *Arthur Symons* 2.00
____HOW TO DEVELOP A BETTER SPEAKING VOICE *M. Hellier* 2.00
____HOW TO MAKE A FORTUNE IN REAL ESTATE *Albert Winnikoff* 3.00
____INCREASE YOUR LEARNING POWER *Geoffrey A. Dudley* 2.00
____MAGIC OF NUMBERS *Robert Tocquet* 2.00
____PRACTICAL GUIDE TO BETTER CONCENTRATION *Melvin Powers* 2.00
____PRACTICAL GUIDE TO PUBLIC SPEAKING *Maurice Forley* 3.00
____7 DAYS TO FASTER READING *William S. Schaill* 3.00
____SONGWRITERS RHYMING DICTIONARY *Jane Shaw Whitfield* 5.00
____SPELLING MADE EASY *Lester D. Basch & Dr. Milton Finkelstein* 2.00
____STUDENT'S GUIDE TO BETTER GRADES *J. A. Rickard* 2.00
____TEST YOURSELF—Find Your Hidden Talent *Jack Shafer* 2.00
____WORLD WIDE MAIL ORDER SHOPPER'S GUIDE *Eugene V. Moller* 5.00
____YOUR WILL & WHAT TO DO ABOUT IT *Attorney Samuel G. Kling* 3.00

CALLIGRAPHY

____ADVANCED CALLIGRAPHY *Katherine Jeffares* 6.00
____CALLIGRAPHY—The Art of Beautiful Writing *Katherine Jeffares* 5.00

CHESS & CHECKERS

____BEGINNER'S GUIDE TO WINNING CHESS *Fred Reinfeld* 3.00
____BETTER CHESS—How to Play *Fred Reinfeld* 2.00
____CHECKERS MADE EASY *Tom Wiswell* 2.00
____CHESS IN TEN EASY LESSONS *Larry Evans* 3.00
____CHESS MADE EASY *Milton L. Hanauer* 3.00
____CHESS MASTERY—A New Approach *Fred Reinfeld* 2.00
____CHESS PROBLEMS FOR BEGINNERS *edited by Fred Reinfeld* 2.00
____CHESS SECRETS REVEALED *Fred Reinfeld* 2.00
____CHESS STRATEGY—An Expert's Guide *Fred Reinfeld* 2.00
____CHESS TACTICS FOR BEGINNERS *edited by Fred Reinfeld* 3.00
____CHESS THEORY & PRACTICE *Morry & Mitchell* 2.00
____HOW TO WIN AT CHECKERS *Fred Reinfeld* 2.00
____1001 BRILLIANT WAYS TO CHECKMATE *Fred Reinfeld* 3.00
____1001 WINNING CHESS SACRIFICES & COMBINATIONS *Fred Reinfeld* 3.00
____SOVIET CHESS *Edited by R. G. Wade* 3.00

COOKERY & HERBS

____CULPEPER'S HERBAL REMEDIES *Dr. Nicholas Culpeper* — 2.00
____FAST GOURMET COOKBOOK *Poppy Cannon* — 2.50
____GINSENG The Myth & The Truth *Joseph P. Hou* — 3.00
____HEALING POWER OF HERBS *May Bethel* — 3.00
____HEALING POWER OF NATURAL FOODS *May Bethel* — 3.00
____HERB HANDBOOK *Dawn MacLeod* — 3.00
____HERBS FOR COOKING AND HEALING *Dr. Donald Law* — 2.00
____HERBS FOR HEALTH—How to Grow & Use Them *Louise Evans Doole* — 3.00
____HOME GARDEN COOKBOOK—Delicious Natural Food Recipes *Ken Kraft* — 3.00
____MEDICAL HERBALIST *edited by Dr. J. R. Yemm* — 3.00
____NATURAL FOOD COOKBOOK *Dr. Harry C. Bond* — 3.00
____NATURE'S MEDICINES *Richard Lucas* — 3.00
____VEGETABLE GARDENING FOR BEGINNERS *Hugh Wiberg* — 2.00
____VEGETABLES FOR TODAY'S GARDENS *R. Milton Carleton* — 2.00
____VEGETARIAN COOKERY *Janet Walker* — 3.00
____VEGETARIAN COOKING MADE EASY & DELECTABLE *Veronica Vezza* — 2.00
____VEGETARIAN DELIGHTS—A Happy Cookbook for Health *K. R. Mehta* — 2.00
____VEGETARIAN GOURMET COOKBOOK *Joyce McKinnel* — 3.00

GAMBLING & POKER

____ADVANCED POKER STRATEGY & WINNING PLAY *A. D. Livingston* — 3.00
____HOW NOT TO LOSE AT POKER *Jeffrey Lloyd Castle* — 3.00
____HOW TO WIN AT DICE GAMES *Skip Frey* — 3.00
____HOW TO WIN AT POKER *Terence Reese & Anthony T. Watkins* — 2.00
____SECRETS OF WINNING POKER *George S. Coffin* — 3.00
____WINNING AT CRAPS *Dr. Lloyd T. Commins* — 3.00
____WINNING AT GIN *Chester Wander & Cy Rice* — 3.00
____WINNING AT POKER—An Expert's Guide *John Archer* — 3.00
____WINNING AT 21—An Expert's Guide *John Archer* — 3.00
____WINNING POKER SYSTEMS *Norman Zadeh* — 3.00

HEALTH

____DR. LINDNER'S SPECIAL WEIGHT CONTROL METHOD *P. G. Lindner, M.D.* — 1.50
____HELP YOURSELF TO BETTER SIGHT *Margaret Darst Corbett* — 3.00
____HOW TO IMPROVE YOUR VISION *Dr. Robert A. Kraskin* — 3.00
____HOW YOU CAN STOP SMOKING PERMANENTLY *Ernest Caldwell* — 3.00
____MIND OVER PLATTER *Peter G. Lindner, M.D.* — 3.00
____NATURE'S WAY TO NUTRITION & VIBRANT HEALTH *Robert J. Scrutton* — 3.00
____NEW CARBOHYDRATE DIET COUNTER *Patti Lopez-Pereira* — 1.50
____PSYCHEDELIC ECSTASY *William Marshall & Gilbert W. Taylor* — 2.00
____REFLEXOLOGY *Dr. Maybelle Segal* — 2.00
____YOU CAN LEARN TO RELAX *Dr. Samuel Gutwirth* — 2.00
____YOUR ALLERGY—What To Do About It *Allan Knight, M.D.* — 3.00

HOBBIES

____BEACHCOMBING FOR BEGINNERS *Norman Hickin* — 2.00
____BLACKSTONE'S MODERN CARD TRICKS *Harry Blackstone* — 3.00
____BLACKSTONE'S SECRETS OF MAGIC *Harry Blackstone* — 2.00
____BUTTERFLIES — 2.50
____COIN COLLECTING FOR BEGINNERS *Burton Hobson & Fred Reinfeld* — 2.00
____ENTERTAINING WITH ESP *Tony 'Doc' Shiels* — 2.00
____400 FASCINATING MAGIC TRICKS YOU CAN DO *Howard Thurston* — 3.00
____HOW I TURN JUNK INTO FUN AND PROFIT *Sari* — 3.00
____HOW TO WRITE A HIT SONG & SELL IT *Tommy Boyce* — 7.00
____JUGGLING MADE EASY *Rudolf Dittrich* — 2.00
____MAGIC MADE EASY *Byron Wels* — 2.00
____STAMP COLLECTING FOR BEGINNERS *Burton Hobson* — 2.00
____STAMP COLLECTING FOR FUN & PROFIT *Frank Cetin* — 2.00

HORSE PLAYERS' WINNING GUIDES

____BETTING HORSES TO WIN *Les Conklin* — 3.00
____ELIMINATE THE LOSERS *Bob McKnight* — 3.00
____HOW TO PICK WINNING HORSES *Bob McKnight* — 3.00

_____HOW TO WIN AT THE RACES *Sam (The Genius) Lewin* 3.00
_____HOW YOU CAN BEAT THE RACES *Jack Kavanagh* 3.00
_____MAKING MONEY AT THE RACES *David Barr* 3.00
_____PAYDAY AT THE RACES *Les Conklin* 3.00
_____SMART HANDICAPPING MADE EASY *William Bauman* 3.00
_____SUCCESS AT THE HARNESS RACES *Barry Meadow* 3.00
_____WINNING AT THE HARNESS RACES—An Expert's Guide *Nick Cammarano* 3.00

HUMOR

_____HOW TO BE A COMEDIAN FOR FUN & PROFIT *King & Laufer* 2.00
_____HOW TO FLATTEN YOUR TUSH *Coach Marge Reardon* 2.00
_____JOKE TELLER'S HANDBOOK *Bob Orben* 3.00
_____JOKES FOR ALL OCCASIONS *Al Schock* 3.00

HYPNOTISM

_____ADVANCED TECHNIQUES OF HYPNOSIS *Melvin Powers* 2.00
_____BRAINWASHING AND THE CULTS *Paul A. Verdier, Ph.D.* 3.00
_____CHILDBIRTH WITH HYPNOSIS *William S. Kroger, M.D.* 3.00
_____HOW TO SOLVE Your Sex Problems with Self-Hypnosis *Frank S. Caprio, M.D.* 3.00
_____HOW TO STOP SMOKING THRU SELF-HYPNOSIS *Leslie M. LeCron* 3.00
_____HOW TO USE AUTO-SUGGESTION EFFECTIVELY *John Duckworth* 3.00
_____HOW YOU CAN BOWL BETTER USING SELF-HYPNOSIS *Jack Heise* 3.00
_____HOW YOU CAN PLAY BETTER GOLF USING SELF-HYPNOSIS *Jack Heise* 2.00
_____HYPNOSIS AND SELF-HYPNOSIS *Bernard Hollander, M.D.* 3.00
_____HYPNOTISM *(Originally published in 1893) Carl Sextus* 3.00
_____HYPNOTISM & PSYCHIC PHENOMENA *Simeon Edmunds* 3.00
_____HYPNOTISM MADE EASY *Dr. Ralph Winn* 3.00
_____HYPNOTISM MADE PRACTICAL *Louis Orton* 3.00
_____HYPNOTISM REVEALED *Melvin Powers* 2.00
_____HYPNOTISM TODAY *Leslie LeCron and Jean Bordeaux, Ph.D.* 4.00
_____MODERN HYPNOSIS *Lesley Kuhn & Salvatore Russo, Ph.D.* 5.00
_____NEW CONCEPTS OF HYPNOSIS *Bernard C. Gindes, M.D.* 4.00
_____NEW SELF-HYPNOSIS *Paul Adams* 3.00
_____POST-HYPNOTIC INSTRUCTIONS—Suggestions for Therapy *Arnold Furst* 3.00
_____PRACTICAL GUIDE TO SELF-HYPNOSIS *Melvin Powers* 3.00
_____PRACTICAL HYPNOTISM *Philip Magonet, M.D.* 2.00
_____SECRETS OF HYPNOTISM *S. J. Van Pelt, M.D.* 3.00
_____SELF-HYPNOSIS Its Theory, Technique & Application *Melvin Powers* 2.00
_____SELF-HYPNOSIS A Conditioned-Response Technique *Laurance Sparks* 4.00
_____THERAPY THROUGH HYPNOSIS *edited by Raphael H. Rhodes* 4.00

JUDAICA

_____HOW TO LIVE A RICHER & FULLER LIFE *Rabbi Edgar F. Magnin* 2.00
_____MODERN ISRAEL *Lily Edelman* 2.00
_____ROMANCE OF HASSIDISM *Jacob S. Minkin* 2.50
_____SERVICE OF THE HEART *Evelyn Garfiel, Ph.D.* 4.00
_____STORY OF ISRAEL IN COINS *Jean & Maurice Gould* 2.00
_____STORY OF ISRAEL IN STAMPS *Maxim & Gabriel Shamir* 1.00
_____TONGUE OF THE PROPHETS *Robert St. John* 3.00
_____TREASURY OF COMFORT *edited by Rabbi Sidney Greenberg* 4.00

JUST FOR WOMEN

_____COSMOPOLITAN'S GUIDE TO MARVELOUS MEN Fwd. by *Helen Gurley Brown* 3.00
_____COSMOPOLITAN'S HANG-UP HANDBOOK Foreword by *Helen Gurley Brown* 4.00
_____COSMOPOLITAN'S LOVE BOOK—A Guide to Ecstasy in Bed 3.00
_____COSMOPOLITAN'S NEW ETIQUETTE GUIDE Fwd. by *Helen Gurley Brown* 4.00
_____I AM A COMPLEAT WOMAN *Doris Hagopian & Karen O'Connor Sweeney* 3.00
_____JUST FOR WOMEN—A Guide to the Female Body *Richard E. Sand, M.D.* 4.00
_____NEW APPROACHES TO SEX IN MARRIAGE *John E. Eichenlaub, M.D.* 3.00
_____SEXUALLY ADEQUATE FEMALE *Frank S. Caprio, M.D.* 3.00
_____YOUR FIRST YEAR OF MARRIAGE *Dr. Tom McGinnis* 3.00

MARRIAGE, SEX & PARENTHOOD

_____ABILITY TO LOVE *Dr. Allan Fromme* 5.00
_____ENCYCLOPEDIA OF MODERN SEX & LOVE TECHNIQUES *Macandrew* 4.00
_____GUIDE TO SUCCESSFUL MARRIAGE *Drs. Albert Ellis & Robert Harper* 4.00

_____HOW TO RAISE AN EMOTIONALLY HEALTHY, HAPPY CHILD *A. Ellis* 3.00
_____IMPOTENCE & FRIGIDITY *Edwin W. Hirsch, M.D.* 3.00
_____SEX WITHOUT GUILT *Albert Ellis, Ph.D.* 3.00
_____SEXUALLY ADEQUATE MALE *Frank S. Caprio, M.D.* 3.00

METAPHYSICS & OCCULT

_____BOOK OF TALISMANS, AMULETS & ZODIACAL GEMS *William Pavitt* 4.00
_____CONCENTRATION—A Guide to Mental Mastery *Mouni Sadhu* 3.00
_____CRITIQUES OF GOD *Edited by Peter Angeles* 7.00
_____DREAMS & OMENS REVEALED *Fred Gettings* 3.00
_____EXTRASENSORY PERCEPTION *Simeon Edmunds* 2.00
_____EXTRA-TERRESTRIAL INTELLIGENCE—The First Encounter 6.00
_____FORTUNE TELLING WITH CARDS *P. Foli* 2.00
_____HANDWRITING ANALYSIS MADE EASY *John Marley* 3.00
_____HANDWRITING TELLS *Nadya Olyanova* 5.00
_____HOW TO UNDERSTAND YOUR DREAMS *Geoffrey A. Dudley* 2.00
_____ILLUSTRATED YOGA *William Zorn* 3.00
_____IN DAYS OF GREAT PEACE *Mouni Sadhu* 3.00
_____KING SOLOMON'S TEMPLE IN THE MASONIC TRADITION *Alex Horne* 5.00
_____LSD—THE AGE OF MIND *Bernard Roseman* 2.00
_____MAGICIAN—His training and work *W. E. Butler* 3.00
_____MEDITATION *Mouni Sadhu* 4.00
_____MODERN NUMEROLOGY *Morris C. Goodman* 3.00
_____NUMEROLOGY—ITS FACTS AND SECRETS *Ariel Yvon Taylor* 3.00
_____NUMEROLOGY MADE EASY *W. Mykian* 3.00
_____PALMISTRY MADE EASY *Fred Gettings* 3.00
_____PALMISTRY MADE PRACTICAL *Elizabeth Daniels Squire* 3.00
_____PALMISTRY SECRETS REVEALED *Henry Frith* 3.00
_____PRACTICAL YOGA *Ernest Wood* 3.00
_____PROPHECY IN OUR TIME *Martin Ebon* 2.50
_____PSYCHOLOGY OF HANDWRITING *Nadya Olyanova* 3.00
_____SUPERSTITION—Are you superstitious? *Eric Maple* 2.00
_____TAROT *Mouni Sadhu* 5.00
_____TAROT OF THE BOHEMIANS *Papus* 5.00
_____TEST YOUR ESP *Martin Ebon* 2.00
_____WAYS TO SELF-REALIZATION *Mouni Sadhu* 3.00
_____WHAT YOUR HANDWRITING REVEALS *Albert E. Hughes* 2.00
_____WITCHCRAFT, MAGIC & OCCULTISM—A Fascinating History *W. B. Crow* 5.00
_____WITCHCRAFT—THE SIXTH SENSE *Justine Glass* 3.00
_____WORLD OF PSYCHIC RESEARCH *Hereward Carrington* 2.00
_____YOU CAN ANALYZE HANDWRITING *Robert Holder* 2.00

SELF-HELP & INSPIRATIONAL

_____CYBERNETICS WITHIN US *Y. Saparina* 3.00
_____DAILY POWER FOR JOYFUL LIVING *Dr. Donald Curtis* 3.00
_____DOCTOR PSYCHO-CYBERNETICS *Maxwell Maltz, M.D.* 3.00
_____DYNAMIC THINKING *Melvin Powers* 2.00
_____EXUBERANCE—Your Guide to Happiness & Fulfillment *Dr. Paul Kurtz* 3.00
_____GREATEST POWER IN THE UNIVERSE *U. S. Andersen* 4.00
_____GROW RICH WHILE YOU SLEEP *Ben Sweetland* 3.00
_____GROWTH THROUGH REASON *Albert Ellis, Ph.D.* 4.00
_____GUIDE TO DEVELOPING YOUR POTENTIAL *Herbert A. Otto, Ph.D.* 3.00
_____GUIDE TO LIVING IN BALANCE *Frank S. Caprio, M.D.* 2.00
_____HELPING YOURSELF WITH APPLIED PSYCHOLOGY *R. Henderson* 2.00
_____HELPING YOURSELF WITH PSYCHIATRY *Frank S. Caprio, M.D.* 2.00
_____HOW TO ATTRACT GOOD LUCK *A. H. Z. Carr* 3.00
_____HOW TO CONTROL YOUR DESTINY *Norvell* 3.00
_____HOW TO DEVELOP A WINNING PERSONALITY *Martin Panzer* 3.00
_____HOW TO DEVELOP AN EXCEPTIONAL MEMORY *Young & Gibson* 4.00
_____HOW TO OVERCOME YOUR FEARS *M. P. Leahy, M.D.* 3.00
_____HOW YOU CAN HAVE CONFIDENCE AND POWER *Les Giblin* 3.00
_____HUMAN PROBLEMS & HOW TO SOLVE THEM *Dr. Donald Curtis* 3.00
_____I CAN *Ben Sweetland* 4.00
_____I WILL *Ben Sweetland* 3.00

_____ LEFT-HANDED PEOPLE *Michael Barsley* — 3.00
_____ MAGIC IN YOUR MIND *U. S. Andersen* — 4.00
_____ MAGIC OF THINKING BIG *Dr. David J. Schwartz* — 3.00
_____ MAGIC POWER OF YOUR MIND *Walter M. Germain* — 4.00
_____ MENTAL POWER THROUGH SLEEP SUGGESTION *Melvin Powers* — 2.00
_____ NEW GUIDE TO RATIONAL LIVING *Albert Ellis, Ph.D. & R. Harper, Ph.D.* — 3.00
_____ OUR TROUBLED SELVES *Dr. Allan Fromme* — 3.00
_____ PSYCHO-CYBERNETICS *Maxwell Maltz, M.D.* — 2.00
_____ SCIENCE OF MIND IN DAILY LIVING *Dr. Donald Curtis* — 3.00
_____ SECRET OF SECRETS *U. S. Andersen* — 4.00
_____ SECRET POWER OF THE PYRAMIDS *U. S. Andersen* — 4.00
_____ STUTTERING AND WHAT YOU CAN DO ABOUT IT *W. Johnson, Ph.D.* — 2.50
_____ SUCCESS-CYBERNETICS *U. S. Andersen* — 4.00
_____ 10 DAYS TO A GREAT NEW LIFE *William E. Edwards* — 3.00
_____ THINK AND GROW RICH *Napoleon Hill* — 3.00
_____ THREE MAGIC WORDS *U. S. Andersen* — 4.00
_____ TREASURY OF THE ART OF LIVING *Sidney S. Greenberg* — 5.00
_____ YOU ARE NOT THE TARGET *Laura Huxley* — 3.00
_____ YOUR SUBCONSCIOUS POWER *Charles M. Simmons* — 4.00
_____ YOUR THOUGHTS CAN CHANGE YOUR LIFE *Dr. Donald Curtis* — 3.00

SPORTS

_____ ARCHERY—An Expert's Guide *Dan Stamp* — 2.00
_____ BICYCLING FOR FUN AND GOOD HEALTH *Kenneth E. Luther* — 2.00
_____ BILLIARDS—Pocket • Carom • Three Cushion *Clive Cottingham, Jr.* — 3.00
_____ CAMPING-OUT 101 Ideas & Activities *Bruno Knobel* — 2.00
_____ COMPLETE GUIDE TO FISHING *Vlad Evanoff* — 2.00
_____ HOW TO IMPROVE YOUR RACQUETBALL *Lubarsky, Kaufman, & Scagnetti* — 3.00
_____ HOW TO WIN AT POCKET BILLIARDS *Edward D. Knuchell* — 3.00
_____ JOY OF WALKING *Jack Scagnetti* — 3.00
_____ LEARNING & TEACHING SOCCER SKILLS *Eric Worthington* — 3.00
_____ MOTORCYCLING FOR BEGINNERS *I. G. Edmonds* — 2.00
_____ RACQUETBALL MADE EASY *Steve Lubarsky, Rod Delson & Jack Scagnetti* — 3.00
_____ SECRET OF BOWLING STRIKES *Dawson Taylor* — 3.00
_____ SECRET OF PERFECT PUTTING *Horton Smith & Dawson Taylor* — 3.00
_____ SOCCER—The game & how to play it *Gary Rosenthal* — 3.00
_____ STARTING SOCCER *Edward F. Dolan, Jr.* — 2.00
_____ TABLE TENNIS MADE EASY *Johnny Leach* — 2.00

TENNIS LOVERS' LIBRARY

_____ BEGINNER'S GUIDE TO WINNING TENNIS *Helen Hull Jacobs* — 2.00
_____ HOW TO BEAT BETTER TENNIS PLAYERS *Loring Fiske* — 4.00
_____ HOW TO IMPROVE YOUR TENNIS—Style, Strategy & Analysis *C. Wilson* — 2.00
_____ INSIDE TENNIS—Techniques of Winning *Jim Leighton* — 3.00
_____ PLAY TENNIS WITH ROSEWALL *Ken Rosewall* — 2.00
_____ PSYCH YOURSELF TO BETTER TENNIS *Dr. Walter A. Luszki* — 2.00
_____ SUCCESSFUL TENNIS *Neale Fraser* — 2.00
_____ TENNIS FOR BEGINNERS *Dr. H. A. Murray* — 2.00
_____ TENNIS MADE EASY *Joel Brecheen* — 2.00
_____ WEEKEND TENNIS—How to have fun & win at the same time *Bill Talbert* — 3.00
_____ WINNING WITH PERCENTAGE TENNIS—Smart Strategy *Jack Lowe* — 2.00

WILSHIRE PET LIBRARY

_____ DOG OBEDIENCE TRAINING *Gust Kessopulos* — 3.00
_____ DOG TRAINING MADE EASY & FUN *John W. Kellogg* — 3.00
_____ HOW TO BRING UP YOUR PET DOG *Kurt Unkelbach* — 2.00
_____ HOW TO RAISE & TRAIN YOUR PUPPY *Jeff Griffen* — 2.00
_____ PIGEONS: HOW TO RAISE & TRAIN THEM *William H. Allen, Jr.* — 2.00

The books listed above can be obtained from your book dealer or directly from Melvin Powers. When ordering, please remit 50¢ per book postage & handling. Send for our free illustrated catalog of self-improvement books.

Melvin Powers
12015 Sherman Road, No. Hollywood, California 91605